A PASSION
FOR FOOD

Other Books by Gerry Shikatani

Lake & Other Stories
Aqueduct
1988— Selected Poems & Texts, 1973-1988
The Book of Tree: A Cottage Journal
A Sparrow's Food

GERRY SHIKATANI

A PASSION
FOR FOOD

CONVERSATIONS WITH
CANADIAN CHEFS

THE MERCURY PRESS

The publisher gratefully acknowledges the financial assistance of the Canada Council for the Arts and the Ontario Arts Council. The publisher further acknowledges the financial support of the Government of Canada through the Book Publishing Industry Development Program (BPIDP) for our publishing activities.

PHOTOGRAPH OF ANDREW MILNE-ALLAN: Renzo Cattoni

A NOTE ON THE RECIPES:
To keep faith with the chefs' individual methodologies, we have kept metric or Imperial measurements (or both) as originally indicated by the chefs.

Composition and page design by TASK
Printed and bound in Canada
Printed on acid-free paper

1 2 3 4 5   03 02 01 00 99

Canadian Cataloguing in Publication Data
Shikatani, Gerry
A passion for food : conversations with Canadian chefs
ISBN 1-55128-070-1
1. Cookery, Canadian. 2. Cooks - Canada - Interviews. I. Title.
TX649.A1S54 1999   641.5'092'271   C99-932059-9

The Mercury Press
22 Prince Rupert Avenue
Toronto, Ontario
Canada M6P 2A7

Contents

For my nephew Paul Seiju Onami,
chef of contemporary and classic Japanese cuisine,
and all past, current and future Canadian chefs
and food producers for their dedication
to the evolution of gastronomy.

Carol Chow

I first heard about Carol Chow during the winter of 1997, when I was briefly in Vancouver. I came across very positive reviews of the work she'd been doing at the Beach Side Café and decided that at some time in the future, I'd want to track her down. Vancouver is a city where the ubiquitous influence of both inexpensive Chinese noodle and congee houses and opulent Hong Kong dining rooms has profoundly nudged Anglo-Canadian food towards the taste tracks down at Pender and Gore in Chinatown and the sprawling food courts of Richmond. It's also a city where talented women chefs are coming into their own as perhaps nowhere else in Canada, and so Carol, a third-generation Chinese Canadian, epitomizes as much as anyone, the direction of Vancouver cuisine. The following year, when I came to scout around for this book, her name naturally came up as among the women chefs receiving consistent praise. Often picked as best restaurant in West Van and the North Shore, the Beach Side has consistently been rated among the very finest by prominent American travel guide *Northwest Best Places*. I went to check for myself one Sunday afternoon brunch at this very pretty dining room, with its views across from West Van back to Stanley Park. With just one salad of hers— peeled small fresh shrimp with pea shoots and a sesame oil dressing sauce, I required no further convincing. I wanted to try more of her food and meet Carol.

I began by asking her about this thoughtfully constructed salad when I had the opportunity to sit down with her in a quiet corner of the Beach Side, away from both kitchen and dining room. It was the lull between lunch and dinner, the sunny afternoon after a more elaborate full-course evening dinner which had left me glowing at the Beach Side.

The approach I like to take is very simple. I don't like to mask flavours of anything. For example, in the thing you were eating, the shrimp is so sweet, you don't want the sesame vinaigrette doing an overkill on it. So, you just want to enhance the flavours— it's the same with the pickled cucumbers— that's more of a texture thing, that helps the whole dish come together... Most of the food I do is very simple. With good ingredients and simple preparation, you end up with a very good product.

Tell me a little bit about your training and background.

Initially, I didn't want to cook. I went to business school for a couple of years, and after that I decided I didn't want to go to school any more. So, I thought about what I wanted to do...

I enjoyed cooking, but I'd never actually cooked as a job— just at home, stupid things like cookies and cakes and whatnot. And I looked into all the different schools and Dubrulle Culinary only took four months to finish at the time that I went. So I thought, well, four months out of my life is no big deal; it's not like the five years for business... so I took that and kept going in cooking and have been in it for quite some time now.

I was born in Vancouver. I've lived here in West Van all my life; I'm third-generation Chinese-Canadian. My dad is from Ashcroft, which is just outside Vancouver, near Kamloops, but my mom is from China.

Dubrulle— that was only a short course.

Yes, it was just from September to January. Then, from there, I got a job at Settebello, which is an Umberto restaurant [chef-restaurateur Umberto Menghi]. He's closed up now, because they unionized, and he didn't want to go unionized...

I worked there for nine months, and I was always looking for something more. I was just doing things like garde-manger, salad preparation, and things like that, and a friend of mine who was the chef at Bishop's called me up and said, hey, there's a position here for garde-manger and I said, great. So off I went and talked to her, and I basically worked my way up at Bishop's— you know— I was garde-manger, then day sous, and then I was the chef. At that point I had only been chef for about a year there— but my time had come. It was 1989-90 or something like that. I was there for about five and a half years.

What was the thing that really triggered you to go to Dubrulle's— to do the cooking?

It was just something I really enjoyed doing— I wasn't even thinking about work. I thought, give it a try— because— I always thought I was going to finish business school. I was going to business school, and one of the reasons I went to Dubrulle's really was that it was only four months. It cost a lot more in terms of money than the vocational schools or anything else, and there weren't any other private culinary schools at the time— right now there are a few more. So I opted for that because it was quick— and I did enjoy it to a degree.

To a degree.

Yeah. [laughs]

Did you find it was really helpful? Had you been able to go in somewhere to start work?

Well, it gave you a basis— you always have to have a basis with anything. People, I think, excel at different times, and I found that the pace at Dubrulle's was a bit too slow— that was the only shortcoming. I mean, we peeled and cut potatoes for two weeks, which I thought was a bit too much. But other than that, they gave you the basis of how to make different stocks and how to cook things and sauces and stuff and you really need that basis. I never had cooked any of that kind of food before, either.

Had you eaten much of it?

Well, yeah, I had. Sunday night dinners we'd always go out with the whole family... but I had never really cooked anything besides steak— I just pan-fried it— but no fancy sauces or fancy potatoes, or anything like that...

When you left Dubrulle's, were you anxious to get going— had it really excited you?

It did excite me quite a bit. After I left there, I didn't have a job— they had tried to find me a few jobs, but I was not willing to take behind-the-counter jobs— I really wanted to get my foot into a good restaurant. Somewhere I could really learn something, at least. Behind a counter was not what I was looking for.

I think what they did when you were in school was instill something in you, maybe too much. Expectations were maybe too high— at least from what I thought. They were always saying, oh, you'll get ten dollars an hour as soon as you get out of school— well, that was ridiculous, because minimum wage was only three or four dollars [laughs]— or something— you know, they're not going to pay some kid out of school ten dollars an hour, and I mean you can barely get ten dollars an hour now. But I withheld and withheld, until my friend working at Settebello called. I checked it out and it looked pretty cool, and again, it was easy, just garde-manger and stuff like that— but it was a step in the right direction.

What they taught me was volume [laughs] and speed, which I think is very important. You have to be a good chef, but, at the same time, you can't be slow. You have to have all the degrees of being a chef.

Tell me about your rise to become chef at Bishop's.

Because I had been there for so long, I kind of stepped in, and it was nothing different for me— I was probably still on my learning curve— which is good and bad— probably more bad for them than for me... It was a great opportunity. Obviously, I do a lot more now than I did before, because I've got my own style compared to then, where I was working with everybody's style I had been shown. But you know, this industry's great because you're always learning.

In terms of learning those other kinds of styles— do you think that was really important?

I do. Quality of the food... even the temperature of your plate— making sure people have a hot plate if it's hot food or a cold plate if it's cold food... garnishing, making sure things are fresh and have nice colour and height. And all those other things you don't always think of... It always tastes great, but eye appeal is very important to people, too.

So what kind of personal style evolved from your various experiences?

Simplicity is what I base all my cooking on; I don't play with my food very much— I like my plate to be hot so you can't have 17 hands in that one plate. You always have to think, how many fingers does it take to put up that one plate? So, depending on the size of your restaurant— you can decide then how many fingers you can have on the plate— this restaurant's quite large, and in the summertime, we're really quite busy, so for me, simplicity is great, because the fewer hands on the plate the better. I don't like to play with my food so much that by the time it gets to the customer, it's stone cold or it's lukewarm.

There's certainly a kind of excitement going around, that there's all kinds of possibilities of taste, ingredients and that— do you think people can get lost in that?

I think you can get lost in it. There're so many options— Vancouver's great for ingredients and that— you've got so many cultures— and Toronto's the same—
    I think anybody can get lost— you can try to play with too many flavours and mask things up— I always believe you add different flavours to enhance the main ingredient in the dish, and not just for that one item it's going to be served with— for example, that shrimp salad you have.

Last night I ate the Chilean sea bass— tell me about that.

That dish came about just because I think sea bass is a very fatty fish and a very soft textured fish. The potato crust is a texture thing as well; it helps to cut the taste of the fat in the fish— and the broth just came to be the broth. It goes very well with the spinach, but it's very simple— the shiitake mushrooms and the shrimp— the broth is a tiny bit of fish stock and chicken stock mixed with some lemon grass, shallots, white wine, salt and white pepper, and that's strained off and we finish it with some butter, the mushrooms and the shrimp— it's not too difficult— you can do it at home.

There's a substantial amount of spinach— it's not crispy spinach, but wilted spinach.

I was in a spinach mode at one point— I love wilted spinach— especially for its mouth feel— which I think is an important thing— again, a texture thing— compared to the fish. The fish is a firm but soft fish. You've got the potato, which is crisp, and the spinach, which is chewy— that's a bad word— but it has a chewy texture. You've got the shrimp, which is crisp— not potato crisp, but shrimp crisp, and the shiitake add a nice flavour; it's all about flavour, texture and heights.

How many flavours do you like to work with in a dish?

I would say a maximum of two. Like— I would never go for an Asian, Indian and French kind of thing— I think that's too much, and people are going, what is it? You want them to find out, but you don't need to have them find out right away. And with three together you're totally going to lose people. There are certain spices that just belong to themselves— and it isn't always good to fuse things with other things.

But you do bring other cuisines— do you do research in those cuisines?

I do— but we've got a great kitchen crew, too— and we're all kind of different— one girl up there just loves her Middle Eastern and Indian food— she has that great Indian background. And Jeff has more of an Italian background, and I guess I have more of a French background. The same with Kimberley. I have two sous chefs, and with everybody together, we work to make something. Even when we do menu planning, we work together— I don't do it just myself. I ask them to bring their ideas, or something they saw, or something they think is worthy, even of talking about. We do talk about it, and we think about what it's going to look like— does it work in our kitchen? That's important. Then, I just take everything home and say— no, not this— or I go, that'll work— but with this— mix and match.

So after you've reflected on all that, and are ready to test out these ideas, do you work alone at home?

I do that more so here, not at home very much, because most of the night I am here. The last thing I want to do at home is big meals.

I like the energy in the kitchen here, because people will say, oh, do you know what would go really well with this? And you're like, oh, yeah— because sometimes, you see a picture in your head and you have tunnel vision and then you come to and someone from the outside can say, hey, hey, hey! If you add this, it will bring out so much flavour. So it's always nice to have team effort. Sometimes you'll say, no, that's the way I want it; I like it that way. But some things you kind of play with and you're not too sure of what exactly you want. Then you work together and come up with something that's fantastic.

Is this a process you learned at Bishop's?

No, not at Bishop's. You know, at Bishop's— Judy was the chef when I was there— and the same with Kim, here— they all planned the menus themselves— so we never really took part in that. We basically did what they said. But I think you have to keep people excited in the kitchen and the dining room— I like them to take part— because, if I just told them what to do, and didn't invite their input, I think that would be pretty boring. *I* thought that was pretty boring; I mean, it's exciting when you do it until you learn it and then you go, okay [laughs], but I like everybody— even when we do the daily special— I like to say, okay, garde-manger— you might have something in the fridge I want to use— so I might say— there's some crab meat in the fridge, and some lemon grass, and blah, blah, blah— and I'll say, deal with that and come back to me in half an hour with an idea— and then we'll work together on that. Before we actually serve that to the customer, we'll plate one to make sure the presentation is accurate— and that gives them more creativity— gets the brain flowing, rather than me saying, okay, make crab meat and do this that and the other. Then, their brains don't work, the creative juices don't flow, because I've just told them what to do. I think it helps everybody in the kitchen, and I think that's what it's about— you come in and teach me something and I'll teach you something— and it's not that personal— I'll teach you something, and you will learn while you're in the kitchen, and that's a continual learning process.

So, you learn from your kitchen team?

Yeah. Kimberley, for example, comes from a very French background. She did her apprenticeship at Crocodile. She came to me almost two years ago, and she's got all these great French background ideas. She's really French, if you want to talk about her cooking. Some of it, maybe, I've forgotten about, or we didn't quite learn it that way. Because it's Alsatian cooking, we didn't quite reach that point in it in cooking school, but it is all learning. Even the guy fresh out of school that I may have doing garde-manger— he says, oh, we learned it that way at school— and I always go, tell me, exactly— and I try to picture it in my head and say okay, then let's try it. Because there are 17 recipes for mushroom soup— and that's probably true for most of the things in the kitchen— everybody's tomato sauce is different— everybody's chicken stock is different— everybody has 17 different ways. When I went to school, they taught me how to make roux— which is a flour-butter mixture for thickening things— and they said, you put butter and flour and you cook it. So when I went to Settebello, and the chef said to make roux, I took some butter and some flour and he yelled at me [laughs], and he said, what the hell are you doing? And I said, making some roux— I was 20 years old— and he goes— you don't make roux that way! And I go, how do you make it? And he says, you use oil, and I said, *oh, okayyy...* [laughs]— this is a cheaper version. Every chef has his own way— but every year you learn something different about how people do things, and that's one of them. There are better ways and there are bad ways— and that was a bad way, I think— but it is all a learning process— and you do learn—

How about your Chinese background— does that play a part in your cooking?

My background? No, not really. I mean, I like Asian flavours, and there's no doubt about that; I love using them, but I can't cook Chinese food. I don't even do it at home. At home, it's probably something like pasta or burgers or steaks.

Did you do any Chinese cooking when you were at home?

A tiny bit, but not very much Chinese cooking— that was my parents... My father more than my mother.

Did you have it regularly at home?

Yeah, about four times a week, and the rest of the time we'd have things like roast beef and steak—

So, what's the relationship between how your own palate, taste bud, evolved, and how you cook?

I like simple food, but I like really tasty food— whether it's spicy— a spicy hot or spicy with spices— or not— but that doesn't always come out in my cooking, because you're not just cooking for yourself, but for other people.

Well, when you use ingredients like, say, halibut, and you're using bok choy with it and black beans— do you think you have some innate sense of this combination?

Probably [laughs] no... I mean, I love black bean sauce.

Because the way we do our so-called Chinese black bean sauce— is not really Chinese black bean sauce, but more tailored to what people want here. Because if they want Chinese food, they go to Chinatown. We tried to serve the real Chinese black bean sauce, but it didn't go off. People found it too pungent, so we ended up putting cream into it and changing it to suit people's taste. So, even though I started off in the right way—

Was it hard to make that decision?

It was, because I didn't want to add cream to black bean sauce. It's absolutely ridiculous! And at the same time, you're also catering to making those kinds of compromises. But they're paying the rent, so obviously they have some say in it, and with the cream, customers have no problems with it; you don't hear any bad comments about it. But without, they say, well, you know, it's a bit strong...

The bok choy we just steam— we don't really stir-fry it— we don't have any stir-fry woks, so... you always have to kind of change things to make people happy and have it work. And sometimes it doesn't work in the kitchen, so you change it to basically adapt it to the environment.

But you don't necessarily have to have those dishes—

But people love it, though.

Or is cooking that more for them?

It's for both. They love it and I love it— black bean sauce and Thai curries, for example— but sometimes you have to change it. Sometimes it's because I particularly don't know how to make it the way a real Thai person would make it. But you have to be very flexible in this industry, and if someone says, it's not like I had it at the Thai Palace, well, this isn't like the Thai Palace. But, if you get a few comments like that, you have to adjust yourself. Obviously, people are commenting for a reason—

Was food very important when you were growing up?

It was family time— for us eating together was very important. When my parents worked we did it every day because we wouldn't see them any other time? We'd sit around the table, and Sundays would be the days we'd go out and eat and it didn't always have to be Caucasian food. We did Chinese, but in terms of Caucasian or continenal we did the Hy's thing and Black Angus... steak houses and things like that... or Italian food. It was always sort of the same places, but we'd make our rounds. It was based on good food and the family around.

That's important?

I think so. Now we're all moved out and whenever we see each other it's always around food?

Do you cook for them?

Oh no! [laughs] I think I've done it once in the last year...
   If it's Chinese, it's usually my mom, with some help from my dad. If it's continental, it's usually my dad— he does Chinese too, but my mom feels more comfortable if it's Chinese and my dad's great cooking steaks, roasts and chickens...

If it's Chinese what is it?

I don't even know— I don't know what you call it... it's not Szechuan, there are dishes that are spicy, but it's more homestyle... I've always liked my dad's chicken with black bean and green beans and my mom always makes a great sweet and sour eggplant dish, usually with pork... that and Peking Duck, I could die for Peking Duck but we don't make that at home. [laughter]

So what would be your comfort foods?

Soups—I love Chinese soups—like broccoli kind of things. They're so simple but there's so much flavour in them. Congees are probably comfort food. I like congee, yeah I grew up on it, yeah, it's not something foreign to me or anything— sometimes beef, sometimes pork, seafood and sometimes with thousand year old eggs?

Carol Chow

You don't make it...

I could probably figure it out but I've never had to make it. It's something you'd go home to eat it? [laughs]

But I also like stew— the winter type of comfort food. Stews are great 'cause it's warm— and it's simple and it's kind of a no-fuss thing. And that's the way I like to cook too. Yeah, it doesn't look like stew but I mean in terms of all the work involved, it's simple, it's good ingredients put together with very little effort and time— but if you use good ingredients and you have a love for the food, you can create something very nice.

So that's really Canadian. You were born and raised in Vancouver. When it comes to local products, say, when you get a nice piece of halibut, and you see it, what do you think of doing?

Simple. A lot of the time, at home, even, I just pan sear it. I don't want to mask it with any flavours. Halibut is so fresh, and it is a very light fish, you don't want to masque it, but just to use butter, lemon or herbs, or tomato and basil is great.

So how did the black bean get into the dish on the menu?

I don't know. It started as a special. I started wrapping up the halibut in noodles with black bean sauce, and people loved it, so it just ended up on the menu like that. But it is a delicate fish— with black bean sauce, too, you don't want anything that's too heavy.

Are there foods that really inspire you?

I really like meat— I'm really big on meats— but also fish. The BC spot prawns are probably one of the best things, and you can't get anything like it anywhere else. The halibut here, too, is a good product as well. There's just so much right now, and not just from local sources. It's really easy to get stuff from Nova Scotia; I do get a lot of my tuna from the East because I think it's actually better from over there than it is from here. And from Hawaii, I should say.

So, you're not a chef who will always work with local when possible?

I believe working with local is great, as long as the product quality is there. But our season is so short that it's a hard concept to have 12 months of the year. You can probably have it for two months of the year on a consistent basis, but to have it for 12... That's kind of hard. You can always have the basic ingredients, say, you can always have salmon, but all the vegetables and fruit? There's just not that much. You can have your root vegetables and things like that, but not the others. I think that's harder to deal with than anything else.

You're a woman chef... there still aren't an awful lot...

There aren't. I don't know why, really, except that I think it's a really hard business, and there are so many old school guys out there, too, that it's hard for a woman to advance in a kitchen.

Except that I never really found it that way, because I only worked in two restaurants besides here. In one of them, I worked under a male chef, but I left of my own accord because I wanted to progress up the ladder, and in the second restaurant the two chefs I worked under were female, but from what I hear from other women— for example, at hotels you don't see any woman chefs— well, Pan Pacific has a junior sous— but I can't ever imagine them becoming executive chef. I think it's too old school— they expect to have a man, and generally speaking a European man— and they fill those positions— but hopefully more women will enter this business, because it surely makes a different kitchen.

In what way?

I think women tend to be a bit more flexible. They have a real calming effect, more than men... I shouldn't say that about all women and about all men, but generally speaking the atmosphere in the kitchen will be calmer, even if you only have a few girls in the kitchen. You can have a male chef, but as long as you have a few women in the kitchen, it changes the atmosphere. It isn't just the boys' club any more.

Carol Chow

When you think of the art and design aspects of cooking, does it affect presentation?

Well, they always say that men like height. [laughter]

Like the towers.

Yeah, the towers of food... I mean, I like vertical food, too, but only as long as when I touch it, it doesn't go all over the plate and fall. And it's like the waiter is scared to bring it to the table, or, even worse, to bring it back to the kitchen. I mean, I like height, but not to excess. It should look good, and the presentation of it should be manageable. People shouldn't have to take their knives and forks and move stuff around just so it doesn't fall over, because then it looks even worse than it did, and half of it is on the floor over by a different table or whatever. I think people are learning this, too, that it's just not manageable. Vertical food looks great, and people go, *wow*, but they put their knives and forks into it and it's a different story. I only have four guys in my kitchen, but three of them are just in the learning stage, so they haven't really got a particular style, not yet, not overly—

Do you think they've been influenced? By seeing other ways?

You have to keep a kitchen consistent— one guy's food can't be totally different from what I cook. People expect a certain style, and if it was way bizarre, he'd have to tone it down a bit, which the guy I'm thinking of has— but he hasn't gone too far in terms of height...

I like the mix. I have three women in my kitchen and I don't like working with just three women. Having a male in the kitchen also changes the atmosphere, and creates a better aura... just a nicer working environment—

When I went to school, it was probably a few more guys than the girls, but not that many. From the class I graduated in, only three of twenty-seven students are left in the industry. But nowadays there are a lot more girls. I've done a couple of tastings at culinary schools, and I see a lot more women— or girls about eighteen or nineteen— and I think that's great. We do need a lot more women—

But it's really a tough business, trying to advance. And the common argument within the industry has been that it's also a tough business physically.

It is.

But that's the same argument used in other jobs when women want to advance...

But like in any another job, too, it depends on the woman. There are a lot of women who can't do what we do— working 12 or 14 hour days, and never sitting down... I can think of half a dozen women right off the top of my head who I know who wouldn't do that, and wouldn't ever want to...

It's physically hard, right... People think you must eat really well, being a chef, but not really. You work with the food and you love the food, but you work with it all day and you just want to go home and have a hamburger, you know? Your tastes really simplify. And for daily food, you really simplify things. This isn't an easy job. It's not just coming here and cooking and leaving at the end of the day; I've got a staff to take care of, there're food costs, there're labour costs... there's menu planning, and costing all the food... It's not a nine to five, come in to work, leave work kind of job. A lot of the time, the rest of the day might be sitting at the computer, punching some recipe out, or doing the schedule, or the budgets...

And it is hard, even when it's slow. It's so funny; people say, you must be so busy, and I say, yeah... I put in the hours whether it's slow or busy; I may *work* harder when it's busy, because there are more people eating... but in terms of actual hours in the restaurant, it's about the same.

What else makes it hard?

Staffing. There's so many restaurants in Vancouver right now that it's really hard to find good people— the wage they're being paid and the hours you put in... it's not easy work, but this is the way it is [laughs]— "Take it or leave it!" You have to do it for love and pay your dues— especially when you're first starting out and making $7.50 an hour.

You didn't start out with this love...

No, it was more of a hatred of going to school [laughs]— there was a love for food but, when I went to school it opened up so many doors compared to what I was used to with my family and going out.

And daily it's different. Something happens on a daily basis. I mean different products come in and the excitement starts again— having chanterelles now, and pine mushrooms— and truffles— it's all seasonal?

What else keeps you cooking?

The challenge— I think it's the stress? [laughs] I don't mean the business end of it but the stress of seven o'clock and fifty people walk in the door. That two-hour stressful period, you're out on a spot and you have all these customers to feed and you're happy with what you did in those two hours and the response you get back— it's like instant gratification... not two weeks later like a lot of things.

There must be things you can look back at and laugh...

One summer evening— it was pretty busy— the garde-manger guy had a cheesecake and he dropped it— and it went... [slaps her hands] splat! It splattered everywhere. It wasn't funny at the time, but it is now. I had this many bills up, and all I'm thinking is, *there goes 50 bucks*... and what about those customers who just ordered cheesecake... and you've got to make up a story, you have to say it wasn't presentable or up to the par of our usual cheesecake. You can't tell them we dropped it! It's not what people want to hear. Most of the time, it's things like that... or things that you're playing with and they flop! There hasn't been enough background done on this. For me, dessert flops are the biggest thing because I do a lot of the desserts here, but they aren't my forte. I prefer not to have to do desserts. Sometimes, when I do try— and I'm not a baker by any means— they turn out... disgusting. I mean burnt on the top and raw in the middle, or, you bring it out of the oven and oh, it looks really good and then all of a sudden, five minutes later, it's *what happened to it?* Because even in school we didn't really learn that much about baking, and I've never actually gone back to school to learn baking. I should, but at the same time I'm not really interested in it. I get by, and the desserts we have are good— they're nothing to write home about, but they taste good and the presentation is good...

But some evenings you must think things are going well, smoothly...

That's a hit and a miss. It's not just my responsibility. The kitchen can't work well if the front doesn't work well; you have to work as a team, and also the reservation book has to cooperate. If thirty people walk in the door at seven o'clock— you know, our kitchen is quite small— we can't feed thirty people at once. If they come in staggered, that's okay, but if they all come in at once, a little mayhem happens... That's like any kitchen. You can only do so much with what you have, and I think we've done pretty well for what we have in the kitchen.

You've been here for quite some time.

Eight years... I've always known when it's time to go. I left Settebello because when you go to work every day and you just hate it and you don't want to be there and you just go and do your job and leave, then you know it's not right. You're not happy, no one's happy, and you create a bad aura around you. [laughs] And the kitchen's grumpy... if I'm grumpy upstairs, then the whole kitchen knows it and the whole atmosphere changes. You don't want that. The same with Bishop's. After five and a half years... even though I was chef for just under a year, and I wanted to do it for longer and everbody was telling me to do it for longer, I couldn't. I just didn't want to go to work any more. And I haven't found that here... Janet's great [owner Janet McGuire]— she's done three renovations since I've been here from the day I started and today the change is 360 degrees. And the benefits— she's taken us to Napa Valley a couple of times, so we learn things there. And she likes to dine out and she knows what it's like. It's nice to work with someone who knows as well... and I think our crew is pretty good, front and back... overall. That makes it nice, too.

But you're not in central Vancouver, where you personally would get more attention... you're still satisfied in West Van?

But this is like family. [laughs] We're so small that people feel... there are some waiters who've been here ever since I arrived— even longer— and Janet's owned the restaurant for 11 years— Mark's [dining-room manager/sommelier Mark Davidson] been here for four or five years... so there are a few core people, and that helps, too— rather than your staff always changing around... Because we have a few regular customers, and they don't always want to see a different face; they want to say, hi, and they know you, and you know them... It's nice to be called Mr. and Mrs. Smith... rather than, oh, I've never seen these people before...

When you go on a trip to Napa what do you bring back?

Inspiration. Sometimes you just get bored with what you do. You might not always copy what they do— because it doesn't obviously work in that situation you're in, but you see different ingredients. They have really neat oils or spices or fruits and veggies that you just can't get up here... different kinds of honeys, like a truffle honey, all that kind of funky suff, different kinds of oils, which we're getting more of now up here. And a lot of organic things, fresh fruits, a lot of Asian things— fruits and vegetables.

So it gets into your food here?

It's always fun to play and I really like Asian ingredients because I think they're so flavourful— whether it'd be Japanese or Chinese, I just think there's so much flavour in it.

What's down the line for you?

I don't know... I know I can't be a chef in the type of environment I'm in now forever. I'm not saying it's bad, but I don't think I could do the 12 hour days when I'm 40. I'm only 32 now, but I feel like I'm 90. You know what I mean— it takes a toll.

And there's so much more I'd like to learn. I've always said I'd like to travel and do little two-month work things in different hotels or restaurants. I would love to go to Asia— like Thailand and Japan, and to learn. Thailand 'cause the food, the culture— the whole thing. The way they live is really interesting. I mean France would be good, but I'd rather got to Asia right now. Asian food to me is so much more tasty— I think that's probably why a lot of our food contains some kind of Asian ingredient. I would like to do that. I think it would be great.

Carol Chow

Carol Chow has been the Executive Chef at the Beach Side Café since 1991. Prior to heading the Beach Side team, she served as the Executive Chef at Bishop's Restaurant for three and a half years. Trained at the Pierre Dubrulle Culinary School, she became Garde-Manger at Settebello Ristorante after completing the accelerated programme. Chef Chow was a founding member of Xclusively BC. She believes in using the finest fresh local products to create meals of deceptive simplicity. Her culinary excellence, dedication and motivation have led to the Beach Side Café's growing reputation as one of Vancouver's finest restaurants.

Carol Chow's
DUNGENESS CRAB AND ROCKSHRIMP CAKES

INGREDIENTS
1 lb Dungeness crabmeat (picked through)
1/2 lb rockshrimp meat
1/4 c red pepper finely diced
1/4 c celery finely diced
1/4 c red onion finely diced
1/4 c mayonnaise
1 lemon, zested and juiced
salt and fresh cracked black pepper
tabasco and Worcesterhire sauce
2 c fresh bread crumbs

METHOD
Combine all ingredients in a large mixing bowl and mix well. Heat a small frying pan with 1 teaspoon of vegetable oil and cook up some of the mixture to test for seasoning. Adjust seasoning to your taste. Form mixture into 3 ounce balls and slightly flatten. Place on parchment lined cookie sheet until ready to use.

Heat large frying pan with 1/4 cup of extra virgin olive oil. When oil is hot, add cakes and sear on both sides. Place in 400 F oven for approximately 6 minutes. Remove from oven and drain cakes on paper towels. (Do not overcrowd pan when cooking or they will not sear properly.)

ASSEMBLY
Place Sorrel Pesto onto a plate using a spoon to spread it around. Place 2 cakes on each plate for an appetizer or 3 for a luncheon.

SORREL PESTO

INGREDIENTS
6 oz sorrel, stems removed
1 clove garlic
1/4 c parmesan cheese
1/2 lemon, zested and juiced
1/4 c roasted pine nuts
1/2 c extra virgin olive oil
salt and pepper
water to thin, if necessary

Place all ingredients in a food processor and mix until combined. Test for seasoning and reseason if necessary.

Robert Feenie

Lumière, Vancouver, BC

A couple of years before this interview, I'd already heard about Robert Feenie. My friend, the poet Sharon Thesen, with whom I've shared many wonderful meals in Montreal and Vancouver, had recommended Lumière as a Vancouver must-dine, and I trust her palate. A past Kits [Kitsilano] citizen, who's traded for The Drive [Commercial Drive], Sharon still has her radar out for Kits challengers to Bishop's longstanding culinary throne. Indeed, Lumière is now firmly entrenched among the best tables of Vancouver. The time of my parachute visit, Robert could barely take a breath because he was in the midst of major menu changes and the food writers were coming fast and furious, from as afar away as New York— the great Barbara Kafka had preceded me— where he'd just been getting splendid reviews for his work revamping the menu at Le Régence at the Hotel Plaza Athénée in Manhattan. We sat down in the dining room just before a private party he was doing on an evening the restaurant is usually closed. Things could have been more relaxed, but on the other hand, this is the reality of a chef's life at pivot-point in the career, his reputation growing across North America. Occasionally his eyes would dart towards the kitchen, his excitement in talking about his experience in gastronomy obvious, but always tugged by the kitchen's seductive call. It was the same enthusiasm the evening before when he'd prepared an extraordinary tasting menu and would come out ever so briefly, to make personal contact with each service, each creation, with enthusiasm and pride.

I knew from the quietly explosive dishes I'd tasted and this all too brief encounter, that one day, we'd meet again in more subdued circumstances, sip wine and talk some more.

You're from the Vancouver area— you're a home-grown chef from here and schooled here. Tell me how you started off.

I started in 1985, and had my first job in a hotel when I was 17. I was working at the Sheraton— at that time the Sheraton was called the Sheraton Villa in

Burnaby— as a banquet boy. I was banquet waiter, and when I got into it, chefs were having some sort of convention there, the BC Chefs' Federation at that time, and there was a gentleman by the name of Pierre Dubrulle at one of the tables I was serving, and Bruno Marti from La Belle Auberge was at the same table. Anyway, I got talking to him because I've always been interested in food— at that time I was deciding, do I go to university or try some other kind of profession? Pierre opened his cooking school here in 1984. I went down and met him and his partner— her name was Diana Becker— and took a look at the school. I was 18 at the time.

I was basically the youngest. A lot of the people who were going to the school at the time— it was a six-month program— had jobs and were looking for something else to do with their careers. But this was something I wanted to do full-time, so I looked at the school and basically finished my grade 12 off and then I went right into the school for six months.

What was it that clicked in this encounter with these people?

I think for me it was always a level of interest I've had with food— it's always been there— it's always been a love affair for me, since I was a kid. And all of a sudden being around the professional environment, it got that much more exciting for me. I started reading books. I started reading about Escoffier, I started reading about Carême, reading about the basis of French cooking— the general love of the great chefs like Bocuse, Robuchon— pretty much everybody— they started to fascinate me. My very first job was working in a small bistro once I finished school. And it was also a kind of fixation as a kid being around my mom all the time— and then being in a professional environment, and from there, going into a situation where I became completely fascinated when I was at the [culinary] school.

What was it in your make-up, do you think?

I don't know. What makes an artist an artist; what makes a hockey player a hockey player; what makes a doctor want to be a doctor? Some doctors probably don't realize it until they're in grade 12— well, okay so I'll become a doctor. Do they love it? I don't know. Is it a job? Do they love it? You don't know... but this is something that I love, and it really has to be a profession you love— it can't be a profession you do for making money. You can make money in this business, but you can't look at it— you have to really really love to cook if you want to be successful. If you want to be at the top of the game— if you just want to be the average joe who gets by day to day, then that's fine, but if you want to achieve a goal in life doing anything— like with cooking, you really have to have a drive.

Take me back to your early food experiences as a kid.

My parents are Irish, so Sunday nights were a big night, right? Sunday night roasts— and things like that— anything to do with being around the table Sunday night cooking roasts, cooking pork roasts, barbecuing salmon in the summer— my uncle's salmon from Vancouver Island, whole salmon— I don't know... just being in the kitchen! Helping my mom, having whole roast of pork or beef or whatever in the oven... and then opening that door once you put all the vegetables in was always something for me. I was fascinated by it. It's the same with making stocks now— it's always my favourite part of what I do here. I love making sauces... that aroma you get, like when you first put all the vegetables in the pan and stuff like that? That to me is the fun part.

It's like that basic thing in common, whether it's La Grande Classique or good bistro cooking?

Pretty much. I think a lot of young chefs get into cooking with the mentality that they want to have the name— and I've been through that phase as well— where you want to sort of be the Bocuse, you want to be the Robuchon, you want to have the book and everything else, but you don't realize the effort and understanding it takes to get to that point.

Cooking is almost like a circle. You start off wanting to do it because you want to be doing something— I mean I want to do it because I love it, but maybe you'll find the odd chef or the odd cook now who starts off because they want the prestige, the limelight, and they start— and you go through the circle, you go through the basics, and then you push past the basics and then you start to create and create and think of new combinations and do all this weird and funky food. I was just reading this book, where Ruth Reichl describes how many young chefs try to do something different just for the sake of being different— and that's all part of that circle when young cooks don't have any guidance.

Is that a necessary step you have to go through?

No, I don't think it's necessary. You can experiment, but you really have to understand flavours, you have to understand balance, you have to understand seasoning, you have to understand the succession of food and how that works. For example, sorbet should be served between the fish and the meat— or is that something that was done in the Escoffier day for a certain reason, and now can we move past that and take the sorbet afterwards... All those little things, and really thinking seriously about people when they're eating... That's when you come to the full circle and you come to understand a little about wine, you understand about where things come from— mussels, for instance— and you understand about the difference between mussels from Normandy and mussels from PEI and the mussels we have here on the West Coast and you understand the difference between the lobsters on the East Coast and lobster coming from Normandy and— langoustine— and you understand the flavour differences, because they're subtle, but you understand— and that takes time as a cook.

I cook by taste and there are some cooks who are technical— my sous is a tech-minded individual— though he does cook by taste... but my mouth tells me what I need to do. I adjust by my mouth.

So you're guided by your mouth, your palate. What were your first experiences of French cuisine in the forming of your palate?

It's always first-time things... I had mussels in Belgium when I was 16, 'cause I was living in Scandinavia for two years— I moved there when I was 15 and came back when I was 17— I went through Europe, experienced what a baguette was in Paris. Experienced— even at the age of 16— what a cheap bottle of red wine was about, with the friends I was with, realized what Brie was, realized where it came from, went to the South of France— I have to be in a place to understand things. Like the wine regions of BC, for example, which I think are really starting to take form. To understand the wine is not just to open the bottle and pour it in the glass and drink it. I think it's about walking around the vineyards and understanding the soil, understanding the people, understanding the smell of the area. You can put a California wine in front of me and I can basically smell it in the glass, you can put a Bordeaux in front of me and I can smell it in the glass, not the particular region yet, my nose hasn't got that much definition yet— or a Burgundy— throw it in front of me and I can tell, or an Australian wine I can tell.

Does that evoke inspiration in terms of food, smelling a particular kind of wine?

Well, yeah— you know Daniel is one of the people I admire right now the most in New York. And I admire Daniel [Boulud] because he's a very simple straightforward man. Jean-Georges [Vongerichten] is a little more extreme, but these guys know that simplicity is what it's all about in food, and not in being difficult; your product becomes the most important aspect of your food. That's what I feel I've learned in food.

For instance, I was critiqued a little bit when I first opened. I was trying to match too much Japanese in my food. Now mind you, Tojo is one of my best friends here and I grew up with Japanese— and he understands. Here's a Japanese man who knows that I've never been to Japan, but I understand the whole circle of Japanese food and a large portion of what Japanese food is all about. I put it in my food because I understand it. I don't put it in my food because I'm trying to be different. Now I don't use soya or ginger or use anything which I feel isn't my food, because it's odd or peculiar or isn't French, because you've got someone like Emile Jung at Le Crocodile in Strasbourg— one of his most famous dishes is the foie gras with the ginger reduction— there's a heavy Asian influence in it.

In what way is that French, in your perception?

That's something, making people understand what French food is— not so much about— you just take a region of France, and you cut everyone else off... People like Robuchon or Ducasse, these guys travel, they go around. Robuchon has a restaurant in Tokyo. Why do you open a restaurant in Tokyo, and why do so many Japanese chefs work in so many French three-stars? It's the simplicity— because of the common comparisons between the two foods. Because you have one area of France, for example, picking up the simplicity, as Tojo said last night, of the one thing and doing it well. I think that's where the French got that idea from— they got away from the big portions and the whole roasts and this kind of thing— like the tasting menus off the table d'hôte. The menus they do in a lot of their three-stars. Going through various tastes— and that's what Japanese food is all about. And now you've got the Japanese incorporating French ideas in their food. That doesn't make it non-Japanese, it just influences the food, and that's the same thing with me. I'm using things all the time on the menu you have in front of you right now. I can walk into a corner bistro and get influenced by food. You can get influenced by anything, you know— whatever you feel comfortable cooking with.

So, do you cook from your palate, or do you cook to some extent thinking about the comfort and reassurance the customer is going to have? What's the balance?

I listened to an interesting interview that Robuchon had on the French CBC three years ago. He said he takes notes— because I take notes as well— not so much on each individual who comes in his door, but what he said was that everyone is different in terms of his palate. I can have four people sitting at a table. Each one has a different taste sensation in his mouth.

Barbara was sitting here the other night. She was saying she's in an affection right now towards tarragon. She loves tarragon. So she was saying with the sea bass dish that I was doing, in the halibut dish I was doing— she was saying, uh, well, maybe a little tarragon in this dish would do well. I think you begin to understand when you're at a certain level, if the fish is cooked properly and has the appropriate accompaniments, has a little bit of texture in it and is seasoned properly, and it's something that someone can eat and go, wow, then the tarragon is simply a personal preference, it's not going to highlight or make the dish better? But it's someone saying, maybe you should put in a little tarragon, because that's what they would prefer, and maybe someone else would say, a little more salt for me— everyone has their own different opinion in terms of what they want their food to be on the table, and I think when it comes to adjusting and when it comes to cooking there's no such thing as perfection, because so many different people have so many different tastes.

Right now I'm reading this book— with Ruth Reichl, Gael Greene and all the other critics in New York— and they all have different favourite restaurants, so that tells you you'll see Daniel and Jean-Georges; they kind of go back and forth, yadda-yadda-yadda, or in Chicago, Trotters [Charlie Trotter]... the third one. I happen to think Trotter's brilliant. And that's what food's like. When you're cooking for people, the expectation for me is that I'm cooking for my palate and I want to make sure I give them the best experience they can have, not so much in comfort, but in an experience. And I think for the most part that's what we try to do here— a little more interesting for people, when they're eating. It's important. It's very important.

But I'm the first to tell you that I love what I do but I recognize the fact that everyone has different tastes and you'll never get around that— ever. That's just part of what happens. So, as a young chef, you don't realize it because someone might not like something and you kind of feel insulted. But in essence, it's not that they don't like what you've done— as long as you put 130% into what you make, what else do you expect? As long as you're not making something so horrific and so disgusting that you sort of have something to ask yourself afterwards... you really have to be on the ball, making sure you're working with the very freshest possible ingredients you have around you.

In French cooking, that's what it's taught me— you go into the market and you're looking at the mussels or you're looking at the so many cheeses, the smell of cheese, you're smelling the bread and you want to have that experience— loving things. There aren't many chefs, especially young chefs, who really have that. They have the ability to have a big head and a big ego but they don't really care for what they do. That's like the difference with a guy like Daniel. Daniel is in the kitchen every day working beside the sous chef every day and their main focus is the food and their customers. That's it, and that's the bottom line when you're cooking. Whether it's French, Italian, Indian, Chinese, Japanese— that's what it's all about— the customer's the bottom line. Not you. Not me, I'm here for my customers. I did this menu not for me, but that's how I like to eat and I want my customers to have that same experience I enjoy.

Who have been important influences to you as a chef— in your past, and in Europe?

Barbara Kafka, who I just met recently, is one of these women who've been around for a long and whom I dearly respect— she has an absolutely amazing palate for a woman 68 years old and in terms of France, definitely— Emile Jung from Le Crocodile in Strasbourg— and Antoine Westermen— but even more so Johnny Letzer, who owns a small bistro called Le Boeuf Mode in Strasbourg— he's the guy who taught a friend of mine here in Vancouver how to cook. He's an older guy who's been around— guys like that have been hugely influential— but it doesn't have to be the namesake guys— it's also guys who make a great steak tartare.

What is it about them that influences you?

Their love— that means their sincere love for cooking— and making a tiède de veau and making it perfect and making a tartare. In a party last night I was asked to make a tartare— whose recipe do you think I used? I got that recipe from Johnny four years ago. So I made it up for some friends last night— best tartare they've ever had. That's what I get— the best from everything— I get the best tartare recipe I can find, I find the best brûlée recipe I can find— and I look around and then it's my own. [bangs table]

You know, I adjust things, but then I say, okay, I like the taste of that and I like the taste of that [bangs table]— okay, put it together. Now, that's what I like— I think that's the essence of what I've got here— working with Emile Jung I picked up— I worked with a saucier for three weeks— François— who's been there for eight years. And Emile Jung is known right across Europe for his sauces— as having the most consistently done sauces. So I spent those three weeks and as a result of working for three weeks— this restaurant has become known for its reductions— the different tastes I have in each one. I have eight, nine to 10 stocks going at the same time—

mushroom stock, vegetable stock, chicken stock, roasted chicken stock, lamb stock, veal stock, you name it— the jus in the short ribs you had the other night— the reduction's from that— what you make the sauce with. I understand all that— and that was from those three weeks. You pick up things from everybody.

That's what great food is about— whether it's a reduction, a light jus, or with seafood, whether it's a natural broth from fish— I think all those things play a huge role in food. What it teaches people is that simplicity is much more difficult to achieve than complication— making a very simple and well-done fish stock. It's the basis.

So you have a piece of halibut. You want to make something with the halibut— what's the best way to do it? Use a bit of chicken stock? Chinese might use a little bit of chicken stock, Japanese might use a little bit of chicken stock. Maybe what I'd like to use is a little bit of fish stock made a little bit lighter, or maybe I'd like to use a vegetable stock. But it's those bases which produce the best product. Eric Lippert with Le Bernardin— I'll say his philosophy, his seafood approach, is very simple, but it's the most successful seafood restaurant in New York and possibly the States because of that man— the mentality. Because of taking up an idea where they were brought up in Brittany— where the mussels have to be the best and the oysters have to be the best— the halibut— and it all has to be fresh and... boom, boom, and on the plate— that's what young chefs will have to realize— that that's what real food is all about. And the seasoning— do you use iodized salt? Last night I was at this place and someone passed this [a salt shaker] to me. I don't touch it. I don't have it in my house any more. The salt we use here is sea salt— and we use it in everything— I use the fine salt as well— in absolutely everything.

Can you run me through the creation of your dishes, like the short ribs— and the artichoke soup I had?

Being winter— it's a big time to braise things now— I've had short ribs many times. I love braised things— well, how did I come up with that idea? Everyone in town right now is doing lamb shanks and I don't want to. I want to do something different. I love the quality of the Black Angus products, so

I said to Frank, let's get this and do a nice braised item. I love celery and root vegetables with braised items, so I put a couple of pieces of braised celery with it a celery purée with it, and that's pretty much how I came up with that. And the sauce— it's all about the marinade, it's all about the seasoning— it's all about the length of time you cook it for— how much marbling in the short ribs. The more marbling, the more it's going to fall off once it's cooked. The leaner it is, the tougher it's going to be— now that type of thing was easy to come up with— but it's a great classic dish, an easy dish to make, but also a very elegant dish to make.

Right now we have a ton of artichokes from one of our suppliers and Frank and I were trying to come up with something— and I love to have texture in things— it's important. An example of that would be the gnocchi— gives it a little bit of texture, and the porcini hash adds a little more flavour, a little more texture to it, and the garlic froth adds a little bit of accent to the soup— and you have a nice clean artichoke soup which is a purée with a little bit of vegetable stock— very clean, very simple?

So that's just my angle on food. I don't think it's so much that I come up with an idea, as I'd rather just present you the product— like I present you the artichoke soup. Or halibut— let's make a very simple halibut— let's poach it, let's preserve the flavour of the halibut. So in any creation we make— for example the soup, it's not about trying to come up with something different— it's trying to take the most out of a product and present it in front of you the best way we can.

The foie gras and scallops is a wonderful combination. They both have similar sweetness, similar textures. It's a perfect combination and it's something in French cooking. You look at— and you see the pairing of it and the accompaniments. I love to use mango, I love to use fruit, I love to use fruit acid and sweet and sour to balance out the sweetness of the scallops and the foie gras— something acidic with it to balance it off. It's the combination of the two I enjoy, and we've been doing that for I don't know how long and people love it. And it's one of those things— if people love it, I'll continue to do it.

Now, cooking in New York... what kind of shift do you have to make in a different market than here where your roots are?

Robert Feenie

I think Daniel summed it up for me when I was there two weeks ago. Great cooking inevitably revolves around the food, the product. When you're at a certain level it kind of gets to be the product. But he has a difficult time getting product in New York— and I've had a difficult time getting product in New York. That's been a problem. And, getting to understand a little bit about what's happening in New York, what the flavours are about, what the textures are about, and what people like and what people dislike— that's been a real learning curve— New Yorkers are much different from people in Vancouver. They are sophisticated, they have a lot more restaurants to choose from, a lot of great chefs and a lot of great food in front of them. So their palates obviously are more well-educated than our palates. I don't mean to say that people in Vancouver don't know anything about food; the big factor is being experienced, right? They have more experience eating.

Does that challenge excite you, then?

Hugely. Much more difficult to be successful there. That old scenario— if you make it there you can make it anywhere is very true. And we're on the right road. The restaurant in New York— we've had a huge turnaround— we got three stars in the *New York Post* last Friday. We've got three stars from another upcoming magazine, and Gael Greene has been hearing some good things about it and has been wanting to come in, but we're holding her off for the time being— things could possibly work out really well there for me.

I believe in what I do. I'm not Daniel and I'm not Jean-Georges, I don't have the same level of staffing as them, but I have the same philosophy and the same belief. Daniel's got 10 years on top of me. But I'm at the right point, I'm probably in the same position as when he first started out in New York as well, right? In terms of my ability.

It's not easy being a chef— have there been any low points, times of self-doubt?

I think the only time I've had doubts— personally, I mean, you have no personal life, basically. That's pretty much what I've gone through. To be successful, whether you're a Daniel or whether you're a Joel Robuchon or

Alain Ducasse, you have no life. You eat, breathe and sleep the restaurant. You have to be surrounded by people who understand it. If they don't understand it, that's why a lot of chefs don't end up staying married for too long because they're usually involved in a situation where a balance is important but, really, at the top of the game it's very very difficult when you want to be in the restaurant every night, sometimes six nights a week, and you've got a family— it's difficult, yeah.

So that side of cooking, I mean doubts? I think— if there was a doubt I had— it's that I knew that to achieve my goal, all of this stuff had to be sacrificed.

Yeah, there were times when I'd take breaks and I'd actually quit. I quit a couple of times. If you ask my parents, it's because of that. I knew what it took. I knew a long time ago. Not quite the first year, but I knew after the third year, like, this, this is going to be hard— the hours, money, going through years of making nothing to make something. Even when I first opened this restaurant, the first year, I gave myself nothing.

What brought you back in those times?

I love it. I really truly love it. And now I have to thank my lucky stars that this restaurant survives. I'm just so proud of what I've achieved here, so that looking back on it, it's worth it. Every week I had to work seven days— every day I got yelled at and screamed at, every day I was told, you're no good. Now I go, okay, it's all worth it. But it could have gone the other way. I could have looked at it and this restaurant could have been the exact opposite and then I don't know what I would have done.

But my dad always had a philosophy and that is anything's possible in life I think, for anyone. And when you know it's there, you can either stand there and look at it or you can go for it. I'm always the kind of person that wants that. And everything I've wanted to achieve, that's the way I look at it— whether it's being the best restaurant, doing a cookbook, or doing a TV series, making sure this restaurant is full six nights a week, or whether it's making sure the wine list is recognized now. I set goals and I achieve them.

Do you think that setting goals is really important for every chef?

Me, I look at being the best from a business perspective, 'cause this city, it's a small town, and being at the top of the game in a 50-seat fine dining restaurant, it's important for me to be at the top from a financial standpoint. If this restaurant was to slide down to fifth or sixth or seventh or eighth in people's minds, then I'd slowly start to lose money because of being a small place. But if it can stay being in the top in everyone's mind, in being, okay, special occasions, if we want to go for a great meal, Lumière's the place, we'll go only once every three months, but that's where we're going to go— as long as I can maintain that— from a business standpoint it's important to keep the restaurant in the limelight or in the public eye. So that the restaurant can stay open and I can continue to do what I dream of doing and that's making great food and having fun doing it.

You're now working on the challenge in New York... do you sit down and close your eyes, think about five or 10 years down the line and set goals that far ahead?

Putting Vancouver on the map from a culinary perspective is what I want to do— it's starting to happen slowly. People like Daniel and Jean-Georges and the other chefs I've met in New York— they're wondering about Vancouver now, and the chefs in Toronto— I mean the central part of Canada now is trying to see what's happening in Vancouver.

When I was a kid I told my mom I wanted people to know what Vancouver was— when I was six or seven— and I almost have— and then Expo '86 happened and all of a sudden, boom [claps his hands] people know what Vancouver's all about. We have people moving here now who love what goes on in this city and I think have the kind of emotion about food. And I want the rest of the world to see what we're capable of— now that's probably going to take another 10 years, but it's going in that direction, and it's going to be a real culinary hot spot in the world, and that's what I want to achieve. I want to be one of the leaders in that so that when people come back from Vancouver they will say— Rob Feenie was part of that. And that would make me feel great, because that's what it's all about— getting other people's recognition, not just for myself but the rest of the group of people in this city.

So, you're really rooted to this place— it's really important to you?

More so now. New York has showed me that. Sure, I like going to New York, and it's fascinating, it's sort of nice to meet these guys, know who they are and yadda-yadda-yadda. I'm lucky to be in my position, I think, in terms of the acquaintances I've had with these guys. But, on the flip side of the coin, I get back on the plane and I come back and I really want to sort of challenge them and say, hey, when you come to Vancouver, we can do just the same, if not better.

So, you're committed to this city?

Yeah, oh, yeah... I'm doing this party tonight— it's not something I usually do, but they happen to be some of my best customers. They wanted the room for the night. Usually I'm sitting in the corner here planning my food. Monday nights are when all the ideas come together, when the restaurant's closed. On my own.

So what percentage is here— and in the kitchen?

Oh, six days a week. I don't know if you've noticed? I've been feeling this pull... it's just part of my nature. If I didn't care about it, I'd probably say let's sit here 'til 9 o'clock.

Is it necessary to travel?

All the time. Any chef in travelling has influenced me to a point where I couldn't, I could not do what I do if I didn't have the travelling behind me. And continue to travel like I want to— like I was talking to Tojo last night, once things are organized with his family— I want to go to Japan with him for two weeks— I love this city. I love going to Toronto and I don't mind saying this— and this may be a little blunt from my point of view, but at this stage of the game, we produce much better food than Toronto right now. That wasn't the case 10 years ago, but I think right now, on the whole, we do. I was impressed with Scaramouche, I was impressed with Canoe. I was impressed with Boba— North 44, Centro— but I still think on the whole, we do better.

What other interests do you have?

I run a lot, cycle a lot. Play hockey. Tons of golf. I'm up early— around 7:30 or 8:00. I need it for my mental space. I need to stay in shape to keep this going— because if I let myself fall apart, the restaurant will fall apart.

[Pulling out a pile of food books] I read all the time. I have a huge library in the back.

Do you find it's important to read about food— about the tradition and to keep up?

Yup, always.

Do you think chefs do that enough?

No. In my honest opinion? Seventy-five per cent of the chefs in this world— I know the 25% I admire— 75% do it for the money. They're in a position to make good money and work nine to five and come home at the end of the day; the other guy does it because his name's in the paper, he feeds his ego and his head gets swelled. The other 25% do it because they love it, they really love it.

I happen to have been blessed with the amount of media we've had, but I still never forget where I've got it from. The moment you think you've had it is the moment you've lost it. Like Robuchon and any of these great guys will tell you— because Ducasse is already looking at the next millennium— if you think right now [bangs table] is the way it is— and you're perfect the way you are, you're finished.

And it takes risks..

Of course. This is a huge risk, this new menu. I haven't seen it anywhere in Canada yet. I know people who do tasting menus, but this is a really bold step for me. Basically, it's all you have now. It's three different menus. But that's a huge risk because it's a lot of work on my part.

Where do you go out to eat here in Vancouver—

Tojo's. Japanese, Chinese and Indian. That's the best.

So— what is it that you're looking for that says to you— that's it— the person there knows what he's doing?

When I walk away from Tojo's, I'm not blown away, but I'm feeling comfortable. Going to Hong's on Robson Street... having, having... I don't go to any other restaurant on my night off because I don't get any inspiration from them. They have their own style, they do their own thing and Michael [Noble] does his own thing but my inspiration comes from Chinese and Japanese in this city. People like Tojo, people like Chef Lam at Grand King Seafood— all these guys— that's where I get my influence. Because... they're good at what they do, they're amazing at what they do. You know, Asians, they've been at it a lot longer than the French. That's where I get my niche. Talking to Tojo— we're talking, we're not joking and laughing— it's serious shit, it's talking about seafood, it's talking about stuff freezing, talking about the local albacore tuna, WHY is it so good, what's the secret. Finding out where they fish, finding out where they get their fish— or going to Vikram Vij's [chef-owner of Vij's, critically acclaimed for its stylish signature Indian cuisine]. Eating some of the stuff he makes— it's an experience for you. It's different.

We eat this food every day. I don't want to go to another restaurant that does the same thing that doesn't do anything for me. Then I go to Daniel— yeah, that's different, because that's what we do, but it's two or three notches above what we do. People have come to New York and compared the two restaurants, but I don't because I'm smart enough to realize that we're not quite there yet.

Robert Feenie

Chef Robert Feenie is the Executive Chef and co-owner of Lumière Restaurant. A graduate of the Dubrulle French Culinary School in Vancouver, BC, in 1985, Feenie worked at some of the Lower Mainland's cutting edge restaurants, including Cherrystone Cove (sous chef), Rim Rock Café and Oyster Bar (chef de partie, Whistler, BC) and Le Crocodile (sous chef). While at Le Crocodile, Chef Feenie travelled to Alsace and worked with Emile Jung and Antoine Westermen at Le Buerehiesel (both Le Crocodile and Le Buerehiesel are rated three-stars in the *Michelin Guide*). Feenie and his partner Ken Wai opened Lumière in November, 1995.

Recruited by Maximillan Schnellenger, Feenie is also the consulting chef for the Crown Plaza Hotel in Toronto, Ontario. Chef Feenie's work in Toronto has brought national acclaim, and he is proud to have placed his sous chef, Ned Bell, and many of his Lumière recipes, at the Crown Plaza. In addition, Feenie has undertaken a monumental task in re-structuring the complete dining experience at Le Regence in the Hotel Plaza Athenée in New York City.

Most recently voted one of the top two restaurants in Vancouver by *Gourmet Magazine* Top Tables Poll, Lumière also received the Top Restaurant of the Year award from *Food Service & Hospitality Magazine* in 1998.

Robert Feenie's
BRAISED SHORT RIBS [for four]

INGREDIENTS
2 lb (1 kg) beef short ribs, cut in 2-inch (6 cm) pieces
Salt and freshly ground black pepper, to taste
2 tbsp (30 ml) vegetable oil
1 medium yellow onion, finely chopped
3 garlic cloves, finely chopped
1 c (250 ml) fruity red wine
2 c (500 ml) veal or beef stock
3 sprigs fresh thyme (or 1 tsp dry)
1 bay leaf

METHOD
1. Trim excess fat from beef short ribs. Sprinkle both sides of ribs with salt and pepper.

2. In a Dutch oven, heat oil over medium-high heat. Add ribs and brown on all sides for 5 to 7 minutes. Remove ribs to plate, set aside. Remove all but 1 tablespoon (15 ml) fat from pan.

3. Reduce heat to medium and add onion and garlic to Dutch oven. Cook, covered, for 2 minutes. Add wine and stir to deglaze bottom of pan. Add stock, thyme, bay leaf and browned ribs. Bring to a boil. Transfer pan to preheated oven at 225 F (110 C) for 4 to 5 hours, or until meat is falling off the bones, turning meat occasionally. Remove meat to plate, keep warm.

4. Strain cooking liquid into large saucepan. Bring to a boil and cook for 10 to 20 minutes or until reduced by half. (You should have about 1 3/4 cups (425 ml)). Taste and adjust seasoning. Serve sauce with the ribs.

Daryle Ryo Nagata

Herons, Waterfront Centre Hotel, Vancouver, BC

I frankly admit that Daryle Ryo Nagata struck a deep chord within me. Like me, born east of BC— he, Prairie-bred and raised— Nagata through his father and his paternal grandparents— holds through lineage the common history of prejudice against Japanese Canadians during World War II as well as the cheerier side of fabulous Japanese-Canadian food concocted from often humble ingredients. Of the same generation as a nephew of mine, they both have mothers of British stock. Daryle was seduced by cuisine, by Europe where he worked, speaks French, and has plied his skills in Quebec and Toronto before Edmonton called him back to the West. Now in Vancouver, where super fresh and super cheap sushi and donburi reigns, and working ostensibly with a palate not so dissimilar from mine, he has gained a reputation for a blending of Occident and Orient, acknowledging, too, First Nations contributions along with herbal medicine philosophy. He's been singled out as a chef at an urban hotel complex for his support of small artisan producers. We met for lunch at the spectacularly situated Waterfront Centre Hotel, a table tucked against the towering glass walls, and its vista overlooking the Pacific toward North Vancouver. It was barely a kilometre from Powell Street, the old Japanese-Canadian Little Tokyo, where my late mother had spent some of her childhood.

I don't think I was mistaken to think that we rapidly fell into a common space of thinking and even gestures at this meeting— which gave me the feeling I'd known the chef for some time, as I began by asking him about his roots.

I was born in Lethbridge, Alberta. I'm the youngest of five kids and I'm half Japanese and half Scottish— my heritage, I would be third generation. My father was born and raised in Ocean Falls. He's a BC man— was— until the war and then he moved to Alberta. He got interned in Alberta and that's where my grandparents ended up settling.

I grew up with my grandma's cooking a lot and my grandpa's fishing—

that type of thing— on my Japanese side. He loved to fish. In Lethbridge, there was a lot of trout, whitefish, this type of fishing, and he had a huge huge garden. There was lots of food from the garden. These are my father's parents. My mom was Scottish, and she actually worked in kitchens, and so, I often got a job working as a busboy or a dishwasher. Then I became a prep cook and a broiler cook, making steaks.

One job was in a trendy nightclub, one of the trendiest restaurants in Lethbridge, where Mom worked, and that was just after high school. But throughout high school I was somewhere in a restaurant, working. I worked two or three jobs at once, anyways, so I always had my foot somewhere.

I was actually going to be an electrician, believe it or not, because I figured it was an honest thing to do. You know kids, when they finish school— What're you gonna do? Well, pick something. I was just getting my final math to go to technical school in Calgary for an electrician degree, and I was asked by the hotel there to come and do an apprenticeship because they knew people where I worked at the Oz Restaurant— and so I went there to work and I didn't start my apprenticeship, and I thought, well, it couldn't hurt. At least it'd be easier to find a job while going to school in Calgary. One thing led to another and I put the electrician idea on the wayside and then really became excited even that much more.

Were you excited before with cooking?

Not terribly excited. I always enjoyed cooking, and I'd cook at home— there were five kids, so everyone had their duties. Ever since I was little we had a schedule up, and whether it was cooking— all of us cooked— or we had to take turns cleaning, washing, gardening, garbage— you know— my mom put us to work. [laughing] You've got to, huh?

So then I had to go to Edmonton to go to school to apprentice, because we'd work 10 months, then go to school for two months, and we'd do that for three years. Mine was at NAIT— Northern Alberta Institute of Technology, and I ended up going there and did quite well. I knew the people in the bigger hotels in the bigger cities had a little edge on me, so I got a job at the Westin Hotel in Edmonton and I moved there to finish my apprenticeship. From there I moved to London, England and worked at the Savoy in London.

Daryle Ryo Nagata

How did that happen? That's a pretty big jump.

Well, as an apprentice, even in Lethbridge, I worked with Swiss people and I always had dreams... As an a apprentice, I worked with a lot of international chefs— Japanese, German, Swiss, Italian. There were never any Canadian chefs. It just wasn't happening then, and I knew that if I wanted to become an executive chef at a quality operation at a major hotel I had to get European training. There were just no Canadian chefs, back then, at any major Canadian hotels. So, I aspired to work at the Savoy because, obviously, Escoffier worked there, and he's the Dalai Lama or whatever...

Was it hard to get a job there?

It actually wasn't, surprisingly enough. I sold everything I had and sent my resumes over to 13— my lucky number— 13 of the top hotels in London and... I'd never been on a plane, on a train, never seen the ocean— the farthest east was Saskatoon and the farthest west was the Rockies. I hadn't travelled much, and I got there and got a place and got my *A to Z* and hit up all the places and got probably three good offers and I took the one at the Savoy.

After that I went to Park Hotel in Guernsey where, of course, Victor Hugo had a little house on the hotel grounds. And then back to the Hilton on Park Lane in London, then to Geneva, Switzerland, to Hotel La Réserve. I was in London and Europe about three years. Then I came back to work at La Nouvelle Réserve, a French-Italian restaurant in Quebec City, which was kind of funny— I'd just seen an ad on the plane for this restaurant called La Nouvelle Réserve and I just applied. After that I went to the Chateau Laurier in Ottawa, then to the Sheraton Centre in Toronto, then I came back to the Edmonton Inn. Then I went to the Hyatt Regency here— and then in '91 I came to the pre-opening of this hotel, before there were any floors or chairs, and I've been here ever since. It's the longest job I've held down. [laughs]

But that was my goal, when I finished my apprenticeship— to work one year, one year, one year, approximately, in different areas. Different chefs have different management skills. Different operations have different clientele— a different abundance of products— or not— and as a sous chef I wanted to do a year and a half, a year and a half, a year and a half.

It was very hard. It was hard to leave the Savoy, it was hard to leave Switzerland. People would say, come on, Nagata, why don't you stay?, you know. It's hard to leave a good thing, there's no question, but I felt that for me to grow to my potential I had to work with other people in different areas, you know? Each time you go into a place it's a huge challenge to prove yourself again. It's easy to stay in one place and be comfortable.

You must be pretty disciplined in your mind, once you get a vision or an idea?

Most definably. I think I have very good discipline. I took a lot of martial arts when I was younger. It's a lot to do with control. In martial arts you need a lot of mental control— I mean, you learn physical control but you have to do it mentally to do it physically— it's all tied in. I think my whole time on my trip what I learned was... I came from Lethbridge Alberta, and it was always, oh, Swiss this or French this, and these people are great. I went over there and the funny thing that I found was that it's not where you're from, but who you are inside.

I saw flunkies over there working in the Savoy. I saw flunkies working in Switzerland with even more experience than me. I've seen good people, too— don't get me wrong— but, it's the drive you have inside. It's one of those things. Be careful what you ask for, you just might get it, and if you try hard enough. I've always been a person to stick by my convictions and support myself in good and bad times and I've never been one to shoulda coulda woulda.

If I do it— if I did it— I obviously wanted it badly enough. If I never accomplished it, or haven't accomplished it, I guess I didn't want it badly enough, did I? And that's what I've always thought.

Did you ever question that when you were doing all this travelling and moving?

Totally. Oh, many times, many times. I thought, what the hell am I doing here? This is crazy!

Maybe I was working for somebody who was a complete lunatic, who really wasn't the quality I expected, but I didn't let that ruin my career aspirations. I stuck with it. Or perhaps, as a sous chef, I wanted to be a chef, and I was frustrated because I wasn't promoted yet and did I want to do this and— yeah, you question, I think that's a definite, but...

You never got to the point of really giving it up? It's hard work...

No, no. It's hard work but it's a great passion. I really get a lot of pleasure out of making people happy and this is one of the few businesses you can actually produce a product and watch someone consume it. I mean, if you sell a car to somebody, he's gone and you probably won't see him enjoy it that much. You might hear from him every now and again if something's wrong. In this industry, a plate is put in front of you. You can see the reactions on the person's face or— often, if you're a chef— you can walk into the restaurant and talk to them...

For me, the team spirit is great as well. I love working in teams and developing a team. My goal as an apprentice was to be a highly competent chef— not just a chef, but a highly competent chef— and to raise apprentices. I have nine apprentices here at the hotel and my last apprentice won the best apprentice award for Vancouver, which I'm proud of, and take very seriously because I like giving back, too. We have to— to raise our own. They're not walking through the door.

So this passion came from all these different experiences under different chefs?

You know, I think the passion grows, every day, every year. I certainly had it when I was an apprentice. I have it today— my resolve— and to me there are different things you can get out of it. Probably, one of the most gratifying things is being part of a team, because you know we do about 1,000 to 3,000 meals a day in the hotel. We have 24,000 square feet of convention space— one multi-purpose restaurant. It's very busy— breakfast, lunch and dinner, room service, outside catering. We have 400 staff to feed— who we take very good care of and feed very well, because they're our guests as well.

You know, the greatest satisfaction is having a great team— helping other people develop and watching them grow. When I look back over the years, I see how much I've grown in a year and it makes me feel good. But it REALLY makes me feel good when I look back over the years and I remember this person or that person and how they used to be and how straight their back is now and how much a huge contributing factor to the team they are now as opposed to before.

Why is that important to you?

Well, I guess I'm a giving person. I suppose— maybe it's a selfish thing— I just get great satisfaction out of pleasing clients. In this industry, if the only motivation was money, there wouldn't be a lot of people in it— you're not going to become a multi-millionaire working as a chef in a hotel unless you're really good at investing. So that's not the motivational factor. For me, the motivational factor is people— my being able to make myself feel good about my customers, feel good about their experiences, to make the team feel good about their experiences with me as the leader. So, that's the biggest part— my team.

Is there someone who instilled that in you— someone you still look up to?

I've seen a lot. I've seen some very abusive people. I've seen people get smacked and beaten up— people slammed up against the wall, slapped around and thrown against the wall, thrown out of the kitchen...

I remember once when I was in Switzerland we had this young kid, his name was Paolo, and my chef de partie— [he was kind of crazy, eh?]— he would say, okay, Paolo, I want you to do 15 dents de lion out of melon de Cavaillon. So he would grab a knife and, boom boom boom boom, show him how to do it. See? Boom. Put it back together and... now you do 15 of them. He wouldn't coach him through this. Then he says, you screw up and you eat every one of them and you have five minutes to get your ass moving. So this is crazy, eh? [laughing]

So this kid's going to fail for sure, right? And he wouldn't let us go near him. And the kid screwed up, and the chef grabbed him and stuffed it in his face and the kid was crying... I mean, crazy... So, yeah, I've seen a lot of good and bad— and I think it's as important to learn from the bad as the good.

I think, as far as kitchen leaders go, probably the greatest leader I've ever worked with was Heinz Wagner of the Sheraton Centre in Toronto. An incredible, incredible man...

Beforehand, I was taught the "make you or break you" philosophy. Heinz, he's very competent, very capable, but he does it with style and class. If you have people do it because they want to it's much easier. It takes more time to get people to do that— a quick fix is to put a gun to a guy's head and say move and do it quickly— but you're going to be replacing staff constantly. You can't turn your back— you always have to be around because you can't trust your staff because they can't trust you. It's not a very good working environment. If somebody was to ask me what's my favourite tool, that would be a well-honed kitchen brigade. It's team effort. I can't do a thousand meals by myself. I wouldn't want to. [laughs]

What makes that up?

I would say that 99.9% of the challenges we have in the workplace relate back to communication. One way or another, communication— communicating effectively. If I say to an apprentice, take this chicken and put it in the Buffalo chopper and chop it up, and he throws it in bone and all and screws up the Buffalo chopper— I could scream and yell at him and call him a loser— whatever— but I have to look at myself, too. Whom was I asking to do this and was I specific, and that's communication...

What I often tell my staff is, figure us out. We spend more time with each other than we do with our wives and our families. I courted my wife for years and asked her to marry me— you really choose to love and be with your wife. And here, you take a job, and you don't really get to choose who you're working beside. You're spending a lot of time with your co-workers and you have to enjoy it and communicate effectively and not intimidate people and discourage them from asking questions— you have to empower them to make decisions and supporting then and give them the right tools to succeed. So, it's a very long process.

It's a balance. There are three areas to look at— there's financial, there's guest service index— the quality of the product and service you're providing— and there's the employee. So, you can be nice to your employee, but if you have poor financial— and you let them do what they want and guests aren't getting a consistent product, that's no good. And if you're mean to all your employees but have great food costs and great quality of food, you're going to be replacing staff left, right and centre— and in this country there are not a hundred better people lined up at the door. It's not realistic. Financially— you can have great financial, but if the staff doesn't get breaks, or you sell something that's not worth it because of saving on your food costs... You need the three— a balance of good financial, good employee relations and good technical product.

Was there something you brought back with you, in terms of your understanding about food, from Europe?

It's something that's been ongoing anyway— and not particularly in Europe. The main thing I brought back is that there's a whole big world out there and we can compete. I can compete on that level, no problem. You have different customers over there. If you start doing something very fancy in Switzerland, which is a very conservative country— you know, *just give me my Zurichoise and don't give me the edible flowers...* I mean, things change there, too. The integrity of the product there is something you definitely bring back— good vegetables, good meat, just good products. You can't make good food with crappy products. [laughs] You have to make sure the stuff you're getting is a high quality product.

Do you think people here get away with inferior products in general?

No, I think things are changing. I think things have come a long way in Canada. I think we have an outstanding agriculture business here. It's a phenomenal business that we have here. We export a lot of high quality products. I buy these beans from this lady in Saskatchewan— who has 30 different types of heirloom beans— and 99% of them she sends to Germany. I buy the other 1%.

How did you find her?

Just through this organization I used to be a co-director of, Cuisine Canada. I've been involved in that and I was the chairman of the food for the conference here called Northern Bounty II, and she was here— I'm always foraging...

Along with having good organizational skills and a well-honed team, a great thing for a chef is having resources and being able to have at his beckon a wide variety of products that are out there. It's just a matter of finding who has them— like this lady who has these heirloom beans or the person who dives for goeduck or who gets the sea urchin for me or the Arctic muskox or the wild asparagus. You know, all of these things— they're out there. It's just finding who has them and developing a relationship with those people. I belong to another organization called Farm Folk/City Folk and that's a another prime example of communication.

I have the chefs banging their heads wondering why they can't get these different types of squash, or whatever it might be— and all these farmers saying, gee, I wish I could make more money in the wintertime or in the fall. Why not have them talk together and say, why don't you grow me these types of tomatoes and these types of potatoes and these types of squash and I'll buy them from you. You know, what a concept! [laughs]

Where does this approach come from— not everybody is doing this...

I feel strongly about supporting Canadian producers and growers and working with them to help them develop their product, market their product. It's very important and I've been a big supporter of the local and Canadian suppliers, helping them and giving them the feedback they need. It's growing— it has grown, and will continue to grow.

It's something that used to be 75, maybe even 50 years ago. With the developments in transportation and communication we see tomatoes in

December and we eat asparagus in wintertime. You can fly it in from all over the world at a reasonable cost. Now people are saying, no, let's go back to eating seasonally, let's go back to eating regionally, and people are doing it. It's not like it's something new, but it's been lost.

Where did this idea come from with you?

I have a passion for Chinese medicine and the ways of foods I grew up with— Daryle, eat this because it's good for this. At one time, people ate seasonally and things were available seasonally because they did certain things to your body— whether bitter greens detoxified your body in springtime because you needed to clean your body system out— because of all the nuts and preserves you would eat in the winter, and the fruit would flush it out in the summer and prepare you for the winter. Pretty much every food or herb has some type of medicinal property to it. It's been a big passion of mine since I came to Vancouver. I think a great deal of it came from my wife, who's very health-conscious. She grew up with an Austrian mother who's very into whole grains and healthy foods and eating seasonally, as they do in Europe. Like I say, it's nothing new, but it's something we kind of lost here in Canada. But I think people are getting back into that.

We did a promotion here some time ago, just as I was starting my herb garden. We had the Imperial Herbal Restaurant here from Singapore and we had the owner, the maître d', the three chefs and the doctor. And, of course, the doctor would come in and take your pulse on the left hand, take your pulse on the right hand, look at your tongue and tell you what ails you. And people laugh at this and think, B.S. So, fair enough. And he was bang on every time— you know, you've got kidney problems, you've got liver problems, you've got problems with migraines, don't you? So you need more ying or you need more yang...

I was into this spa thing for a while, but I've never been one to count calories. I don't believe the Canada Food Guide is what it should be. I think it's driven a lot by the Canadian dairy farmers, grain growers and cattlemen. Yes, I believe people should eat balanced diets, but there isn't one diet that fits all. People come from different backgrounds. Some shouldn't be eating dairy at all because there's too much mucus in it. Some are okay with it. Some should be eating grains, some shouldn't. You have to listen to your body and I believe strongly in that. That's my passion— eating seasonally, eating smart, a little bit listening to your body and getting back a little bit closer to the earth— less processed food...

You've just moved into a new menu. Give me an example of what you want to offer people.

One of our great dishes would be the chicken pot au feu. It's got roasted squash, pumpkin gnocchi— all the root vegetables are in it. It's quite seasonal. Again, it's one thing— I have a business to run, too, so people still demand certain things. I can't only run a hotel here with seasonal product and say, no lettuce because it's out of season here and it comes from California. So sorry. [laughs] But there are certain things we can do.

We have giant sea scallops here. They are from near Alaska— the Prince Rupert area— large scallops. And you have the salmon dish here. It's lightly pan-fried, it's natural— a little salt and pepper and a little bit of citrus or butter on top of it.

You mentioned your background— your grandparents— your grandfather's garden. Does anything come back from those days in your approach?

Oh, yeah. Some of the greatest memories are of harvest time— tons of lima beans, picking through those and— pulling a carrot out of a garden, washing it, and putting it in your mouth— there's no flavour like it. I mean there's flavour there... tomatoes...

For me, tofu, making fresh tofu, the smell of tofu— listening to the blender going— and the smell... I make tofu for my kids at home. You can buy tofu, it's a good product, but it's totally different if you make it fresh, and especially if you make soya milk, which my kids love. I make warm soya milk— you get a little bit of carob and a little bit of maple syrup and, man, it's the healthiest chocolate milk or hot chocolate, you can come by. And it's fresh soya milk.

So, you're going back to your present day life and your background—

That's right. They're great memories, and many studies say the most powerful memory that you have is smell— more powerful than anything. People will often walk into an area and smell something and have a déjà vu about when they were a little kid in the apple orchard, or whatever it might be. And it's often triggered by smell. So, [laughing] because I work in a kitchen, not that I sit there and daydream about my childhood all the time, but often, you know, I look at food and I have great respect for it— great respect for the products we have, and we treat them with respect and make sure my suppliers realize that.

You spent a lot of time with your grandparents on your father's side. Do you have very strong memories about that food? You ate a lot of Japanese food?

Lots. One of my favourites in summertime is making fresh somen— and icy somen and... I mean, it doesn't get much better than that— umeboshi, which not everyone likes. At home I eat a lot of Japanese food— making inari sushi and different types of maki roll, tempura and sukiyaki, miso soup— udon noodles.

I used to watch my grandma cook all the time. For me, one of the exciting things, as a little kid, was standing there watching my grandma cook. I don't know why. I just [laughing] thought it was cool. How she would take the little obliment out of the egg with a chopstick. I thought it was amazing. How she would prepare stuff— okara, for example. When I make tofu I save the okara and then have cold okara on hot rice. It's the kind of peasant food that people would normally throw away. Tofu is very high in protein but very low in fibre. Okara is very low in protein but very high in fibre because you separate it when you're making it. I enjoy that.

We have a Japanese breakfast buffet here— every day— and for special meals and for special guests I'll use some of that in my cooking.

"Fusion" has been used to describe some of your food. Is it influenced in particular by Asian food?

Daryle Ryo Nagata

Probably more so for me because of my background. It's kind of natural for me. It's really part of my style. Instead of making a regular consommé en croute, I would perhaps make a consommé of ginseng chicken— a chicken that's grown here that's fed ginseng and vegetables— so it's a ginseng chicken. It's a kind of elixir. A consommé of that and put in it some shelled soya beans, some wolfberries, which are good for your eyes— it's Chinese medicinal medicine— and instead of covering it with puff pastry, cover it with a spring roll wrapper and make a stamp on it with, for example, Valentines, a heart with an arrow through it, or a Chinese signature, and tie it with a gourd. Then, when you bake it, you have a nice stencil on it. Then you just hit it and crack it open instead of a big puff.

Instead of your typical bombe Alaska we do individual bombes with a mixture of green tea ice cream, raspberry sorbet and mango. On our fresh sheet we'll have a sample plate— so you'll have some maki rolls, some tempura vegetables, spring rolls, maybe a little bit of kimchi— I do a lot of East Indian cooking. I love curries, I have a great passion as well for many of the areas in Asia— Thai, Indian Malay, Singapore— not just Japan— satays, all that kind of stuff...

In terms of palate— not just out here in BC, but everywhere, there's a trend towards introducing very Asian elements. Do you think you have a different approach because of your background and your own palate?

That's a good question because, for me, I don't cook for my palate. I cook for my guests. I think it's important where you live, knowing who your clientele is. For example, with catering— you have a banquet for 500 people or convention coming with 2,300 people. I don't want them to send a regular menu. I expect the catering manager to come and ask me, are they 300 women from Japan or 300 Texas oilmen? They're going to eat different things. They're going to want different things. In the restaurant here we have a large number of Asians— Japanese, Chinese, Taiwanese, etc. They love seafood. They love these different types of lotus root, and gai lan and bok choy. One of our most successful dishes was a spring roll which we stuffed with pomme purée and some Asian vegetables served fried with a red Thai curry sauce on the bottom with a Chilean sea bass. For me, I think it's important to realize who your clientele is. I say I don't cook to my taste— yeah, to some degree, naturally it will come out in my style— but I try to anticipate. And I think I have a good idea of what my clientele wants. I'm not the type of person who makes, for example, here in Vancouver, osso buco. I put it on the menu— you can make the best osso buco there is but you're going to sell maybe one a day. What's the point?

When I was in Quebec City one of the biggest sellers was a cervelles de veau. You put that on the West Coast here, people aren't into it. Sweetbreads? They're not really into it. If you were a small French restaurant where people go for that, fine. But if you're in a hotel restaurant— we're more of a Pacific Northwest or BC regional type of restaurant here... Again, you have to listen to your clients.

One of our most important tools is our fresh sheet. It has about eight different items. Some of them we keep weekly, but about half of them we change daily. From there we get a great idea— the way we word it and the type of feedback we get— of what the customers are saying. I can make the best scallops, but if the customers aren't buying it and the customers actually don't like it...

So where is the balance in terms of a chef's personal vision and innovation and the reassurance and comfort that the customer seeks?

I think you have to listen to your customers and you also have to educate them. If I want to educate my customer on the latest BC emu or BC ostrich, I'm not going to put out a big tournedo of ostrich— a big four ounce piece of filet of ostrich— we will often buy it like that— as their dinner. What I'll do is put out a trilogy of lamb, which they love, beef tenderloin, which is safe, and a little satay of ostrich. They'll buy it like crazy because it gives them an opportunity to say, hey, I tried it and it was pretty good.

You can bring them on that way. So, there are ways of getting the feedback you want. It's easy to be complacent. It's easy to say, if it ain't broke, why fix it? Especially with cuisine. There are classic dishes and they're fine, but there's innovation as well, and people want to be excited, people want to try something new— and you don't have to get too kinky about it.

Daryle Ryo Nagata

Do some chefs get too kinky?

Most definitely. And there are some chefs who bastardize cuisine in many different ways; they take a dish and completely destroy it— the integrity of the ingredients of a dish— having 15 different flavours in a dish— a dish that has this taste and that taste and this taste and that taste— so many strong flavours coming at you that in the end, someone asks, how was your dessert, and what did you like about it, but you couldn't even figure it out. Certain flavours you can mix together that marry nicely and make a complete taste.

With your Scottish- and Japanese-Canadian background, do you think you might have any kind of advantage because you understand the potential and integrity of certain ingredients and cooking techniques— say, if it was Japanese?

Oh, yeah. When I say I don't cook from my palate— it's not entirely true, because, subliminally, I do, though intentionally, I don't. There are certain cuisines, certain ingredients, that you have to know how to use. If you aren't educated about them, if you don't know what a good olive oil is, you won't know what to do with them. And if you don't know that, you'll have a hard time cooking Italian cuisine. If you don't know what a good semolina pasta is, you'll have a hard time cooking Italian cuisine. Or risotto.

You do find all kinds of exotic ingredients listed on menus of young chefs straight out of school...

You see that. People can write what they want on paper. But can they deliver it? That's the challenge. One of the things for me, and my wife always kind of wonders— I'll never order pasta in a restaurant unless it's a very good restaurant, because pasta is very delicate, and if you don't know how to cook it properly, if you don't do it properly, it's ruined, it's disgusting. It's got to be done right. I won't order pasta unless I know there's a good chef who knows pasta.

If I go to a— because I have kids— into a restaurant— I'll kind of [laughing] look at the restaurant and say, I wonder what they could do best— and that's what I'll order and [laughing] I'm usually quite successful at it. But don't expect me to go to one of these family restaurants and order. I'm not saying it won't happen— people do things well and people have things on the menu that perhaps are ego things that probably shouldn't really be there. I can be— because I'm in the business— not necessarily snobby, but picky, as far as what I like... But, by the same token, I'm very appreciative of what it takes to produce a quality product, so I'm not a snob when it comes to that.

.   People often say— my chiropractor says— oh, gee, you know, a friend of mine invited a chef over to dinner— god, geez... can you imagine? It was funny because I remember my mother— before I was an apprentice, when I was quite young, a dishwasher— she came home and said, oh, I got this new job. I'm working at this place and there're three Swiss chefs there— which is a big thing for Lethbridge— and she says, could you imagine their parents when they come home for supper; can you imagine how intimidating that would be? Maybe, subliminally, wanting to make my mom proud of me, I became a chef— who knows, right? There are a lot of head shrinks down there probably narrowing it down to something close to that, but, like I said to the chiropractor, if anything, when I go to people's houses, I can really appreciate the love it took to make the meal and I don't judge people at all, well, he should have garnished it with this, he should have...

But on the other hand, if you're going to a place and paying for something... well, then there are different expectations. If I'm going to a restaurant and I'm paying good money for something, and I feel I'm getting ripped off, I'm not getting value... I'm not one to cause a stink, but I'm not going to come back. I simply won't.

Do you think enough people cause a stink?

No. Especially Canadians. Most Canadians— and, in fact, that's a problem with our industry— do not complain. We take complaints very very seriously. And we have very few here. But when we do get them, we phone them up, we follow up and thank them for their feedback and take action, whichever way we can. It's very important.

Daryle Ryo Nagata

When I talk to other chefs they talk about a certain number of components to make a dish— how about you?

I never really thought of that. I guess it comes naturally, but, there's the eye appeal, there's the taste, and you need to have colour on the plate; it's got to look presentable. When people first see it they are going to form an opinion— a first impression. If it looks like something palatable, then they're going to get excited about it and, if it tastes good, they're going to enjoy it. I don't really try to get complicated about the food. Maybe it's wrong.

But how about numbers of flavours?

Well flavour-wise, it really depends on what it is. For example, a curry. You need 15 to 20 different spices to make a good solid curry. Nothing wrong with that, right? But certain dishes have delicate ingredients in them and you have to be careful that they're not overpowered because the seasoning or spice that's supposed to enhance the product has now taken over the product— and it's not what it really is. If you have a scallop and you have some vegetables or whatever, there are certain things to bring out— to give it something. But, if it's overpowering, you've lost the whole idea of it— unless it is your idea to completely take it over with that flavour.

It's a great honour to work in a place like Vancouver. The multiculturalism here really allows us to have a wide variety of products at hand. Chinatown is full of all these vegetables. We have Greeks, Italians— so we have all these great olive oils brought over, and so on and so forth. We have a wide variety of products available right here in Vancouver. Of course, the ocean is here, we have great fruit growing, and I really get a lot of unique berries, like Chinese gooseberries, kiwi grapes the size of a gooseberry. I get them from a special guy in Delta. Every year, they usually call me first. We have red currants, black currants, white currants. We do a lot preserving here. I really enjoy preserving and drying all our own fruits. The kiwi grapes are great— they're a little bigger than a grape, and you cut them in half and they look like a kiwi and they taste like a kiwi. Salal berries, which the Native Indians... I have a great passion for Native North American cuisine. I enjoy making pemmican and making bannock and serving it in modern fashion.

We'll often do a VIP function where we'll turn the ballroom into a longhouse and we'll get all the native art, totem poles and trees, and visitors really like it. We'll have some Mounties standing there and stuff— those are some of our really popular ones.

I know there can be problems and failures in the kitchen— but there must be laughs, too...

We always plan for the unexpected. You have to. I like to have fun at work and they're always things that are funny. There is a joke with the apprentices, a classic. You send the apprentice two blocks up to Hotel Vancouver to get a soufflé pump if a soufflé is falling. Or send him across the street to the Pan Pacific for a "long stand"— and they just tell them to stand there. Or give them a bunch of caraway seeds and get them to chop them in half lengthwise— or mince flour—

Often there's humour we find in the day for our own sanity.

Well, it is tough work— and hard on personal life, isn't it?

It can be. For many years when I was an apprentice my sole concentration was on my professional life. I always said that if I did have a successful professional life, I would never have a successful personal life.

I remember dating this girl. I had dated her throughout my apprenticeship and she moved to Edmonton to go to university. We had gone out for four years, but then came the time I had to travel, which I knew I had to do. I told her she couldn't come with me because I didn't want her to follow me around— I mean I loved her, but I didn't want her to follow me around and not pursuing her dream, even though she didn't know what it was. That was tough.

And, you know, I've always been able to excel in anything I've done. I've often thought, if I really want to do it, I've often done really well in it. I believe very strongly in visualization. Playing lacrosse as a child I always visualized... before it was in the news I used to do it all the time. I'd close my eyes and dream how I would do something the next day— how I would score the goal, how I would do this— or how I would work the next day.

Before I even walked into work, I would know exactly how many steps I would take— turn left, get this, walk over here, grab three spoons, one ladle, six pots, two of these one of those, go over here, open the fridge, grab six limes, two lemons, two tomatoes, boom boom. I always like to make it a science. I've always been a strong believer in planning. It's very important.

So, I've always excelled. I remember, in Switzerland, I lived in Geneva— or just outside it— and we'd do the Autostop sometimes— or a straight walk, and it would be half an hour if I missed the train on a split shift, and I always did a lot of walking and thinking. I remember walking back— how in two months I had become in charge of garde-manger. My chef de partie was gone and I was in charge and how I was doing really well but realizing that I wasn't really happy because even though I was doing well, beyond everybody's expectations, I knew deep inside that I could do a lot better, and for some reason, walking on that road, it hit me, [snaps fingers], my personal life sucked. And not only did it go that way, but it went the other way. If I expected a good professional life, I better have a damned good personal life.

So, from that time on, it became a new priority of mine. People who think they can keep their workplace at home are fooling themselves. Things happen in our lives, right? And you have to marry it together. There are times I work 16, 18 hour days— seven, 12, 15 days in a row sometimes. But there are some days when it's sunny out, it's not that busy and I take the day off with the family— and why not? Every year I take a month's vacation.

Some people say— how can you do that? Well, first of all, I train my staff well— if I can't do that then I'm not a very good trainer— and not only that, I need to shut myself off if I expect to grow every year. I need to get out of the box, to get away from it— into something else— my family. I think I balance it very well— and it's not by chance. I make a conscious effort, because if I don't, I know I won't succeed professionally.

Where do you see yourself— five, 10 years down the line?

I don't think I'll be here in five years. I'd be surprised if I was here in a year or two. It's going to be one of the toughest places to leave. But you have to cut the umbilical cord sooner or later. [laughs] I probably see myself moving into a director of food and beverage— and then, I would see myself being a director of operations and being a general manager of a hotel. Then again, I can see myself being an executive chef all my life.

It doesn't interest me to open my own restaurant. You know, it goes back to lifestyle. I work really hard and here I can take a month's vacation every year. I get a salary, I get dental. If I have a problem, I phone human resources and put some ads in the newspaper; I phone an engineer to fix my stove. I have the utmost respect for people who run their own restaurants, but for me to take a bunch of money I have in my assets and throw it into something to maybe make what I make here in the first year, it's not worth it to me. It really isn't. And it really doesn't excite me, because I like a lot of variety and a lot of different things. I love cooking, but I also love dealing with people. I love organizing teams. I like the industry as a whole. I love talking about it with people like you— to share things with other people. That they're also passionate about it is also a very exciting thing. It's a very great satisfaction. As satisfying as cooking for somebody. I like talking about food, and the things you're passionate about.

Are you excited about the way things are going in Canada?

I am. Canada, I think, is really coming of age. I think they're really starting to support and take an interest in their local community farmers, and I see that growing. I think they see the importance of it. The quality of cuisine in Canada is outstanding. You talk about Jamie Kennedy, John Higgins— there're equally as many on the West Coast— and in Montreal and on the East Coast. There are a great number of talented chefs. Today, an apprentice can finish his apprenticeship and get the training that I had to go to Europe to get— well, didn't have to— but it's very doable in Canada now. Nowadays you don't need to go... you can get it right here. That's an accomplishment in itself— an indication that we're headed in the right direction.

Daryle Ryo Nagata

Daryle Ryo Nagata was born of a Scottish mother and Japanese father, and enjoys combining regional ingredients from various cultures as he specializes in Canadian cuisine; incorporating his own philosophies on healthy eating while protecting natural simplicity of taste and look have become trademarks of his. He is the Executive Chef at Vancouver's Waterfront Centre Hotel.

Chef Nagata has recently planted a 2100 square foot herb garden on the hotel's third floor terrace where he grows fresh herbs for use in his recipes and fresh garnishings. Chef Nagata feels a strong desire to pass on his gift to others and thus maintains active involvement in the development of apprentices.

When asked what he wishes for Canadians, Chef Nagata said, "To eat seasonally, to return to our connection with the land and to practise all the age-old forms of preservation from drying to pickling."

Daryle Ryo Nagata's

CHARBROILED FILET OF BABY COHO SALMON WITH A WARM SUNDRIED CRANBERRY CAPER VINAIGRETTE [for six]

6 x 4 oz boneless baby coho filets (skin on)
4 tbsp sundried cranberries
2 tbsp capers
1 tsp garlic (finely diced)
1 tbsp shallots (finely diced)
2 tsp thyme (fresh)
2 tsp pink peppercorns
6 pieces lemon wedges (skinless or rindless)
6 pieces lime wedges (skinless or rindless)
1 tsp chives (finely diced)
2 c red wine vinegar
4 tbsp canola oil
3 c water
2 tsp cayenne pepper

METHOD

Charbroil or barbecue filets of baby coho on medium-high heat for approximately 3 minutes on each side, and serve with warm vinaigrette on top, either on a salad or with potatoes or rice and vegetables.

To make vinaigrette, simply mix all the ingredients together in a jar, shake well with the lid on and refrigerate for at least a day. To heat up the vinaigrette for serving, pre-heat a sauce pan on medium heat for a half a minute and add the vinaigrette.

ROSEMARY & THYME SHORTBREAD COOKIES [makes 8 cookies]

INGREDIENTS
3 tbsp unsalted butter
1 1/2 tbsp fine granular sugar
1/2 c all-purpose flour
1 tsp thyme (freshly chopped)
1 tsp rosemary (freshly chopped)
1/2 tsp flower petals (fresh)

METHOD

Cream the butter and sugar together with a wooden spoon or electric mixer until smooth. Slowly add in the flour, herbs and flower petals. Mix until consistency allows the formation of a small ball. Roll out the ball to 1/2 to 1/4 inch thick. Cut out desired shapes. Bake on non-stick paper or pan at 325 F for 15-20 minutes or until slightly brown. Cool and dust with sugar and serve.

Michael Noble

Diva, Metropolitan Hotel, Vancouver, BC

The name of Michael Noble first entered my files in 1996. I was living in Paris at the time, but I was back in Canada on my way to Japan via Vancouver where I had an assignment to do a guide-to-the-city piece for a magazine. Diva, and Noble's designs for it at the Metropolitan Hotel, then undergoing renovations, was still a few months off, still just a vision. When I returned to Vancouver in 1997 and then again in 1998, Diva had become that vision turned, according to the critics, Top Table success both years. I was interested to hear from Michael Noble, who had steered this from floor-plan to this important elegant address which expressed the evolution of Pacific Northwest cuisine. He has spent most of his life as a Lower Mainlander, and is of that generation of chefs who came on the heels of the important classically and European-trained chefs, to spearhead local cuisine in a city and, in fact, province where there's been probably more fierce pride in regional food and wine than anywhere in English Canada. The cooking, rich in flavours and sensory surprises, is in his hands, judiciously anchored, much like Diva's design itself, where the au courant kitchen is surrounded by a room of solid sophistication. I met Michael in Diva, for morning coffee. It was that quiet before the energy started to go in full tilt for the day's lunch and dinner service.

He seemed mellow, relaxed after the high energy of the night before, when he'd overseen dinners of a chef's table, mine among them, from Diva's open-to-view kitchen.

I was born in Calgary, and lived there till I was about 10 years old. I've lived in Vancouver since about 1970, so it's really home.

Where'd you grow up, whereabouts?

Just south of Vancouver, and I actually live out that way again, so I've kind of never really left that area. I think I'm pretty lucky to have grown up in a city that I can actually do this profession in. I have all of my family here, so it means a lot, having a wife and three kids, to have all the grandparents in the same area, and all the aunts and uncles. I think it's important to have that balance in life.

You spent the early part of your life in Calgary, and now you're known for your signature cuisine of the Pacific Northwest. What is it, actually?

It's a tough type of cooking to define, but I think the most important thing about it is that it's very much rooted in both the products and the ethnic influence of the Pacific Northwest. I really believe in using, and kind of featuring, as many local products as I can, and I live in a good area to do that. The obvious thing is the seafood, which can be one of the most inconsistent things to be able to depend on getting local and fresh. When you tell people that, they think you're crazy, but it's a lot of political stuff. We have wonderful growers, and on top of that, such an ethnic mix. The obvious thing is the Pacific Rim, but that extends into high influence... you've got Indian... there's a lot to it. I don't think Pacific Northwest cooking is anything new— we're not recreating the wheel— we're only customizing the wheel to what our local bounty is and to what our most direct influences are.

I think it's a very natural approach. It was interesting being part of the Canadian Culinary Team and having the opportunity to travel and cook, and talk to chefs from, first of all, all across Canada. That was really the first time I'd ever done a lot of that, and it was absolutely amazing... I thought, when we went to Toronto or Halifax or Ottawa or wherever, that the cooking would be the same as what we do here, but it's really different. I find the cooking in the Eastern part of Canada to be a little more complicated, more layers of flavours and so on. Here, we're a three to five component style, and I don't think that's only my style. I find that's pretty indigenous to a lot of chefs in BC. Very uncomplicated, but complex at the same time; not necessarily obvious flavours going together, but yes, flavours that do marry well. We maybe take something traditional and then put a little twist onto it.

An example might be our braised lamb shank on our dinner menu. We actually marinate the lamb shank with Szechuan spices, cook it off, and then put the lamb shank on a whipped potato made with scallion oil. It's traditional, but then it's got some of our Pacific Northwest influence.

Take me through a 30-second summary of the evolution of Pacific Northwest.

It's really tough to put a date or to say exactly, but we started something like this... Some people who mentored me, in different ways— the first one probably would have had to have been Kerry Sear. I originally worked with him in 1987 at the Four Seasons in Vancouver. He has since moved to Toronto and now is in Seattle. He's English, but he did a lot of his cutting of teeth in the cooking profession here in BC. He had some maybe overly "interesting" combinations early on in his career, but I think then mellowed some of those out to kind of do something unique, again rooted in traditional methods but with some unique twists. Bernard Weber and I go back all the way to my apprenticeship. He's Swiss, but a very forward thinking Swiss. Nothing against the Swiss, but that's something pretty unique. He has a real passion for cooking and I think you can develop your cuisine through passion as well, by not being comfortable with the status quo, by looking for what's new and interesting— not to mention the fact that technically he's a wonderful cook, and I think all good cooking, no matter where it is, is based on technique. It all goes back to Auguste Escoffier and the boys way back in France. You can't break those rules without going off the track the wrong way.

The man I look up to as "my mentor" is Bruno Marti, with whom I was also involved on the culinary team. We go back a long ways. Bruno is a chef who taught me to be a little more spontaneous. I worked with Bruno directly only for about five months. We worked together in his kitchen at La Belle Auberge out in Ladner, south of Vancouver. We had some nights where... he has an à la carte menu but he loves to have people come in and say, Bruno, we have 50 dollars per person, just go crazy. And we had some nights, just the two of us in the kitchen, because maybe we were open only with 10 or 12 reservations, and then had walk-in after walk-in up to 50 or 60 people. I remember one night in particular when, out of doing 55 covers, we might have done 45 covers, and so we were constantly creating menus out of what we had in the fridge. That helped me develop a talent for being able to walk into the fridge with half an idea and then complete the idea, and I think that helps in the evolution. And I think you never stop learning. I've got an incredibly passionate and talented brigade, and I think I can learn from every member in that brigade. It's kind of an apprenticeship that never ends, I suppose.

Is that a change in terms of the way executive chefs operate, or do you think that's always been the case?

I think that executive chefs now have to put their egos aside to a great degree, and I think to their benefit. It's a very competitive business and the ratio of good cooks to cooking positions open is very imbalanced, so first of all you have to put your ego away, because if you're a madman you just don't have good staff. They find somewhere better to work. That's sort of the philosophy of the '90s anyway, even the new millennium, that the communication, the development of people, all of that also makes a good kitchen, because if you get good staff, you should try and keep them. You can only do that by developing them, by communicating with them, by giving them freedom to grow. But giving them freedom to grow also helps us to be better than just me saying, this is my menu, you guys cook it. When we develop a menu, I even get some of my senior line cooks involved, because ultimately they have to buy into what they're cooking. If you kind of just say, here's your menu, cook it, how much are they going to buy into that? Whereas if you get them involved in the development process... They've all worked for great chefs, too, before they came here, so even though they may not have a fully developed sense of what their style is, they may interject with a sauce, or a starch, or a garnish, or a why-don't-we-do-it-this-way that can take a dish from 90% to 100%.

Even talking with my sous chefs... we can set and develop the menu, the five of us, plus a couple of line cooks, and that menu just grows... The lamb shank is on my mind, so I'll use that as an example. For one thing, to serve a reasonably sized portion of rack of lamb, we can't do it within our price-point that we want to be at. I think if cooked properly you can do a lamb shank at any time of the year, and that's been proven out by the sales over the summer menu. We wanted to do a lamb shank, and you kind of automatically think of the Italian way. My restaurant chef, David Griffiths, is very into ethnic products, whether it be Mexican, Thai... and he's very well-versed in those, and he said, well, why don't we do something with Szechuan? We have so many good cooks that right away we just said, yeah, you know, that will work. We don't really have to go through a lot of development process— maybe a little with presentation or a fine-tuning here and there, but we can take an idea, walk out in the kitchen, cook it and sell it to the guests that very night, and it will be a success. And that's talent. That's not my talent, that's the talent of all the people from the sous chefs to the line cooks. Even our most junior positions in the kitchen— we still give them responsibility, because that's going to help them grow, and that's going to make us better ultimately.

So that creation, is it a mixture of both trying things out in the kitchen as well as book research and shopping research?

We're pretty current with what's on the market, and I think that's what's maybe developed Pacific Northwest cooking over the last six or eight years. It's been that sudden availability of so many different ethnic products, even more so than it was 10 years ago. So we always kind of know what's on our market; certainly we follow trends. Just recently we spent a weekend in New York just dining out, which was a real sacrifice, since we had to eat and drink good food for a whole weekend, but that's sort of how we stay ahead. Our menu items sort of develop over what we do on a daily basis, whether it's on our regular menu or our special items. We're constantly giving a lot of free rein to the cooks to have a look at our market lists— see what interests them— let's bring it in. They do the initial creative process and then we step in and take a dish to the next level as sous chefs or as managers, together with the staff. Then when we go to make a new menu, it's kind of a best-of from the last season's specials for Diva. That becomes a new menu.

You must have reflected on your own approach and philosophy...

Yes, my approach, more than anything, is uncomplicated. I just don't like food that looks over-prepared, over-handled, kind of too played-up on. We did go through a bit of a phase where we were a little bit vertical, not by the intention of wanting to be like anyone else, but because we had three or four flavours layered upon one another. I like always to see a little clean plate between the food and the rim; that automatically makes the food start in the centre and kind of go up. We've toned that down a bit. I guess we went through a phase where we deep-fried just about everything to make a little straw, or a little hay, on top of the dish. We still do that sometimes, because I like dishes with texture, as well, so we have a lot of soft components, a lot of soft mouth feel. It's nice to add some kind of a crunch, that caramelized flavour you get from a deep-fried carrot or something to highlight a dish. That doesn't say much about my philosophy, but more than anything, it's clean, it's got to make sense from a technical cooking standpoint. I never do the weird combinations... I never combine beets with black beans, for instance, because to do something new is not my philosophy. To do something that works, from a flavour combination point of view, is. So it's fairly straightforward, not traditional but I guess clean, based upon traditional lines, then adding something interesting to bring it to another level.

So, with that philosophy, you had this project called Diva. Can you take me back to starting at square one?

Well, it's been a dream come true for me, as a chef, because there I was at Four Seasons Hotel and this job at the Metropolitan, which happened to be right across the street, kind of fell into my lap. I wasn't looking for a job, but Metropolitan took over this hotel, they have a philosophy which focusses on food and beverage selling the hotel, and I guess they wanted a Canadian-born, Canadian-trained, forward-thinking, young chef, and I fit the bill. So there I was. I came on to really an operation that didn't exist, because the space that Diva is in now was actually kind of a tacky mid-80s design cocktail lounge. We served food, but from an upstairs kitchen, our dining room... I just didn't want people that I knew coming into it, to be honest... well, they did, but fortunately they focused on the food, which took some time to evolve as well.

We essentially took this tacky bar right down to concrete again. I was part of that whole development process, and it was fascinating. Normally, when there's a new restaurant, they build it and then they hire you two weeks before opening and say, here's your restaurant, go to it. In a lot of cases the kitchen is designed by an architect who's never cooked, so that's your first headache, which oftentimes can be insurmountable. I was able to come on here at the Metropolitan and hire some of the key members of my team for that development process. So I had at that time my executive sous chef, Ray Henry, I had my restaurant chef already hired, and I had a key member of my line brigade, Chris Mills. We were part of the development and the design of the kitchen. I sat in on the twice-weekly meetings with the architects and the owner, Henry Wu, and the general manager, and the food and beverage director, to say, what is Diva going to be? How is it going to look? What kind of shape is it going to take? What kind of cooking are we going to do? What kind of wine are we going to serve? What are the colours going to be? We were able to design as a team a kitchen which... granted, it could be bigger, but I've never worked in a kitchen that works so well from a logistical point of view, and that's because it was designed by chefs. We developed a style for what Diva was going to be, but we were able to hit the ground with our feet running. When we opened Diva we were already at full speed as far as what we wanted to cook, and so the first menu wasn't a developmental menu. I would cook the food that we cooked then now and still be very proud of it.

We always sort of had an unsaid, or unwritten, mission statement, always looked at what we're doing and said, is that really Diva? We've always had a focus to not follow trends, but try and be at the forefront of setting trends. Not setting trends, but doing something maybe a little bit more risky, a little bit outside of what people traditionally have done, and done successfully. It was a huge challenge to take what is really a hotel restaurant and make it a restaurant in a hotel. Diva has its own personality, its own recognition outside the community. We're now selling our catering product off the Diva name. It's all about being innovative and not thinking like hotel people. We oftentimes try to think like entrepreneurs, and then that maybe brings a little black ink to the bottom line which then keeps your owner happy, which then allows you to go on thinking the way you do.

Thinking about what you've developed here, how does that connect to your early European experiences— Switzerland and I know you were in Monte Carlo.

Out of those times I probably got an even deeper respect for traditional, technical methods. You know, what is a good butter sauce and how do you make it? How do you cook fish properly? That more than anything. I already had a lot of the passion already, but... there was a time when Canada didn't have an identity in cooking. As a Canadian, unless you had European experience, you didn't get the opportunities.

Do you think that's changed?

Oh, absolutely, and that was another thing that I learned in going to Europe. Hey, we cook pretty well over here, if you take everything into account. In Europe they have brigades of 40 for a restaurant this size. Here we have a brigade, for a dinner service, of five or six, we cook just as well as they do in Europe, and that was really what I learned, that traditional methods of cooking still work. I learned a lot more about them, but I also learned that I can be happy cooking in Vancouver, being successful at it. I guess the challenge is to hopefully be a part of the movement to take Canadian or Pacific Northwest cooking to another level. Over the last few years that's been starting to show, not only myself, but a lot of locally raised and trained chefs who have settled in this area.

If you consider the palates of the chefs themselves between here and Europe in terms of what cookery's about and also those of customers, is there a distinctive difference?

Well, I think, in Europe, because they have so much history... I mean here we call history 100 years. Over in Europe it's hundreds of years, literally, so they have such traditions established, and living and working in countries like France or Switzerland, you see what a big part of their life food is. It's not just at the restaurants, but it's living in people's homes. They take two hours for lunch in France, to this day. I couldn't imagine that system here, it's such a competitive kind of atmosphere here now that they couldn't do that, but there it's still a big part of their life.

As far as the chefs go, I think we're a little more creative here. A lot of European chefs now look to North America; even maybe some of the most famous ones look toward North America for inspiration. I guess they realize that we do have good technical basics here, because they have to acknowledge their countrymen and so on who have come to North America to live and work. You look at any of the gourmet magazines in Europe now, and they have articles about California cooking, or what's happening in the States. There's a lot of interest in that, so the tables have turned to some degree. There's still wonderful cooking going on in Europe, but they follow tradition almost to a T. Look at Paul Bocuse's restaurant; he's still got filet of sole with Hollandaise sauce. You couldn't do that in North America and be successful.

Let's turn the wheel back a little to Calgary before you were 10. What were your food experiences?

They were very little, actually. I didn't eat spaghetti with meat sauce till I was at least 12 or 13 years old, so I guess I come from a very classic Canadian background. My mother is a wonderful cook, but she's always cooked supremely traditional Canadian cooking, so much so that spaghetti with meat sauce didn't enter the repertoire until I was a teenager. I always looked forward to Saturday nights. We were members of the YMCA, so every Saturday afternoon we went swimming as a family, and then we would go home, and we had hamburgers, and potato chips, and we watched *Hockey Night in Canada*. I mean, how much more Canadian than that can you get? And probably every Tuesday night, on alternating weeks, we would have liver and onions; the next week was pork chops. It was well-prepared but very standard. Although I did develop somehow an enjoyment in the kitchen. I still have memories of my grandmother, who is of Swedish descent. We visited my grandparents often, or they visited us, and she spent a lot of time in the kitchen. I have quite a sweet tooth because my mom has always done a lot of baking— cookies, cakes— she makes her own Christmas cakes.

So, we're still talking about care in the kitchen.

Yes, and I guess as a result, in the summertime when I was a kid and I was bored and hanging around watching TV, I started making cookies and cakes and lemon loaf, because I like to eat it, too; so, hey, when I get hot cookies out of the oven, you always have to try one. I sort of got initially, maybe not to my own consciousness, interested at that age, and then as I got into high school I needed, in Grade 11, a course to fill out my curriculum. So I took a course, and I did like most Grade 11 boys will do, I just jacked around with my friends the first semester and maybe made a C+ average or something, and then in the second semester I made something one day that came out perfectly and I was excited about it. And so I went through the same course in Grade 12 and actually was the top student in that course, and by that time I'd decided I might like to pursue cooking as a career.

Most Canadians leave high school, and kind of flop around university for a few years before they really figure out what they want to do. I knew what I wanted to do, and so I got into professional cooking at a very young age. Being 19 or 20 years old and already into an apprenticeship is pretty unique for Canadians. And so I was probably too young to know... in fact, when I first got into the cooking business I wasn't so sure if that was for me, because I didn't have the passion for it yet. I had some basic skills, but it seemed like a lot of stress and a lot of unpredictability and a lot of things that, as a young person, most of the time you can't really deal with. I still remember asking myself, is this really what I want? Getting yelled at by my chef and not really knowing why they were yelling at me? It's not an easy profession, but I go back to Ben Weber; he was the first guy that I worked with, and he was only a chef de partie at that time, but he had incredible love for cooking. He taught me how to love cooking, and from there I kind of went into my European experience, and then I worked with Bruno Marti, then I was back with Ben Weber again at the Canadian Club at Expo.

He taught you how to love cooking?

He taught me how to be cooking on the line when you're doing 130 covers, and you've got bills pouring out of the machine, and you've got 20 racks of lamb cooking and you're trying to get all that together, and love that. To actually get that exhilaration of being in the weeds, so to speak. It takes a special type of person, or personality, to enjoy it. I don't like the boring status quo, and I don't think many people that work in the kitchen do. All the way from the point where you come in and you're already in the weeds, because you were busy last night and you're going to be busy tonight, and you have to make all your mise en place again, but Ben somehow taught me not to freak out in that situation. He would come with me to the stove and teach me how to make sauce, and there aren't many people who know how to make sauce any more. Good sauce, that's a feeling, too; there's no recipe for good sauce, it's a feeling for how-to, and the basics, so he taught me: don't panic. In fact, he used to laugh at me when I was kind of upset because, geez, I'm in the weeds and I'm not going to be ready for service, and he would just stand back and laugh at me, and I learned to laugh at myself in that situation, and figure out that being uptight was not helping me.

And that's just developing a professional approach, where you can take all that pressure in stride and then go into service and handle that pressure. There was a time in my career when I was a bit of a pot-thrower, and I just didn't have the coolness that it takes. When I see people that have that problem now, I can relate to how they feel, and help them. And I think even to this day, I'm still learning, but it's that professional approach that I try to instill in others now, because I think that makes a difference in the food that gets placed in front of a guest. If you're all scattered and not taking the pressure in stride, the product's going to show that.

Were there certain foods when you were a kid, maybe you still like them, stuff that really turned you on?

Well, I still love to barbecue hamburgers, believe it or not.

Do you still do the potato chips, and that whole thing?

Oh, yeah. Actually, I guess we're a little more health-conscious now. But when I make hamburgers I don't buy extra-lean ground beef, because that doesn't make a good hamburger. I buy lean beef because there's nothing worse than barbecuing a hamburger that doesn't make any smoke, you know it's not going to have any flavour, either. Other foods I love— sweets— I just love chocolate. On very difficult days when I don't have time to eat, and you get that sort of lightheaded feeling, I just head right for the pastry shop and grab a handful of bitter chocolate, because it gives you the energy you need, and it also puts a beautiful flavour on your palate that, if it's a good chocolate, is going to be there for an hour and a half. You only need a couple of ounces and away you go. So, even though I don't have a lot of pastry experience, I love desserts, I love sweet.

I didn't eat spaghetti until I was 12 years old, but pasta is one of the best things for me, and that's what we cook a lot at home, too. I don't have a pot-washer at home, so I like things that I can do in one pot. We do a lot of one-pot pasta, when you do that kind of thing, you learn about feel, about cooking, about flavours, about going through the fridge and pulling a bunch of stuff out that maybe you didn't buy intending to be part of pasta. It becomes that way because you know that it goes well together.

So principles from here at Diva, that you use here apply...

Any time you get near a stove. It's the same thing.

You talked about spaghetti and meatballs. Was that sort of your first exotic food experience, or even, we had this thing called fancy food or exotic food?

Yeah. It probably took me even longer than that to really come into contact with what I would consider to be exotic food, or different food. It was probably even to the time when I was into my apprenticeship that I had first contact with something that might be considered a little different.

I do remember as a family going to one of those Japanese restaurants where they cook on the grill in front of you, chop chop chop chop, which, for me, was exotic— I mean, a whole bunch of fried bean sprouts. I don't know why we went there, because it wasn't really in our family's tradition to do that, but I guess my parents had heard about this neat experience. Maybe my dad had been taken there on a business lunch, and we took the whole family, but to me, compared to what I was used to eating as a kid, that was like, totally exotic.

But even my first experience with spaghetti, funnily enough, was on a soccer exchange. We would have a team from Seattle come up and stay at our house, and we would go down two weeks later and stay at their house.

Michael Noble

I felt sorry for the mother of the kid that I was billeting with in Seattle, because I guess she wanted to cook something that you can be sure a kid staying with you is going to like. She figured, well, spaghetti with meat sauce... I'd never had it. I'd had noodles before, so I said, maybe if I could just have the spaghetti without the sauce? Of course it had no butter, no oil, no nothing on it, it was just like a lump of starch, very difficult to eat. I must have come home and recounted this nightmare to my mom, and she must have looked into the whole spaghetti and meat sauce thing. Maybe we went to the Spaghetti Factory or something. So then we learned to enjoy it, but I really have no first recollection of interesting or different food.

It probably wasn't until I really got interested in the passion side of cooking... because, really, when you get into your apprenticeship, you still remember spending hours pushing the meat down on chicken drumettes for hors d'oeuvres, and doing chicken liver wrapped in bacon, but I wouldn't have any part of the actual preparation of the chicken liver, the banquet chef would sear it all off, give it to me with a couple of cases of bacon, and I'd lay out 900 or 1,000, 1,500 strips of bacon and wrap up the chicken liver in there. The cooking part isn't your job yet, it's just all of the grunt work, so it's not until you get into some of those more interesting stations... or maybe you spend three or four months cooking breakfast, frying eggs, that's not exotic, either. It's a bit into your apprenticeship before you actually find out what a scallop is, or what a lobster is, and what to do with it.

That's a far cry from that spaghetti with no sauce, that's a far cry from the Culinary Olympics and your success at the Bocuse d'Or competition. Take me through that experience.

The whole competition thing was something that I kind of avoided for a great deal of the early part of my career. I mean, even as an apprentice you can get involved in culinary competitions. I was more interested in learning how to cook. I didn't really have an interest in learning how to cook plastic show-food. But I guess in the back of your mind you always know that you haven't done it all, or you're not totally well-rounded until you've competed.

The first major competition that I competed in was Bocuse d'Or in 1995, to earn the right to represent Canada at Lyon, France. At Bocuse d'Or I had to win a Canadian cook-off, which was in the late spring of 1994. That was my first time competing, but it was a hot competition, a competition not only for presentation— 50% of the mark was for taste— so I felt like, hey, I can do this. I didn't really have any idea whatsoever how to put food on a platter, but I won the Canadian cook-off because my food tasted the best. The judges felt, even though I didn't have the best presentation, I had by far the best flavour, and that they could teach this guy over the next eight months, before he goes to Lyon, how to put the food on the platter. So, as a result, I practised like crazy for eight months, I mean, I had European sea bass for one platter and I had veal rack and sweetbreads and kidneys for the other platter, and I practised so much that after that competition was over, if anybody asked me for a menu idea using veal, or kidneys, or sweetbreads, I was brain-dead, I just drew a blank because all I could think about was what I had done in Lyon. But we practised very, very hard, and actually had a sixth-place finish in Lyon, and it just so happened that my mentor, Bruno Marti, was in Lyon, and watched me cook there... finishing in the highest ever placing for a Canadian. He was already engaged to manage the 1996 Canadian Culinary Team.

When he formed the team, he had a lot of great cold competition people. He felt he maybe needed some more hot-kitchen cooks. He had Ben Weber already on the team, who is a great hot cook. The Culinary Olympics are now slowly evolving from 80% of the scoring toward the cold competition, to now, more to the hot side. Even so much that part of your cold table has to be reproduced to be tasted by the judges. So, he felt that I was a good fit, at least initially, as an alternate member. As the team evolved, I became a full member doing hot and cold. The biggest single memory is the hot competition, and in Berlin where we won a gold medal. I was responsible for the main course of our three-course menu from the point of the cooking, the sauce, all of those things. I love cooking in front of people, under pressure, and then being judged for it.

We got back from Berlin in mid-October of 1996. In January of '97 I was back in Lyon for Bocuse d'Or '97. Because I came back from Bocuse d'Or '95 and said, gee, we need a Canadian chefs' federation to develop some kind of a plan where we can pre-select the next representative for Bocuse d'Or and to take to the present competition, to experience that. I set up a competition to pre-select Canada's 1999 representative because the Bocuse d'Or is every two years. Robert Sulatycky, who was selected to represent us in January of 1999, came to observe the '97 competition, so, as a result, I competed in '97— not because I'd won the right to do it, but because I was appointed by the Federation. So I went right out of the Berlin competition into training for 1997 Lyon. I didn't do as well. I finished ninth, mainly because I think I didn't have time to prepare and really fine-tune my cooking for Lyon. But I think that whole experience made me a much more well-rounded chef with the ability to say, I went in and I cooked on the world stage three times. Those competitions are really idea exchanges where you get together with, well, in the case of Berlin, there's 32 national teams, so you get together with chefs from all over the world, and exchange ideas, and see their styles, and maybe you pick up an idea here or an idea there. You go to Lyon and you do the same thing; you're cooking hot, then you... The interesting thing in Lyon is that every one of the 22 competing nations is given the same principal food products to work with, and it's amazing to see the spectrum people through which people take those two products and what they do with them.

It sounds pretty exciting.

Very exciting. You're basically rubbing shoulders with some of the grandfathers of cuisine, Paul Bocuse, Pierre Troisgros, Roger Vergé, I mean, all of Bocuse's cronies come to Lyon, at least for the official photograph. And there you are, with people you've only read about, and one of my biggest single memories of international competition... Bruno Marti was on the floor with his video camera while I was competing and I was dressing my fish platter, and I didn't realize till I saw the video, that while I was working on my platter, Paul Bocuse was standing right in front of me, watching, he's looking at the food, he's watching what I'm doing, and then he looks up, and he gives kind of a nod of appreciation or approval, and I mean... what a souvenir to have, to have one of the most famous chefs there looking at what you're doing, and at that time, really, I was an executive sous chef at Four Seasons. I was anonymous.

Let's turn to how you create a dish... the process.

How does a dish evolve for me? Essentially, the first thing is to find the basic ingredients, for instance, our smoked Alaskan black cod... we don't repeat dishes from menu to menu, but once in a while you come up with kind of a signature dish. I've cooked the smoked Alaskan black cod for probably 10 years now, all the way back from Four Seasons days, but always a different way; and when I— if you want to call it that— create a dish, I like comfortable food, not comfort food, but I like food that looks and feels and tastes good, so I think about the richness of the smoked cod— it has such a beautiful luxury to it, the large grain, the smoke, the slight salt content. But then, not to overcomplicate— so roasted leeks become part of the mashed potato, but then, sauce... I mean, already you have rich flavour, you've got rich potatoes— what do you do for a sauce? Certainly not a butter sauce. A vinaigrette is one way to go, but everyone has done that, too. The way we always constantly evolve, we bought one of those natural juicers to make vegetable juices and so on, so we'd been playing around with it, and... what goes well with smoked, salty cod and this roasted-leek whipped potato? I thought, gee, celery would be nice. So we said, well, why don't we just juice celery and make that the sauce? We took that— it was a little bit too sweet— so we added just a hint of rice-wine vinegar. It was celery juice, rice-wine vinegar, no butter, no cream, just a little salt and ground white pepper. We put that around the mashed potato in kind of an oversized soup plate, and what a comfortable plate of food to eat. As you eat it, the celery juice with its nice flavour combines with the roasted leek potato, almost to make a very thick soup, but then this rich, flaky fish! Very simple— complex to the point of the celery and the smoke and so on— but just wonderful flavours going together.

What percentage of that is working on it in the kitchen, and doing it there, or somewhere else, or at home?

I think I thought of that dish at home. We had pretty much the skeleton of our menu together, but we hadn't come up with our smoked cod dish, or we had decided at the last minute to add it. So, because I wasn't around my brigade at all, and I kind of had to put some thought process to it. I thought of the dish but I knew at that time that it would taste great. I came in to work and I said, what if we do this? I think we ran it as a special that night and it was a big hit, and just went on from there. When you have experience and you've cooked for a lot of different chefs and you've cooked a lot of food... some of today's young chefs skip over that part, standing at the stove with a saute pan in your hand. You have to put in that time to have a feel for the food. The more filet of salmon you pan-sear... while you're doing it, you develop a feel for what goes with it. You see that it's rich, it gets a nice crust on it... It's cooking and eating that makes a good chef, not reading a textbook. You need the basic technique, but you need to handle the food every day, and that's maybe part of our strength here. As chef and sous chefs, our management team handles the food every day and we cook every day, so we're really hands-on; ideas come from holding food in your hands.

What about your palate ?

I like textures; I like a complex depth of a few flavours together, but also the mouth feel. There's nothing better than a good mashed potato. There's nothing better than a good soup. There's such a thing as good and bad soup. You can boil up a whole bunch of vegetables, blend them up, add a little salt and pepper, and have a bad soup. You can make a good soup by giving it depth. Good food is like good wine. You have great initial flavour, but then the flavours change as they reach different parts of your palate. A good soup, you feel that in your stomach, that warmth that it gives you, much like a great dish with a great mashed potato gives you... it gives you a warmth, a good feeling. So palate is more than just taste. I think it's feeling, and good food puts you in a good mood.

But does the diner think about those textures?

It's probably an unsaid thing, but I think it adds to their enjoyment of a food. Going back to that smoked Alaskan cod, you can poach that cod, but for me there's nothing better than pan-searing it or grilling it, because you get this wonderful caramelized crust, so you have another dimension, "A" in flavour but there's also "B" in texture, in mouth feeling. And maybe it's some of those unsaid things, or those things that a guest sitting at a table doesn't perceive, but somehow they enjoy it; maybe they don't know why, but they know that they're enjoying it, and that makes them come back.

There's passion in this profession, but has there been a time when this wasn't all that fun, when you were in the kitchen?

Yeah. It's a very demanding profession. There've definitely been times in my career when I've thought, gee, there must be something easier than this, because I do have a family. I have three young children and they're not going to be young for much longer— they grow up so fast— and I have a wonderful wife— that is my big enjoyment, spending time with my family. There are definitely times when you are so busy at different times of the year... I just spend too much time at work, because I have to. We run 365 days of the year here. Essentially we serve food 24 hours a day, so it takes an incredible amount of time.

And do you take work home?

I don't like to take it home. This business has a pretty high divorce rate. I'm lucky to have a life-partner, my wife Frederique, whom I met when I was apprenticing. I happened to meet her at the time when I got into this passion side of food... I started to come home excited: wow, we were really busy tonight, but it was awesome. So she, before we made that life-commitment to each other, already understood what this means to me. Some chefs, they get married and their partner doesn't really understand why they do this, or why they spend so much time, or why they have to be here. Sure, I come home and talk about my job, but that's a natural thing; if you have a good relationship you're going to bounce things off your spouse. And my wife, she's not afraid to speak up... she'll put me in line, she'll say, that's not your style, or sometimes she'll come to Diva and she'll say, this dish doesn't really work for me; she's not afraid to say that, and that's great. I guess I've grown as a person to the point where I realize that there are a lot of days when I just need to walk away and leave my work at work. It's important to have that balance. If I don't have that balance I can't be good at work, and I can't be good at home either.

Michael Noble

So I do a lot of things that discipline me to put time aside for my family. I coach my son's soccer team, I'm involved in coaching hockey, I take my daughters to their soccer games, I help out with their practices and so on as much as I can. I feel you have to make those commitments. Otherwise, in this business at least, you're always going to say, well, I'm too busy, or I have this to do or I have that to do, and so I can't be home. But now, I leave every Monday night at 4:30 because I have soccer practice at 6:00, and that's the most important thing every week. Certainly, if we have something very important going on in the restaurant, I can miss soccer practice one week, but you always have to put things in balance and perspective, I think.

Can you recall a specific night when you got a real high because things were really going well, and what was that like?

Oh, there've been countless nights like that. For me there's nothing better than working the pass on a very busy night when you've got an outstanding brigade working with you. They all know their jobs extremely well, they're all in place, you've got awesome specials going on, and working in an open kitchen especially, you can feel how much people are enjoying what you're doing. Yes, you have a lot of stress to deal with, you have a lot of bills coming in, but those nights are clicking. There may be nights when I'm here helping out with a chef's table, coming out and describing each dish to the guests. I mean, there's a lot of nights like that, where you just get this incredible high from what you're doing. Actually, if we were to say, a special night that you remember more than any, we did two nights of grand opening parties for Diva, where we did a set menu; we had about 110 invitees for each of those nights. That was right in the infancy of Diva, and we came up as a team with an incredible menu, and we had it planned down to the last carrot and shallot. Both nights just clicked incredibly. We always get much more excited when we're cooking dishes we've never cooked before, and they come out. That's part of the challenge. You can always do what you've done before, but to do something, a combination, or a dish, that you've come up with and it works perfectly... You have to be organized and spontaneous at the same time. There are spontaneous chefs who have no organizational skills; I don't think they are as good as they can be then. I do spend some time in the office, because

I need to plan for the future. Sure, I could spend every day, every minute in the kitchen, but we're not going to progress anywhere as a team if I do that.

About the future, what are your visions of where you're going to be in a couple of years or 10 years down the line?

I honestly don't know. I'm really happy doing what I'm doing now. Certainly I need growth, too, so I'm always going to be looking for areas and places to grow to, and I think I still have a lot of those places in my job right now. Way down the road, I guess I've always had a dream of having my own restaurant. I'm not unlike a lot of chefs. Maybe it won't be a fine-dining room, but I believe I can have a business one day where my wife can be involved in it, my kids can be involved in it, if they choose to. My kids, indirectly, have been exposed to a lot of different foods. The more time you can spend as a family, the better off you're going to be, and if we can have even more of that balance, I'd much rather have a bigger balance toward the family than toward work, so if we can work that out for the future... you still have to make a living, too, so I think it will take sort of an innovative time, idea, place, and some luck. Hopefully I'm not going to be so involved in what I'm doing on a day-to-day basis that when something pops in my mind, or I see a place or a possibility... I know we won't be afraid to go after it. Because what's better than working for yourself?

Just a last word for people thinking about going into the business, students, or young chefs?

Try and learn that passion as early as you can, but before that, learn the basic technique. There are excellent cooking schools out there, but the more time you can spend in your basic training, the better off you're going to be and the higher you can fly. I often get people who maybe aspire to be cooks, or they're getting out of high school and they don't know what to do but they think this might be it. We do a lot of student placements. I may get mature people who are looking at a second career choice, who want to have my opinion on where they should go. I always equate your career to building a skyscraper, an 80-storey building. If the foundation is weak, you can only go maybe 30 storeys, but if you have a good strong foundation, the sky's the limit, really. Because everything I do now is based on what I learned in the early stages of my career. I still make Yorkshire pudding using the same recipe I learned in cooking school in 1979. So you always learn things and you take them forward, but the more times you can repeat making soup, making stock, making sauces... The more you can do that, over a year period versus a three or four month period, the better you're going to be, and the better your career can be. But you really never stop learning. That's the thing, don't close your mind to learning. If you become a chef, don't get arrogant and think you can't learn any more, because what makes the profession so great is that you really never stop.

Michael Noble

Michael Noble was born in Calgary, Alberta. The first Canadian to ever compete on the Japanese television show *Iron Chef* (aired to 22.5 million Japanese viewers), Michael Noble, Executive Chef at Diva at the Met (Metropolitan Hotel, Vancouver) was honoured as 1997 Chef of the Year by the BC Chefs' Association. National Chair of Bocuse d'Or Canada, he was a member of Culinary Team Canada 1996 at the Culinary Olympics in Berlin, Germany. The team finished with three gold medals, one bronze and two overall bronze medals with a final standing in sixth place. Noble was Canada's representative at 1995 Bocuse d'Or World Cuisine Contest; his sixth-place finish represented the best finish ever for a non-European country at that time. He managed the Canadian team at Bocuse d'Or 1999 to a best ever finish by our Canadian candidate (fourth place).

Michael Noble's
NOVA SCOTIA LOBSTER, AVOCADO AND OVEN-DRIED TOMATO RISOTTO IN A PARMESAN TUILE

PARMESAN TUILE
150 g grated parmesan cheese

METHOD

On a baking sheet lined with parchment paper sprinkle the grated parmesan to form round disks. Place in a 365 F oven and bake approximately 5 minutes until the cheese is melted and slightly golden brown. Remove from the oven and let the disks cool slightly. Drape the melted cheese disk over the back of a cup and let cool to form the tuile. Set aside.

RISOTTO
200 g Arborio rice
400 to 500 ml lobster or chicken stock
1/2 shallot, diced
2 cloves garlic, chopped
75 g butter
1 bay leaf
175 g lobster claw meat (cooked and cut into strips)
1 tomato (oven-dried and cut into strips)
1 avocado, diced
60 ml reduced lobster glacé
50 g parmesan cheese, grated
2 tsp chervil, chopped
white pepper
salt

METHOD

In a shallow saucepan, over medium heat, sweat off the shallots and garlic in 50 grams butter. Add the Arborio rice and continue stirring until the rice is warm and looks transparent. Add the warm stock, a ladle at a time. Continue stirring constantly. When the risotto simmers, reduce the heat and add the bay leaf and a little seasoning. Continue adding stock until the rice is al dente and creamy looking. Stir in the remaining butter, and the parmesan. Finally, add the lobster, oven-dried tomato, avocado and chopped chervil. Season to taste.

Serve in the parmesan tuile, drizzled with daikon sprout oil.

Patrick Alléguède

The National Club, Toronto, Ontario

Of all the chefs here, I've known Patrick Alléguède the longest. In my early years as a dining columnist, my brother, a veteran purchaser in the restaurant trade, told me of an extraordinary chef he was working with, introducing such things as duck confit and magret at that time, years before they began appearing on Toronto menus. For many years a good friend of Dominique Toulousey, the famed chef in Toulouse, Patrick has arguably the most profound understanding of foie gras of any chef in Canada. A pheasant and blueberry terrine he once made remains a legend in our family and frankly, I am hard-pressed to find better terrines than his anywhere I've travelled and stayed in France. With his family in Capdenac-Gare in the Southwest, I got a firsthand feel for French cuisine. His ceaseless curiosity about food and uncompromising quest for quality illuminated for me my responsibilities at the writerly end of gastronomy. He was the first to point out the role of my mother in my own caring about food. While raised with tradition, he learned his metier during the evolution of Nouvelle Cuisine, and he regularly reconnects to that background when he sees family in France. I was living in Paris, when he and his wife Tara, sun-drenched after family visits to the south, met me in the city. "Where can I go to see what's happening with food?" he promptly asked. It was late, near closing time. Why not La Grande Epicerie of Au Bon Marché, I thought, now the Left Bank gastronomy supermarket of choice. And off he charged through the aisles, looking, sniffing, at one point, like a good disobedient Frenchman, breaking open packages just to explore.

Two years later, at their home in West Toronto with Tara sitting in the corner along with their new baby, I began by asking him what he was looking for on that brief stop in Paris.

It's amazing to measure the evolution of people. We don't talk in France about *mondialisation*— but more a European— opening up of Europe. Because before, France was very— the regions. Paris was the gathering of the regions,

Patrick Alléguède

but not so much a gathering up of the whole of Europe. There was so much Spanish food there. You know, it's kind of amazing. I didn't expect it, I expected more to see the products of Brittany, Auvergne, Champagne, Burgundy, Provence— but things from Italy, from Germany— I didn't expect that.

But you were also looking at the packaging of the food— I remember you were even tearing [laughs] some open to look at it—

You know, now, food doesn't sell by itself. You need the packaging— people want more— I guess it's linked to pleasure. I guess if you put just a baguette— people like to see some frills around it. They like to buy it— but want a little bit more. You know, you want to buy your cake but— *whiiih*— the packaging seems to be important— especially in North America—

And in France?

People would grab something more for the quality— for the gustative quality, not for the eye appeal.

So what did you see there when you were seeing this—

Well, the evolution. I saw that the French and Europeans are really taking on the American way. It's not a very good thing. You know, you have to let the product talk by itself. Like before, people used to go shopping just with a basket or with a bag— there was no plastic bag— nothing. They used to put the fruit and vegetables on the scales and dump it in your bag. Now you have papers— when you add up all this packaging— I mean, what are you buying...?

I personally feel that before, people used to buy the products just by the touch of them. It was very important. When you go to a market in Paris— people ask you when you want to eat your avocado or your fruit, and they select for the ripeness... Now, to put that into your bag, they hide the products— it's totally different. We have changed. Everything is packaged, for the look... the young people don't have the knowledge our parents used

to have in food. There is a big change in the way of feeding themselves. They don't have time to cook, first of all— so they buy everything— the soup in a box there— they just have to warm it up. People don't have time. Both the father and mother work. Before, my mom was at home. She had time to cook lentils for three hours— now you buy lentils— they're cooked in 15 minutes— you don't need so long to cook beans or lentils.

So you often think about your early experiences?

For sure. That's very important. When you used to eat something, it was tasty, it was always the right consistency, it was proper. You know, for pleasure— and I think food is only pleasure, basically— it takes a long time— it takes a maturing time, like a stew. Nowadays, you buy a stew and it takes how long to cook? Half an hour? Before, the stew used to simmer a long time— mostly because people were putting the stew in the morning on the stove, simmer it, and they could go away to work in the field and come back at 12:00 and it was ready. But I mean there was a reason, and the meat tenderized— the meat gets all the unctuous flavours. If you cook it too fast, you don't have that. You bypass the process.

What do you remember?

The smells, the smells— the kitchen, the whole house used to smell of what you were going to eat at lunch time— so imagine yourself— put into a box like a house and just smell from 9:00 to 12:00— you were hungry and you were ready to enjoy the food. And you knew what you were going to eat— the sausage, or whatever. If I was at my uncle's, my grandmother's or my mother's— I think the lentils were one thing— because that was a different flavour, like the beans— the stews, also, depending on the vegetables she was going to cook. There was Swiss chard, the carrots— the flavour was different, the smell was different— also the way they used to cook the old hens— the chicken— pot au feu— you could smell that for hours, because it was simmering on the stove for three or four hours— so you knew when they were adding the different vegetables— the leeks— you could smell the leek flavour, the turnips...

Patrick Alléguède

And you could identify—

And I still can now in the kitchen, when they cook something, when they cook the turnips or whatever. I think for me the fragrance, the smell, is very important. Not only in the food, but I can smell the smells of the seasons— fall, summer, spring— you can smell the difference— Mother Nature... you smell the leaves— especially in the fall, I remember way back. You could smell the leaves and some different flavours of the moisture of the ground. The temperatures— the cold of the night, the warm of the day— you have a different smell, different touch.

It's a signal that you have a change of seasons, a change of vegetables, everything changes, and you see changes to your body, also. If you come into the fall, you have the smell of the mushroom, and you think mushroom, you're already open to cook with mushroom. I mean, what does the fall mean? It's hunting season, so... the fowl, the game— it's very important.

So you grew up in a big family— brothers and sisters— what was it that it was you who ended up going into cooking? Do you remember when?

I was seven years old. To see my mother make the pies, the cakes— preparing the food— and I think my grandmother, you know, I remember when she used to cook rice, they didn't call it risotto— but it looked kind of like a risotto, it was a soft rice. All these things for me were wonderful. It was pleasurable to eat; that food tasted good. It had kind of a meaning, you know.

My grandmother used to have a big chimney— no stove, no gas stove. A big chimney, and she used to cook on the wood. It was chemistry— you adapt this, you adapt that, you end up with a product that is totally different. That's magic!

So, that's like a little boy or girl when they see magic.

Well, I didn't go to Disneyland at that time...

Yeah, yeah... [we both laugh]

Magic had a different meaning... I mean the way you could transform something that came from the ground into something that you can have pleasure to taste— there's a kind of a magic there. And the guy who does that, who practises that magic— he's a hero!

So when did you tell your parents you wanted to cook?

I was seven. Actually, I wanted to be a pastry chef... uh, pastry something... I didn't know that was a pastry chef or what. I mean pastry was all that chemistry, because you take butter, flour, eggs and sugar... man, the things you can do with that. And it tastes good... oh...

Did you help your mother?

She always had a piece of dough for me to work with. It didn't always turn out properly, but at least I started to do something. And I was always attracted by bread. And I remember it took me so long, to understand what bread was about. The first piece of bread I made was so hard [laughing, bangs his fist on the table] nobody could get their teeth into it. You have to understand, it's basically just flour and water and some little animals— creatures to make— I mean, that, too, is magic. I was very very young.

I had an uncle who was a charcutier in France, working on pigs and transforming the pigs in San Probatier, a little village next to it. So I spent my childhood working there. When I started to go there I was probably one or two years old. So from the pigs screaming because they were slaughtered, to the final product of the sausage, pâté and all that... I lived it all, I know it. You have to help, you have to work. There was no Nintendo game at this time, huh? Nintendo was playing with a knife and a leg of pork, there.

I don't know if it was always exciting; it was exciting, but work. I did it because we were seven kids and my mother and father— that's where I was spending my vacation. But it was interesting, I learned a lot— even when you make a sausage— all that— you mix broken meat and fat, seasoning and all that... you let it dry at a certain temperature, a certain weight, a certain wind, and here is the final product.

Patrick Alléguède

After that I decided to go to hotel school for three years in Toulouse. And before I went, I went to work in a restaurant for a good summer, and there I was doing menial work at first, and little by little I was doing the pastries and cleaning the chickens, and after that I was doing omelettes. It was a restaurant, a nice restaurant where you had foie gras and all those sorts of things. At first I was a helper, but I picked it up fairly fast and I was loaded with more and more work. And after that I went to Toulouse for three years.

It was intense training, very intense. I learned all the catering from the waiter to the dishwasher, the pot washer— you had to learn everything. All the basics, all the theory. You didn't have to watch too much. You had to do things. Not like the schools here, where you have a mirror and you have to look at it.

And the summer you had to spend working in hotel and restaurants as a co-op. I went to Biarritz and Massif Central— and one year as a waiter and one year as a cook. After that I studied pastry and worked in different hotels and resorts. So in the summer, you go to the seashore, and in between summer and winter you go to Paris to work. And you go for winter to the resorts and then you come back to Paris. You have four different jobs, basically... you move around and learn lots. I did that until I was 25.

I wanted to do pastry— that was my choice, but I developed some flour allergy so I had to stop. I liked that because it was interesting. With so many different aspects— from the bread-making to the breakfast pastries to the ice creams, the spectrum is very big— and all the decorations, the sugars, the chocolates, the pastillages— decoration things— it's amazing.

Well, I was talking to Nicolas Jongleux in Montreal and he said he started with pastry, and that going into other restaurants, it helps.

Yeah. That gave me an edge. Definitely. It still gives me an edge— to know pastry. Because sometimes, a pastry guy is off in his own corner, unconnected with the chef; it's kind of a different trade and it was in France especially; it was two fields. I never really had that problem because I was either/or, you know. And one summer I switched and went to the cold kitchen— garde-manger— in a hotel.

So you did this travelling around until you were 25. And after that?

Well, then after that I settled in Paris and it was time to make some money, and I went into Le Crillon in Paris and Le Meridien... and there I learned a bit more and I managed to advance. At Le Crillon I was in the pastry shop still, making all the petits fours and all the delicate little pastries. At Le Meridien I was in the kitchen... I was kind of a *tournant*— filling in for people on their days off. So I went from the sauces, to the garde-manger— I was rotating chef. And then I went into a hotel where I was chef-saucier— I was making all the sauces— for fish, meat. That was very serious because the guy was a very good chef, Mr. Barbier... Barbier de Seville... and he was with the company which owned *Devoir* and Tour de France... that scared me a bit. That's probably why I decided to go to Canada.

That organization... you become one of them. You don't have any freedom after. You have to follow their way and they send you to their friends around France... and you do what they call the Tour de France.

That guy struck me because everything was in detail and everything had to be done in a certain way... from scratch. Everything from scratch, you don't cut any corners. When you got a rabbit, the rabbit arrived with the skin and everything, and you had to bone them, and skin them, and keep the blood, very very important, very thorough. You had to process all the sauces in a certain way... that's where I learned that's where the quality comes from. Definitely... hand-cut quality. And I think I'm still under that kind of influence, which you know in some ways is a drawback, because sometimes you have to let go to be more efficient.

Some people talk about the lack of freedom and not being able to move around too quickly as a chef.

No, you can't. In France, you have the tradition, you have the establishment, you have to follow the pattern. It's like a staircase, and you cannot jump the stairs— it doesn't work that way over there. You have to go each step at a time... I think that has changed.

But with that guy it was like that and he wanted to send me to somebody in the Val de Loire and after that, that guy would have sent me to somebody else, I said, hey, oh, oo...

I didn't see it as a necessity. I am a maverick, maybe, I don't know. I like to do things my way. But there, I felt I was used, because you work lots of hours, and hours don't mean anything. You start at eight in the morning and you're there at 10:00, 11:00, 12:00 at night.

You don't have a life. You have basically been born what you've decided to be. If you're a cook, well, tough luck, no family, no this, no that. It's like entering into a monastery. Forget the rest, you're there, that's where you belong. You're a monk, you're a cook-monk. You couldn't get anything else. You can see that very early in the kitchens.

Your job still is most important. Work, family, and your country... so work comes first.

So did you have second thoughts, then?

No, because I like what I do. For me, it was my job, it was very important. It's still important... Somebody in the back [referring to his wife, Tara] is saying the job goes before the family.

So you came to Canada?

I had a friend who had come to Canada and he sounded very happy. It was a way to go away and experience something new. I think it was reaction against the establishment. You didn't have any control over yourself, depending on someone else to get you somewhere, to give you a job. Who needed it?

I knew it was going to be a bit tough so I came to Quebec. Jesus Christ, what a cultural shock that was. When you come as a chef-saucier— a respected professional— and they put you in front of the grill to make hamburgers and grilled tomato and mushrooms which are not even washed, french fries which come out of a frozen bag... gee. I thought I was wasted.

It was at L'Hotel La Concorde. It was a nice hotel, nice place, busy. But man, Jesus Christ, these guys were using mushrooms out of the box, not even washed, in omelettes, and I said, Jesus Christ, that's pretty disgusting... I didn't care, because you have a transition, you have that kind of experience, you have to learn, and there I wasn't in a position to be the boss; I was starting at the bottom again. So, I said, well, that's what you want, so let's go...

It went pretty fast... I started to go up the ladder when they saw that hamburger wasn't my type. They put me in the restaurant and... I lasted there two years, and then I came to Toronto.

So what did you think about the quality of the food in Quebec at that level?

Once I moved out of that coffee-shop atmosphere— yeah, they had a small restaurant there which was quite good. We decided to implement a kind of Nouvelle Cuisine— with a French flair, I must admit. Already I had an idea of what North American cooking was all about. At La Concorde we did lots of banquets— a thousand people and so on so, you knew what volume was— and that's something I didn't really experience that much in France— not so simple— just to throw a piece of meat on the barbie and serve it with a baked potato. The frozen chicken, you thawed it out and roasted, convention-style at the hotel. I didn't like that cup of tea. I couldn't believe that people could have pleasure with things like that... even if you're a businessman talking about business and bottom line... man, what stops you from eating something you enjoy eating instead of having to eat something that, I don't know, is kind of a suspect quality.

In Toronto, it was worse; it was money, it was just productivity, and push, push. I arrived at the Harbour Castle and I was on the commission side and it was a big-volume restaurant. But there, with all the cooks, we tried to give quality, also. We had more leeway to do better food.

But isn't that the dilemma in North America in the big hotels where they still want to have a fine restaurant?

The problem is that there's no personality— there's no personality. The problem with the big hotels is that people want to make money selling bedrooms, because it doesn't cost that much to sell a bedroom. That's what a hotel is: to put people to sleep one night or two nights— but not to feed the people. To feed the people is part of the service you give to the guests. They don't want that to cost you too much.

But they like to have a fancy restaurant.

Well, sure. But when they put their noses in the books they know it's going to cost them money, so they don't want that.

Well, you've been doing this for many years and have been an executive chef for many years. How do you do this when you know the bottom line? There's something to learn for a chef about this balancing act...

It was tricky at first, but for me, if you manage to get the costs you want, if you're in line, to produce the food and make the customer come back also. So, I don't know... maybe because I was born into food, I don't know, I breathe food all my life, I read books on cooking all my life... maybe for me it's like for you walking. You don't know how you walk, somebody asks you how you walk and you say, well, I don't know, I put each foot in front of the other. For me, cooking is the same thing. I do it. [Laughing in disbelief] I do it like that! I don't know. But for me, giving costs and good food has never been a problem. Now, how do I do it? I don't know. It's a feeling, it's a touch. How much salt do you put in? I don't know, just look.

Can this be taught? You've always had so many apprentices and young people in so many hotels and restaurants?

It's a slow process. People have to breathe like you. But you don't always have apprentices who are going to be as good as you are. They have to become their own, also. It's a slow process. They're going to learn more in watching how you do things... In the pastry side you have a recipe to follow, you have measurements and you have to scale everything. In cooking, you don't scale, you know. How much salt do you put in there? Well, it was a dusting... How much wine did you drop in?... One ounce... but you never measured it, so is it really one ounce? When is meat cooked? When is a fish cooked? Well, okay, with your finger, you touch. But there're a lot of things experience is going to teach you. Like, I know, my guys... if they're going to do a sauce, it's never going to be as good as if I make it. Why? I have no idea, and they don't know why either.

So is this to do with the difference in training here and in France or is it more basic?

In France, the training is very long. You hone your skills very slowly and you don't specialize. You have all kinds of learning experiences. Whew... I remember, when you get deer, you don't get a piece of deer. You get the whole animal, which you've got to hang up in the kitchen and you have to pull off the skin and cut the animal. You have a different approach, a different feeling. I don't think people here... In some hotels there you receive half a calf or half of a steer, so you have to break it down, you have to know what to do, that's another point... Maybe I can manage food costs and all that— with any piece of meat or ingredient, I use everything, I don't dump anything in the garbage. All the by-products I use. That's something you learn. I was lucky to be where I was at the right time, because I remember we had this half a steer coming into the kitchen. Man, you have to break it down and these chefs, too, at the time, I learned from them, what to do with it— a consommé of beef, bones, stocks. Nowadays you buy everything. You know the guy gets a strip loin, there are no more bones.

But you have to sell the food. You were probably the first person to introduce the food of the Southwest, things like duck confit here in Toronto. Is there a responsibility to teach customers from your vision and taste, or for food costs are you forced to produce what they want?

No, no, no. You always have to excite the customer, excite the curiosity of the customer. The North American was very stereotyped— he eats certain things, he's shy of experimenting. So, what do you do? Either you teach and in teaching customers you don't make that much money and it's always frustrating, or you aggravate the customer, you provoke the customer. And I think nowadays the people are getting used to it. Fusion cuisine is a very aggressive way of cooking and I think the customers are starting to get used to it. But I think at the beginning of the '80s, man, these people they just knew salmon, halibut, chicken wings and beef... and pork chops.

So you think fusion's a good thing?

Yes, but I think we're going too far. That's the extremes. From one extreme we jump to the other extreme in a very short period of time. Nowadays you look at the menus and man, they take something— you're going to find some sushi with different mixtures that don't have anything to do with sushi and you're going to find some spice from South America mixed up with something from Asia... I think you have to follow some kind of rule there. You can be flexible in the rules but you have to respect the product. And I don't think we have people who respect the product nowadays.

It's kind of scary. In the States, it's the same thing. There is no conscience, there is no background, there is no history, there is no culture— so these guys, they don't have to respect that tradition that we have in France. They come out like a jack-in-the-box, you know? Put something weird with something a little weirder.

I was in the Los Angeles basin. Over there people are different, that's for sure. Different because they've just come out of their macaroni and cheese from Kraft and they go into the restaurant where I think the food is more part of the decor— in going out, it's like the maître d' has to have a big smile and smell good, and, like the shaving, the food has to look good and not be too aggressive. The fish is not allowed to taste fishy.

People are not curious, they're not that interested, they stay with that iceberg lettuce. For them, it's top. In France, you have five or six different lettuces to choose from every day.

In Canada, it's a little bit more open. I think it's coming, too, if you go to New York— I saw a little more European input in Los Angeles. I mean Los Angeles is very far from Europe. It's like in Montreal, you're probably going to see things done in a more traditional nice way than you see in Toronto— it's definitely in the pastries. The pastries are not 12 feet high, they are more what we expect in Europe. Tasty, not so sweet. It's like the chocolate. You can sell in Montreal chocolates that you can't sell here. Here, you need sweet. It's funny that, too, huh? In California it was very sweet, too. Dressing— sweet— I don't know why they put sugar in there— pastries were very sweet, and everybody wanted to be on a diet.

I think people— if you want to surprise them and give them good food— for sure— you have to go beyond their expectations. You have to know what they want and for me it's been to "kick it up a notch," so they were always thrilled. And I think that's why it was so easy for me to introduce a new product.

Now, you also spent some time in Beijing?

I was there for at least three months. It was to open a North American restaurant. In Beijing, the cooking was very poor. The fun was not in opening the restaurant but in looking at what people were doing— how they eat. Lots of restaurants on the sidewalk. They were limited in cooking facilities. Lots of woks where you boil, fry inside— and either they do pasta— because it was in Beijing there wasn't that much rice— pasta or bread dough. Very greasy, not too much meat, but they use the whole animal there— from the feet to the beak to the intestines. It was very interesting to me because when people don't waste food, it's always very important, very interesting. How people become very creative in using all the parts— it's very wonderful. There they used everything and they used lots of vegetables and the vegetables were very good.

But I didn't learn a lot there. Basically you fry or you boil. Those were the only two concepts. But I knew some of the guys in the kitchen when they were preparing the staff meals Chinese style, they knew how to do it, the way. But as soon as we were trying to train them to cook the North American way they were incapable. But to cook their food, they knew that. They had no problem.

To break the habits is very difficult. For me, a guy past the age of 23, it's very difficult to train because the guys start to be set, the metal is cold, you cannot bend the person. It's very difficult to train somebody who already has a mind of his own.

So are people cooking from their own palate?

I personally find that in North America, it's more interesting to cook with a farmer than somebody from the city. They have more respect for the produce.

You later went and worked in St. Louis. Tell me about that?

We stayed there roughly a year. It was a different life. I don't like it there. Gross. Everything is fatty, big, huge... ugh... the food— cheeseburger soup... [we laugh] Can you imagine, the ladle was standing up in the soup and that's the way they like it. And they eat massive amounts of food. The first time we went to a restaurant there it was supposed to be the best in town. A pasta place— man, the plate was so big I thought it was a platter. It was a platter! There was enough for four people, but there was no quality. It was huge but, how can people be thrilled eating that? What kind of pleasure you would have to eat that? I don't know. I couldn't relate to these people. If you don't have pleasure, what's the point? For me, even with a hamburger you have to have some pleasure, even a sandwich, even a soup, a salad— the simplest thing— you have to taste something, that simple thing has to have something to tell you. Even a piece of bread. How many bakeries did we try in Toronto? Massive amounts of bakeries. A piece of bread has to have taste, has to have something to tell you. And I think it's respect for the guy who is the baker. How can I respect the baker if his bread tastes like Weston Bread... the bread doesn't have anything to tell me; I don't like it. Why should I put that in my mouth? For convenience. Well, sometimes you have to. But I'd rather have a piece of dry bread that I'm going to soak with a little bit of cold water than to have bread that isn't going to taste of anything. Many times Tara goes to buy bread at Dimpfelmeier's, that white bread... I cannot swallow it. I'd rather have a piece of stale Italian bread and soak it in water and eat it.

So for a dish in a restaurant or if you're making something for yourself, what are you looking for?

Flavours, taste, I want an association of flavours—

But what did you mean then about certain aspects of fusion?

It's a masquerade. It's a masquerade because your main product is totally degraded by other flavours which come conflicting with it. You know, if you take the main product— for example, a breast of chicken which already has to have some taste— you have to enhance that breast of chicken. Complement it. Make it look good. Make it look better than it could be... so you have to choose either the vegetables, the sauce, the ingredients of the sauce to make that breast of chicken look its best.

And where's your guideline?

I think it's your gut feeling. It's in your guts. You know, you will find, because of your background, different ingredients than me. It doesn't mean that your ingredients or the way you're going to make it are going to be worse—

The philosophy is to create a balance. That was the way I was brought up. I was trained. It's a very fragile balance. If you put too much garlic in, you overkill everything. If you don't put in enough— well, something's going to be missing. To manage to bring the cooking of the product to where it's not really overcooked, not undercooked. You overcook your chicken breast, and all the flavours come out— how is a person going to eat it? It's going to be a dried piece of cardboard. And also the season— when you cook a breast of chicken in the summer, it's not going to be the same in the winter and in the fall or in the spring.

So, in the springtime, I list the products, the animals I'm going to cook for the banquet and the products which are seasonal.

Right now we have morels, fiddleheads, dandelions, you have fava beans. You have some budding vegetables, because fortunately in North America, spring is viable all the time with the plane— and when you have that, what else can you associate with it? Sea urchin— maybe we could do something with sea urchin— the product could marry well with the white meat and the flavour, so could I do something? Could I take frogs' legs, maybe— yeah, maybe frogs' legs, it's springtime— they start to jump all over the place, maybe frogs' legs, yeah, maybe that's going to be something new. Snails. Maybe a breast of chicken with snails. And after that you have to create the contrasts in texture. If you take the breast of chicken, well, what do you think? It's mushy, you have to chew it— could we get something crispy? That would be fine— or maybe something softer or maybe something crunchy. If you put it with fiddleheads, maybe you're going to have that crunchiness. And if you put something with morels, and all the water is going to come out and it's going to give a nice middle flavour and something soft with it... The middle flavour is penetrating, it's woody, it's nice. All these things have to be taken into consideration.

So you're saying that texture comes second, and you think first about flavour?

For me, the taste, and after— you know you have pleasure when you eat, when you put it in your mouth, and it's all the same way you eat it, chew it... it's like a cow always eating the grass and the grass, the same grass... your palate is not challenged. A breast of chicken is going to take you about 15 minutes to eat, but if you put something crispy— like, for example the crispiness of the bread, like a nice crusty bread. It will challenge the monotony of eating that breast. So the guests are going to be more interested, it's going to bring another pleasure. In the pastry department, cake can get boring, it's boring to always eat a crème caramel— people like that, it's comfort food, but could we bring another level— crème caramel is always soft and nyum-nyum-nyum-ny... okay, you don't need your teeth. Well, maybe we should put a cookie with it, something crunchy— you don't always have that monotony. Maybe the vanilla has to be a different tasting vanilla— intense flavour— you're going to bring from the fresh beans. Could we put a bit of zest of orange, maybe, just to break that caramel-milky taste and bring another level? See, all these considerations you have to bring, especially nowadays— the desserts are becoming very complex. In North America, especially, you have all the berries. The berries here are very acidic because they don't have time to ripen in the plane. What can you do with it, you know? You have acidity, so you have to find some acidity with the cream or with a mousse, and all that is pretty soft, so you bring something that can be crunchy, or a little bit more dry, like a biscuit which is going to be a little bit more impartial but still restore that feeling that you want to again put your spoon back into the plate. That's a challenge.

So you challenge the customer... do you want to challenge yourself, too?

Sure. For me, no status quo. What was good today could be improved tomorrow and we have to find a way to improve it. I don't think perfection is a place where you arrive— it's a journey, you know? So, always you question yourself— how can I do better? And you always have to find a way.

You know it's a way to stay young; you don't always keep repeating yourself. There's not that many ways you can reinvent the wheel, but you always have to find a way.

So at different points in your life you came to different stages?

Yes, yes... Sometimes, at first, I think love had lots to do with it... when I was younger... all the girls you try to... love, love... they help you to bring pleasure... you want to please them, you want to please people, make people happy, and you have lots to give— and maybe I don't have so much to give... I don't know... [calling out to his wife] Tara, can you leave the room, please...!

Plus life has become more eclectic and it's becoming more difficult to create, to find combinations, not creating crazy combinations, but to find associations to break down the routine.

But at the same time you say it's a... gut feeling.

Right now, I'm drained. I can feel it. I can feel it, I'm drained of all creative energy. I'm tired, I'm going through lots in the past three weeks [he and Tara have a newborn] and I can feel it. It's very painful. So you tend to copy, you copy whatever you come up with. Sometimes you have a period of time when you don't come up with things. It's like you when you write. I bet you have times when it's very difficult.

But you have to go through it... to keep going if you're a chef. It's not an easy thing...

It's not easy. I find when I used to go closer to Mother Nature— in the woods, by the ocean— California was noisy, there was always ocean, beaches... it was more easy to create. You had a confrontation of cultures. You had the Spanish and you had the White and for me there was more expression out of that. Especially because I was working with Spanish people, and they brought their ways of cooking and they knew products and it was more interesting... challenging.

But right now, I'd like to get close to Mother Nature, the farmers— you know the Lot [region of the River Lot in Southwest France, where he was raised], you go and visit the markets... that helped me a lot. And now I don't do that... so it's tough.

Can you tell me about a recent dish which you have created?

I think the combination with sea urchin because it's a product nobody really handles very well. They never think about it, it's an ugly piece of thing that Canadians still really haven't mastered that much— besides Japanese restaurants— and even if it's a Japanese restaurant, it's part of a sushi, they don't really know too much about it. And I think that product needs to be put in the open, it's a challenge... We did quite a few things with it. We did a soup and we did scallops. People were very surprised. It's very easy— you cook your scallops with some white wine and a bit of cream and at the end you pour your sea urchin and you blend all that together and you make a wonderful sauce. The colour is orange... the flavour, it's kind of... uh... [laughs] people don't know. It's orange and that strange flavour— what's going on? The other thing we did was the ostrich. Ostrich is a new product also, and people don't really know about it; it was easy. We had to introduce it as a surf-and-turf and it was a very successful affair. So we had two sauces, lobster tail and the ostrich, and put it in a nest with a glaze of balsamic vinegar, and lobster coulis around it.

You have to tease the people, so we put in a piece of ostrich, rare— and it went well. So you have the balsamic which is a kind of acidic, full of flavour, and you associate this with the mellowness of the coulis of the lobster. And the crispiness, because we use a special kind of dough, which is something from the Middle East, like a vermicelli— and it's interesting and nobody knows about it.

Another thing we did was a quail. Now people are bored... they eat them grilled. But Moroccans have a b'stilla which is a kind of a cake with crisp layers of pastry and layers of parsley with scrambled eggs— you put in your quails, your pigeon breasts, and on top, some almonds with sugar and some orange water, and you bake that in the oven. And we did that but on a small scale in the leaf of pâté à brik [a North African pastry] which is very crispy, and we served that with some greens... that, too, they liked. And if you take the bones of the quails and you make a reduced jus, and we did a saffron pimento vinaigrette. The Moors, the Spanish— that part of the world. That was great. Nowadays everybody puts some goat cheese with everything... we didn't put in any goat cheese.

Some chefs talk about a number of elements in a dish. Do you have your own ideas about that?

There's another point. Depending on whom you're cooking for. You have some people who know about food. I have a customer at the club who is very well-educated. You don't need to put so many things. You have a main product, cook it well, two garnishes, three garnishes... that's it. But nowadays, more and more you can see people want so many different conflicting products. My job is to please them. You have to add more different flavours; maybe too many. Far too many. They don't want to taste simple. Look at foie gras— foie gras was good by itself. A little bit of pepper, a bit of aspic... that was it. Now you have foie gras, you have figs, you have... What are you eating? You don't know. You have lost your main product. In France, you have it a lot simpler. They go for products— one sauce, one garnish, and that's it.

They give the centrepiece— the most important thing on that plate is really that product. Sometimes, you know, in North America, your main product doesn't have taste, so you have to bring it some life.

That's another concept. What is centre stage on your plate? It has to have taste. Like when I buy my chicken from Quebec, because they have lots more taste than in Ontario— whatever we find on the market here. And that's very important. It's like the salmon— your father was a fisherman. If you compare the salmon you were eating 20 years ago and what we have now— most of the salmon is tasting the same. Every restaurant has the same salmon coming from the same or different farms. And yesterday, we were talking about smoked salmon and we found a salmon from Gaspésie which we're going to start to bring in, and the flavour is totally different. A nicer salmon.

How about emotions? How are they in your cooking?

It's very emotional. Personally, when I cook, it's a part of myself. It's a message. I have pleasure cooking and that pleasure I want to transmit through the cooking to people. That plate I'm preparing is a plate of pleasure. I hope the guest is going to have pleasure, and it will be all that he was expecting to eat, and be like a little bit of a smile, a ray of sun, this moment of life. For me it's a transmission of pleasure, to make you happy. When I cook for us, it has to have pleasure, it's part of me, I give you part of my existence, my heritage, my culture... for sure.

I don't think people notice this stuff. I don't think people realize that. Especially in North America, for most of them it's refuelling energy.

It's the pride to make them discover where I come from, where I am. What I believe in, in the matter of cooking. I'm not at ease cooking Argentinean food, I don't relate to it. I don't know these people. For me, it's passing along part of my childhood, the people I mingled with when I was a kid. The village I grew up in, you know? When I select that bread to give you to eat, it's because it reminds me of things I experienced before.

As soon as you get back to France, does that sense of your own heritage from the Southwest... because you grew up in the charcuterie with the foie gras... come back to you?

Yes, yes. A lot. It's 10 pounds more at the end. No, it's a satisfaction. I think it's the child in you who gets to come up again to life. I don't think people can just say, well, I'm not a kid any more. I think you always have a piece of you that remains young. Which remains the child you were when you were 12, 14, 16... and I think that person will come up again. It's like when you revisit a place where you were born— you know, it's not the adult. It's the kid who is again there, who is alive. You have memories, going through that. I remember when we went to see an aunt, and she cooked a pot au feu—

and that flavour of pot au feu, you know... put me so many years back, when my grandmother was alive, and I could see memories. When she was cooking that rice— man, I never had rice like that before and I don't think I'll ever have rice like that again.

As soon as we go back over there, it's to take a duck, roast it with olives— simple— nothing else. Just very simple. It's more simple food than what I'm using in North America. A lot simpler. Like rabbit. We would put just a few mushrooms in, with a bit of ventrêche, a little sautéed pommes meli, a few mushrooms that are around, and that's it, nothing else. And the bread, of course the bread. And a glass of wine and it's satisfying. You don't need truffles, you don't need foie gras— no, it's just plain. When you go and eat foie gras on a farm at my brother's— a nice piece of bread, foie gras— that's it. You don't need the confit or the coulis of figs, curry or whatever the powder— don't give me that, just give me the foie...

With your long background in charcuterie, when you make a terrine, what are you looking for, is there something in the seasoning, the combination of the fat, the meat...?

[laughing] He's going to get all my secrets here... Yeah, the seasoning is pretty standard, because you're always seasoning it at 18 grams of salt per kilo, your two grams of pepper, you put in some wine. I think the seasoning is a bit the same throughout...

It's the marinating, the slow cooking, it's all these little details, it's the equipment. You don't cook it in aluminum, you cook it in cast iron— all these things are important. I don't know, do we do something different? I don't really realize it. Yeah, when I make a pâté, the different mix of meat and fat, the marinating, a bit of garlic, a bit of onion, the parsley. But I don't think that's anything really fancy or like when Paul [my nephew, chef Paul Onami] told me— you remember— when you made that hare terrine with blueberries. Wasn't so fantastic. For me it was not. For him it was. I don't know why. Well, right now what you see is a lot of mushy terrine, and they grind everything just to hide the fat. I think a terrine is like another product, you've got to take the meat and the liver and you have to let it express itself. You're going to help it out with a bit of spice, a bit of seasoning and wine and some bay leaf, maybe some juniper berries— but I like all the game and venison to be cooked with juniper berries because I think that makes the meat sing— gives it a little woody flavour, and maybe the aroma. Now, you have to put a crust on it? I don't think so, but... just a little bit.

You've been doing this for many years... Do you ever have times when you doubt— this is not for me?

Sometimes I do. But I don't think I would be happy if I stopped. The problem nowadays with cooking is you can't really feed a family. It's tough; you don't make much money.

It's hard, because you have to work when other people enjoy themselves. When you work is when people want to eat. They have finished working, so you end up on the opposite schedule and to find a family that is going to be happy with that is going to be difficult. The divorce rate is very high. It's tough on a family and you work long hours. You work vacations. Christmas. There's never been a Christmas Day off. New Year's Day off doesn't exist.

But more and more you see the cooks and chefs are young. Because it's very demanding. There's always lots of things happening. You never know if your fish delivery is going to be on time or an hour behind schedule and throw off all your preparation.

Sometimes it was hard to make a living. Could you find another way? Especially in North America.

Even now, sometimes I wonder— is there not another way to make your living than that? Like last night, when I went home, it was 11:00, and the night before it was midnight. What am I going to do? Am I going to be a millionaire? No, never. I see people who just go to work at 10:00, finish at 6:00, man... but there is pleasure.

The next day you feel better. When you have a bad day, the next day it's better.

Knowing that you have made somebody happy. Oh, hey, that was great! It makes you feel better. That's a reward, because once the plate or the meal has been finished, you have to start all over again. It's not like you're going to put it on a wall there and look at it for hours, or years. It's over. Once the guy puts his fork into it and finishes it up, your job is over; you have to stop.

And you have to be ready at the same time of day because you take breakfast in the morning, you take lunch at lunch, and dinner at 8:00. You have to be very disciplined. You cannot tell a guy, well, I'm sorry your lunch is not ready; come tomorrow morning; I'm going to have it then. It doesn't work. Yeah, you have to have discipline.

Well, the last time you went to France you went to the South to visit the land of the Cathars... is that related to your feelings of cuisine du terroir that you have?

I think, yeah, probably, because these guys were so close to Mother Nature. The Cathars were at the turn of the first century, Millennium, it's a religion that was competing against Catholicism, and the religion had taken over the South of France, Italy, probably Switzerland... these guys believed in a different way of God and a different way of life. They were very simple, dedicated to different values; pleasure didn't have much room there for anybody. But I felt very close, maybe because I'm trying to find another way of life. I am bit disillusioned with all this philosophy, maybe I want more to be at peace with myself than to be materialistic, to be a capitalist, socialist, what does it mean, all these things? I think we have to live closer to the environment— but, no, it was very interesting and it was moving when I went to visit where they used to live.

It was feeling at home; it was like something inside you is magnetism, which is talking to the environment.

It seems to come, you know, when you talk about food and when you really get into your guts— yeah, that's probably from the same place, from within yourself. For sure, if I had to cook in Mongolia, I don't think I could really relate. I would be totally disconnected. Japanese cooking, for me... that's why I don't really try to do it— I wouldn't connect, I wouldn't have anything to connect. I don't have veins? I don't have... I cannot. It's not on the same level.

So with Mount Segur, it's very much inside of you?

Yeah. Even when you do a recipe, you can connect with it because your roots are there.

It's so you're very content when you eat that food; it's very tasty, it's not the cliché; they give you real value, they don't work on perception, the true value of the food. Here in North America, everything is perception. How you perceive it— we're going to do it for you. It's like the wine in California. In France, a Bordeaux is made like a Bordeaux, not what these guys want to drink. In Europe, you do a thing because that's the way it is. I can remember in a winery in California— well, here we have market research to know what kind of Chardonnay they want to drink. Or this year it's Cabernet Sauvignon, okay, we're going to make Cabernet Sauvignon. I was kind of surprised. I mean, the grapes— what is this grape? I dunno, we're going to adjust them...

The food is the same. Try to predict what next year you're going to sell, and we're going to make it. It's a bit like fashion.

Maybe I'm still very traditional, myself. Very much so. But that's what I like to eat, too.

Patrick Alléguède

Born in a small town in the Southwest of France, the oldest of seven children, Patrick Alléguède knew at an early age that he wanted to be a chef. He attended the Ecole Hôtelière des Pyrenees in Toulouse, where he received his culinary degrees, and went on to win the Grand Prix National des Desserts at the age of 20. His apprenticeships took him to resorts all over France. He then worked as a chef in the famed Hotel de Crillon and Hotel Meridien in Paris. After coming to Canada, his work took him to the Hotel Loews' Le Concorde, then Los Angeles, Chicago, St. Louis and Beijing. Currently Alléguède is focusing on the transformation of a Toronto private business club into a gastronomic stop for its members.

Patrick Alléguède's
LE DOS DE SAUMON AUX LENTILLES, TOMATE CONFITE ET BEURRE
AU SAFRAN [OAK PLANKED ROASTED SALMON ON A BED OF
LENTILS, CONFIT TOMATO AND SAFFRON BEURRE BLANC]

INGREDIENTS

FOR THE SALMON
4 x 180 g salmon filets, scaled, skin on
2 tsp olive oil
coarse sea salt
ground pepper to taste

FOR THE LENTILS
60 g green French lentils
1 small diced onion
1 small diced carrot
1 small diced celery branch
1 crushed garlic clove
1 bay leaf
1 branch of thyme
1/2 litre chicken stock
1 tbsp olive oil

FOR THE TOMATO CONFIT
4 vine-ripe plum tomatoes
2 tbsp olive oil
1 clove garlic
3 chopped basil leaves

FOR THE SAFFRON BUTTER
2 finely chopped shallots
4 tbsp Noilly Pratt vermouth
4 tbsp dry white wine
1 pinch saffron
75 g sweet butter

The day before: soak the lentils in water and immerse in water a 15 cm x 30 cm oak or cedar shingle.

Prepare the tomato confit: preheat the oven to 300 F. Peel the tomatoes and cut into quarters, eliminating the seeds. Toss with remaining ingredients and course sea salt. Lay on a baking sheet lined with silicon paper. Cook for 3 hours in the oven; avoid browning. Refrigerate until the next day.

Drain the lentils. In a pot, sweat in the olive oil, the lentils, chopped vegetables and garlic. Cover with chicken stock. Add bay leaf and thyme, coarse salt and pepper. Simmer until done. Add additional chicken stock as needed.

In a sauce pan, reduce slowly the shallots, vermouth, white wine and saffron by half. Whisk in the butter cubes. Correct seasoning and remove from the heat.

Turn on oven broiler. Lay the four salmon steaks, skin side down, on the oak/cedar shingle. Rub with olive oil and sprinkle with coarse salt and pepper. Bake in the middle of the oven, under broiler. The salmon should be slightly browned when done and pink in the centre.

On dinner plate, put two tablespoons of lentils at centre and display the salmon on top. Place four teaspoons of saffron butter around the salmon as petals on a flower. On top of each puddle of sauce, display a wedge of tomato confit. Decorate with chives or basil.

John Higgins

Chiaro's, Le Royal Meridien, King Edward Hotel, Toronto, Ontario

When I went to Spain in June of 1998, I'm grateful that John Higgins was part of the small group invited to discover the food of Spain by that country's Trade Commission. He arrived in Toronto just before I moved to Montreal and so all I knew of him was the high esteem those who know food in Toronto held for him. It's a treat to travel with a chef, to watch the sense of awareness, the looking, the touching, the breathing in of the perfumes of a plate of food, the seconds of reflection as food is moved in the space of the mouth— things John does as a matter of pleasure and learning. I also saw the totally unpretentious approach he has, too, impatient of pretence, while his work world is that of lofty-priced first-class hotel cuisine— and indeed, he once cooked at Buckingham Palace. The respect he showed towards the food and work of honest, hard-working chefs, showed how much his own food and palate is about the search for taste and the rudiments of seasoning. He looks for different ways of presenting satisfying tasty flavours, elegant colour and shape, eschewing complicated ostentation: food where one need not endure a chef's overbearing persona. I recall how that first morning of our trip, on a transfer at Heathrow, John as well as Jamie Kennedy ordered the heavy-duty full cooked English breakfast in the plebian airport coffee shop, digging into it with gusto, while most of the food writers went tamely to breakfast. They ate with down-to-earth sensual pleasure.

I got the feeling John wanted to talk about Spain as we sat down for breakfast one morning in Chiaro's at the hotel, and my ears willingly perked to the ready when I asked if and how the experiences in Spain had become woven into his chef's culinary passage.

Oh, I think so. Thinking of Spain, I think of the good times, and of the basic foods there. I've told numerous people that the best foods I've ever tasted, travelling in Europe, were in Spain. By far.

No matter if you go to a little hole-in-the-wall tapas bar and you're getting the sautéed potatoes with squid and bacon or you go for a nice meal, there's a lot more love and affection. France is the same, I think, but Spain impressed me much more. Very very very very simple food. Nice people; they please. It was very, very enlightening. I've come back here with a different feel for food. What's difficult is trying to explain what it was all about— the experiences, and the feels, and the touches and the smells— to people here. People still have a hard time getting that sort of understanding of food, and that's what makes it difficult.

How do you express that, then, in terms of what you do?

The only thing that you can do, really, is to try and keep the simplicity. And a lot of what I enjoyed about Spain was the simplicity. The dishes weren't complex, and that's really reflected in a lot of my cooking. You can almost call it a French brasserie style. In Spain you would get possibly a piece of fish, and vegetables, and that would be it. Or you get a piece of meat and that's it. And almost the same thing, in that you get pot au feu, you get a jarret d'agneau or you get a sole meunière with maybe steamed potatoes or something else. Very simple, very basic. I was thinking about the lunch we had the other day, [which John had served to those in the group to Spain], and the main course was just salmon, tomato, olive or sea parsley. Nothing else. There was nothing fancy, nothing "Wow." I just wanted to try and cook it simply. And I think sometimes the problems that we have here, the hotel here and in general, is that it has to be fancier, bigger and better than everywhere else. That's not necessarily the case, and I sometimes have a hard time with the cooks, trying to make them understand this. If the mashed potatoes are seasoned right, to perfection, the liver that is sautéed off and is kept pink if the guests ask for pink, that's what success is. It's not building it higher and bigger and better than everyone else.

The hard thing is, it's almost like trying to tell a Frenchman or a Spaniard to cook North American style food. Unless you've been there, savoured it, felt it, touched it, visualized it, it's hard. It's hard for someone to understand the way the food is there, or the way it is in Europe or the way it is in South

America, if they've never travelled, possibly, or never been outside of Ontario, maybe outside of Canada.

The way you talk about it as such a physical kind of thing, does it say something about what the relationship of real food is?

Yes, I think food is powerful. It's a perfect medium. And it's just the visual. You see it, "Wow," you stop, you smell it, "Wow," you stop, you're eating, you say "Wow." It's the wow-factor. And it's very difficult to explain. A lot of it is senses— the touch, feel, smell, and taste. And that's what, to me, food is all about. No different than when you go to McDonald's. You walk into McDonald's and you go "sswhihhh" [sniffs deeply]... I'm in a McDonald's, because there's a certain smell, there's a fat there, there's a fat sometimes that you smell, just like at Kentucky Fried Chicken. It's the fat that gets your palate going already— that defines the food. It's very difficult to define the food and express that to someone who has no idea how we can talk about a simple tomato sauce. You know, you go to Italy, you get thick, thin, medium, chunky, hot, spicy, and that's difficult. And I think the thing is that sometimes cooks in general don't do an awful lot of research. I don't necessarily think you have to go to Spain. I think it enhances your knowledge by going to a country like Spain, or going to California, or wherever you want to go. But you can pick up a cookbook— and I think this is the secret to being a chef or a cook— and I don't think there's any right one... An old college teacher of mine, Mr. Hogan, used to say, "There's no such thing as great recipes, only great chefs." A lot of it is— you visualize something, you see it, someone has told you about it, and you can duplicate it. And that's a gift. It really is a gift because sometimes I see the cooks that we have here, or cooks I've worked with other places, or even in Team Canada, and you can tell them something and they don't really grasp it.

Sometimes people say to me, "It's okay for you, you've 20 or 15 years' experience." But I had this when I was in the kitchen only four or five years. We're talking about it like there's a love and a passion in it, and it's interesting to meet people who have the same passion. There's very few really good friends who would go into expensive restaurants. I go to cheap restaurants, and it doesn't make any difference. Good food's good food. Sometimes that's one of the questions I ask staff when I bring them on board, be it front of the house staff or back of the house staff, "What's your favourite restaurant to go to?" I don't really care if they say McDonald's, to tell you the truth. I'd ask them, "Why do you go to McDonald's?" "Oh, I like that big taste because of this and that!" and that's what you want, the excitement.

In Spain, was there one particular thing that you felt really in common with the people there, or one particular place, or experience, or person you met, where you really sort of connected?

Three or four things really connected with me. The first meal we had in Spain was very much of an eye-opener, because there were eight people, and maybe two or three of them had been to Spain before. This simple, basic food tasted so good, it was just like "Wow." It just brought everyone together. No one had really had that sense of bonding, and this food just brought a whole group of people together. We talked about it, and it was like, wow, you couldn't do this in Toronto because of X, Y, and Z, and that's what it's about. That's what food's about. Bringing people around the table and saying, this is what life experience is about, breaking bread. There's a significance to that. I think that was one of the best experiences I've ever had, at the restaurant in Madrid. And it was interesting, going into this three-star restaurant, El Bulli... That experience was... comme-ci, comme-ça. Why was it comme-ci, comme-ça? The food was all right, but the chef was conceited as hell, the china wasn't the best china, it wasn't three-star, and I think again it's the visual aspect. I've been in three-star restaurants before, and this wasn't really a three-star restaurant, it was just a lot of hype and whatever else. Bullshit sells sometimes. That wasn't a great experience.

Definitely it was something different. The person had done a lot of different things, the seawater sorbet, the jellies, there were about four or five dishes I thought were exceptional. But the experience of the whole thing was, ah, it was okay. I could have gone for some fritatas or something else, something simple, and been just as happy.

Other experiences I thought were exceptional. The night near Barcelona, we went to that restaurant.... There were only two or three cooks in the kitchen at the time. Basic food, nice variety, good flavours and tastes. I think it was great that every time you went somewhere else the food would change. The ingredients were basically the same— olive oil and garlic and parsley, and sometimes eggs— but it would change— heavier on the sauces, maybe more on the fish, more on the salads. They wouldn't have as many spices, but the flavours and the textures would change. That was very, very interesting. But I think what I learned on the whole was, keep it simple.

In my little notes I have this thing written about simplicity in terms of asking you questions, and I remember you talked a lot about salting...

Yeah. Basic things. I had a staff meeting here last week. I said, you know, guys, the key to success is not Joanne Kates writing in the paper whether you're good or you're bad. The key to success in cooking is salt and pepper. Salt and pepper. You can put seasoned salt and you can put herbs on it, but if a dish doesn't have any salt and pepper it's not going to go, and I don't care where you go. Even if you go to the worst restaurant in the UK, they can seriously overcook the food, but as long as it tastes okay, they're not going to complain. And most people will send food back if there's no taste. And they won't come back again. That's the biggest thing. I'm very much the same with the cooks here. Make sure you taste, you taste, you taste. But I don't think they teach that at college any more. I think that's one of the scary things. A lot of cooks or restaurants in the business— I call them grill chefs or prime chefs— and what I mean by that is that they go into a restaurant, a lot of them in Toronto, and all they do is grill steaks, grill peppers, zucchini and grill swordfish, with a salsa and this and that, and there's no real cooking technique. You take something to your grill, you season, salt and pepper and that's it, that's easy. But the amount of salt and pepper you put on a piece of steak or a piece of swordfish on the grill is completely different than you'd ever do if you'd done a braised dish in the oven. You've got stock to be concerned with. Then you put wine in there, then you put vegetables, mirepoix in there, then you put the stock in there, and you have to season more to get more flavour out of all those things. That's a lot of the lack and the void that we have in the industry. It's just the basic things, making a good pot of soup, season it to start with, because it never tastes the same when you season it at the end, for some strange reason. It's just those basic things, it's scary. I get worried.

You're still talking about simplicity...

Something as simple as coq au vin— it's a very simple, basic— a farmer's dish, red wine, chicken, mushrooms, bacon— lardons— some onions. But the format for the dish is very simple. You've got to cook the wine and make a little sauce with it, but that's five times harder to do than taking out the best steak and the grill. Because you have to make sure the chicken's cooked, you have to make sure it's not overcooked, you have to make sure the taste is there, the red wine has penetrated the flesh a little bit, so you have almost the gamey flavour from the wine, and that's difficult to do. A lot of people don't understand that. I like things like coq au vin. It's a good wholesome dish to eat, and it's so simple and so tasty. But in some restaurants and hotels— to make a real true coq au vin you have to marinate the chicken— they think you can make a coq au vin within an hour, and that's ridiculous. People have to take an interest in understanding dishes, in understanding the history of the dish.

You know, it's like Sautée Marengo, named after the Battle of Marengo... and they don't even braise it and it's supposed to be braised. They think they can grill it, or think they can sautée the chicken off finished and put the sauce over it. I hate to get back to Spain and back to Europe, but I think people understand it a lot more. This is the idea of preparation. They don't cook any better than we do over here, they're just much more traditional and pass it along more.

So, is that possible, are we talking about some sort of ideal thing for people who are more passionate about...?

Yeah, I think it's for people who are more passionate, but you don't have to do this all the time. I think you can do it once a week. My best friend, he's a mechanic, he loves to cook. And he's good, but it's just as a fun thing. I think sometimes it's just taking the basic things and doing them well. And it's no different with a hamburger, or fish and chips, or bacon and eggs. It's the same thing.

So does this come right down to the shopping, for people, do you think?

Yeah, and again it's shopping for... it's like making a sandwich. You either go and buy Wonder Bread or you go and buy bread from Ace [small local baker]. You're talking 20 million miles of difference. You're talking a price difference as well. I think that's where a lot of the comparisons are made. How cheaply can I get it here versus there, instead of having a small piece or maybe one slice of bread, or one sandwich rather than three sandwiches.

Quality over quantity...

For sure. But I think that, luckily enough, here in Canada there's a lot of good quality product out there. A little bit more expensive, I think. That's where even the organic farmers rip people off, I think, by charging the real prime for the product instead of maybe just charging what they could charge, get people used to buying it. Sometimes I think they feel they have to get a return on their investment real fast.

Go back for me a little bit, to growing up. Where are you from?

Just outside of Glasgow. Basic family. We had no fancy bells and toys. We got holidays every year, just myself and my sister, my mother and father. Very small family, very much working class. My father always worked overtime to pay the bills. He was a steel-worker; my mother was a nurse. As kids we were very fortunate. We always got nice Christmas presents. But one year— I think that's maybe why I'm realistic about a lot of things— I had to wait two years for Christmas to get a set of golf clubs because they couldn't afford it. You get to appreciate things a lot more. That's what I have from my parents. My mother used to cook. She was never the best cook in the world... she was okay. She used to cook on a Sunday, cakes and sponges and that. She was pretty good at that, actually.

But my granny, my grandmother, she was a good cook. It's interesting, if you take something like minced beef, and she'd cook it for three hours or something, very very slowly, but her minced beef was the best in the world. It tasted so good. You cook at a lower temperature for a longer period of time. It's the same as when you cook something in the oven overnight. The protein doesn't harden as much, it's softer, it's much more moist. I mean, they were a big influence in my cooking to start with, and I think the biggest thing was that some of my aunts and uncles were very supportive, you know, you want to become a chef, wow, that's a good idea...

How old are you talking?

Ten years of age. I knew where I wanted to go when I was 10. I wanted to work at Glen Eagles. A lot of people were very supportive. Some people said, you want to be a chef? That's a dead-end job. But I had visions of being a chef at Glen Eagles and this and that, but I was aware at different times, of my friends saying, a chef? What do you want to be a chef for? You queer or what? You different? You off the wall or something? But it wasn't an accepted thing then, and someone coming from my neck of the woods, a working-class neighbourhood, it wasn't something people would have done. They either worked in the pits, the steel industry, some sort of heavy industrial thing, or a factory or out on the road or something else. A few people were, ah, what are you wasting your time for? And I was, screw you guys, I'll show you who can do it and who can't do it. I was very much focused on the vision of where I wanted to go.

I knew I wanted to work at the Central Hotel in Glasgow. It was the place to work in the west coast of Scotland, great training, a Michelin-star restaurant as well as a hotel. I went to Motherwell College first of all, which is just a couple of miles from the house, and I got a super, super, super basic training there. When I look at George Brown College here in Toronto, it's a disaster. There you would get Dover sole— this is what I mean by feel and touch— they give you a Dover sole, a real Dover sole, it costs a lot of money, you filet a Dover sole, you make a dish, you make a Dover sole doré or Dover sole bonne femme. There'll be 10 or 12 Dover sole, and 10 or 12 people in the class, so you see 10 different versions. The teachers there had all worked in major hotels and major positions, very, very knowledgeable, they really inspired me. Mr. Hogan was a nice, nice, nice man. He was 67, 70 or something when he finished teaching, and he was telling us, "When I worked at Buckingham Palace, when I worked at Glen Eagles, when I worked here and there..." And I just took the opinion, if he can do it, I can do it. And that was it. Focus, vision, and I said, I'm going to go to the Central Hotel first. I applied to the Central Hotel— there were about 130 applicants— and I got the job.

I wanted to go to Glen Eagles and eventually the company did transfer me after I finished my apprenticeship, to Glen Eagles. I was 19, and I knew then that my mission in life was to work at Buckingham Palace. So I say, Ma, I'm working at Glen Eagles and I want to go to Buckingham Palace, and it was like, you must be nuts. [laughter] So, halfway through the season at Glen Eagles, I wrote to Buckingham Palace. No jobs. Wrote to Buckingham Palace. No jobs. Wrote to Buckingham Palace. No jobs. Then it's the '79 season at Glen Eagles and the chef was saying I'd done such a good job, I was only 19, he agreed to send me to the Windermere Island Club in the Bahamas for the winter, to be the chef. I went, holy shit, what the hell, it'll be a disaster. Never went. Couldn't get my visa. Then they phoned and said my visa was in London. I said, well, maybe not, I don't think I'm going to go. The next day my mother got a letter from Buckingham Palace asking me to go for an interview.

How many times had you written them?

Three or four times. Perseverance, you know, squeaky wheel gets the oil. Kept on bugging them. Went down to the Palace, they offered me the job.

And then, before I went to Buckingham Palace, my mother'd received— a beautiful postcard from Canada, this beautiful road with a fall scene, beautiful blue skies. I says, I'm going to go to Canada and work as well. So, I was at Glen Eagles, Jack, the baker, was friends with Chef Merard, who was a chef at Four Seasons. He says, you want to go to work in Canada? He's looking for good guys. I said I'd love to go but I'm going to go to Buckingham Palace first. So he says, go to the Palace. Tell me when you're going and I'll organize it. So, needless to say, Gerry, what happened is I went to the Palace, worked at the Palace for two years, phoned up Jack, he got me in contact with Chef Maynard, and I came to Canada.

I was only coming for six months, but then the first night I arrived here... I was at the Inn on the Park, up on Leslie. It wasn't Buckingham Palace, but there were a lot of other facets to the kitchen... I was in the Café de l'Auberge, but then you'd see the Harvest Room and the banquets and you'd say, oh, man, this is a nightmare. So my buddy told me there was a Four Seasons downtown [Yorkville], so I said, I'm going to stay here for a year and then I'm going to the Four Seasons downtown. By the end of the year I had a job at the Four Seasons downtown.

But you soon went to the Four Seasons in Washington, DC. Why?

The chef there was a great guy and it was the best place to train. I heard a lot of stories about him even when I went to Yorkville, and he was a Scottish guy. Being Scottish it was even tougher for me. He was a disciplinarian, Chef McNeil, and he told me, "When you come here you do it my way, and if you don't want to do it my way, well, you can just go back to Canada."

I went there for the first three, four, five months. It was a nightmare. He was on my case all the time, 24 hours a day. I worked from five in the morning till 11:00 at night, day after day after day, and, you know, there were times... A few times I thought, I've got to get back to Canada. I don't need this shit in my life. But I'll tell you something, if I wasn't working for this guy, he wouldn't have pushed me to the next level. Everything I've done since then, really, has been a reflection of him. He pushed and pushed and pushed me.

What kind of ways?

Just realizing what your potential really is. Getting the best out of you. Thinking about food much differently, thinking about the customers much differently. It's not just the food, it's the customer. You have to look at him— what does he or she want, what do they need? Sometimes, chefs in the kitchen tend to make dishes or menus that reflect us. You have to make something that reflects the guests. Why do they come? Maybe they don't like sauce with their french fries. Maybe they don't like french fries. Maybe they want more roasted dishes. Get out there in the dining room, speaking to the guests, understanding the business aspects, understanding how to run the kitchen better, taking control, ordering costs, and just a host of other things. Understanding wines, going to different restaurants in the city, checking them out. Why were they good? Why were they better than we are? What can we do to improve? That chef was just the most amazing person I've ever met in my life. Aw, this guy's God. And needless to say, I came back. I left Washington. I was there for two years. My girlfriend stayed here. She was great. She'd come down every couple of months to see me.

The chef who was at the Four Seasons Yorkville went to Sutton Place. He asked me to come back as executive sous chef and I worked there for two years. It's funny. My old boss came up, and he said to Chef McNeil, "I don't know what you did with him in Washington, but you never sent the same guy back to me. It's a completely different guy." Even my girlfriend said I'd changed. My life had changed somehow. Everything. Just a complete change of my life.

Do you think that happens enough among chefs?

No. I think it's people taking an interest in someone. The last two years, I haven't spent as much time with the cooks as I should because I'm involved in other things. I spend time with the cooks who are really interested, and some of them don't want to develop themselves, and if they don't want to push themselves that much harder, why should I do it? Before, I would have spent a lot of time with them, coached them, taken them here, done this... I mean, I still took one of my young guys out to Edmonton. I took him to the competition in Chicago with me. I still do that. Whereas before, I'd have done that with nearly every single person in the kitchen.

Some people say, and certainly in the old days, or the old school, that there is discipline, there is really working hard and being pushed, but

there are some chefs who are just totally out of hand. Is there a new way, or is there a middle road?

I think there's definitely a middle road. I'm very much... not exactly disciplined.. more self-conscience, I think is the best phrase. I'm going to give you a prime example. Last night the guy made mashed potatoes for the fine dining. They were nice, they looked good and everything else, but there wasn't enough salt in them. So I said, I just did a meeting last week. I told you guys why can't you... I'm always putting it back to them, rather than saying, this guy never made this. This guy never made that. I just tell them, you're chef de partie here. Take pride in your cooking, because in this job, for you to be successful, and all these other people you're working with on the line, you have to be good at it, and care, and if you don't care about it, you're not only letting yourself down, you're letting me down, you're letting everyone else down, and the guests. So if you don't want to do it for a living, that's it. I've caught the same person maybe two or three times not seasoning things, so now I'm going to put the pressure up, or, using peer pressure, to try and get them to understand. If you shout at someone, they say, oh, he was just an asshole, she was an asshole. I think if you use words that are much more relevant to the actual issue, and put it right across like, you're affecting someone. Beforehand, people were screaming and shouting. It's just a different approach.

So, there are problems you see in the industry?

I think the sad thing is a lot of places have changed. There's no discipline. Discipline is a strong word. A lot of places I go into there's a lack of interest. Look at the city. I think it's Canada's major city, financially and whatever else, but when you look at it how many great, great hotels are there in Toronto? How many great, great, great restaurants? Where's the industry going in 15 years, 10 years, five years? I wonder at times.

You've had the rare experience of cooking at Buckingham Palace for the Royal Family. That must have been a totally different kind of cooking situation.

The great thing was you got to serve them first hand. A lot of things that you read in the press is hocus-pocus— it never happened. Made up to sell newspapers.

For me, it was the urge for a guy from a working-class neighbourhood, simple taste really, to go there and see, and like, wow, this is what it's really like. That's again... a vision. It's saying, I want to go there. I want to see what it's like. And the nice thing about it is, maybe we never had any fancy cars or stuff, but I can say I went to Buckingham Palace and I've danced with the Queen and seen the Queen and cooked for the Queen and met princes and that and everything else. A lot of people sometimes look down their nose and say, you're only a cook, but there're all different levels. It was fun to get to see people, to get to see what they like to eat, and to see history. You see something that's been done for years. You'd see pieces of china that are priceless. There was the aspect of going different places, working different castles, which is very, very intriguing, and you go in and see something and you say, wow. I wonder how long that's been there for. I wonder how many executive chefs have been here. Why have they always done it such and such a way? Or you stay in dungeons, or you stay in a different part of the castle. It was just the most wonderful experience. The food was very simple, but cooked well.

How big a staff was there and what was your job?

Twenty cooks in the kitchen. I was a Junior Royal Cook, so I was like a demi-chef, a chef de partie type thing. A lot of fun. Some guys were the best guys I've ever met in my life. Do anything for you. But again, things had never changed rapidly, the same food year after year type of thing. And for me, at that time of my life, I was only 20, 21, there was a big, big world I wanted to see. And I'm glad I've done it. Even the executive chef at the time, Peter Page, told me, "You stay here for a year or two and then you disappear. You go someplace else." And that's what I did.

Were you doing big dinners a lot of the time?

No. You get into the small. You cook for two or three Royals. Sometimes you cook for the Queen or you cook for the Duke or someone else.

Sometimes they'd eat separately, because they'd be going to a function or doing something else. It depended. What I mean by staying the same is you do the garden parties through the summer, or the same sort of menus. You do the Sunday lunch— it could be a poached lamb with roasted vegetables. It could be a poached lamb with carrots, or something else. It was always very interesting.

The quality was very, very good. What I really enjoyed was... when you're travelling and you're in Scotland, and you go for a walk, or you go down to your room near the stables, and you turn around the corner and the next thing the Queen's coming. It's like, whoa... this is really the Queen!

It's exciting. One day I was out for a walk in the afternoon and Princess Anne comes with a dog, and so I say, "Hi, good afternoon, Your Highness," and all that, because you have to say, "Ma'am, Your Highness," and all that. Yeah, I was nervous. They were always very, very courteous, very accommodating. The biggest thrill I think I ever had was to dance with the Queen, at Balmoral Castle. It was a Scottish country dance, so you pass partners. There was the Queen and the Queen Mother and I always remember after, I got home and called my mother and said, "I danced with the Queen tonight. Wow, it was great."

I've never been a person for material things in life, to a certain degree. That kind of thing, no one can ever take away from me because it doesn't cost anything. It's just an experience, but it's worth so much. And the same thing when the Queen Mother was here in Toronto. I got to do all the cooking for her for five days. And the cooks, the footmen, all knew me from the palace. And the Queen Mother's staff would come from Balmoral Castle to Windsor Castle with us, so I knew all these guys, Reggie and the whole crew. We had a bit of a party time, and then when they came here to Toronto Reg told the Queen Mother, or a lady-in-waiting told the Queen Mother, that I was from Scotland. So the lady-in-waiting comes and says, "The Queen Mother would like to see you in the next half an hour or so." I says, "Okay," and the next thing I was making the afternoon tea stuff, and the next thing, who comes into the kitchen but the Queen Mother. She comes in and starts talking and laughing and the whole thing. And that was nice, you know. They didn't have to do that. And at the end of it, it was funny. She gave me a set of silver cufflinks with ER engraved on them. It was nice, because all these other people saying, "What did you guys get?" and I'm saying, "Oh, I got these silver cufflinks." "Wow... ahh... oooo!" [I laugh] One guy offered me $5,000 for them since then. I wouldn't sell them. It's not the money. It's an experience. It's like, while in Spain, we didn't eat at the best restaurants, but it was an experience. Everything's an experience.

Before you decided you wanted to be a chef, was there a dish, a food, a "Wow," that happened?

Yeah, I'll tell you what I used to love, two things that my mother used to do for me. When I was sick, we used to always get scrambled eggs, and she'd make them in a bain-marie so it was always nice and light and fluffy. And she'd make, I used to call it cheese and ham pie, which really is a quiche lorraine. And those were the two things she'd make that were, "Wow." I couldn't eat enough of it. This was good. And they're so simple. Scrambled eggs and toast, when you're not well. I'd say, "Oh, when can I have scrambled eggs again?" "Well, when you eat that it has to go right down to your toes, and it takes a long, long time." "I think it's in my toes already. Can I have more?" [laughter] It was like that.

Obviously you got inspired by working with Team Canada; you have a real commitment.

It's been a great experience. I've been involved since 1997. It's been peaks and valleys. There've been learning experiences. In Scotland we won the World Championship. I'm co-captain. It's very rewarding, but you have to be able to sacrifice your own personal time. When we go, you're off the plane, you're in the kitchen, you work. Fifteen hour days, you go to bed, you work maybe one day a 30, 35 hour shift straight. You go to bed, you go to the awards ceremony, you may have an evening off, and then you're back on the plane. Why do you do it? I think to push yourself. I enjoy the company of my fellow team members. It's a learning experience. It's nice to see the progression. It took a lot of time for the team to click together. You can see we're getting better and better and better, and you get to know each other. We haven't spent that much time socially, apart from over a beer maybe once or twice or so. By the end of my term it'll be five years I've been doing this. It's a long time. But it's been fun.

What's a competition like?

We do two segments in the competition. There's the cold and there's the hot. For instance, I'm in charge of the Menu Gastronomique, and maybe another restaurant platter. I will put maybe six plates together. That represents a menu you'd eat in a gourmet dining room. And it's well-balanced. It's nutritional. It's simple to do. You could do the same thing for 50 people. It looks good, it should taste good, the proteins are there, and it can weigh no more than 650 grams, which is difficult. You have to use interesting china, plus, my part of the cold table has to be relevant to my fellow team member, so the whole table when you put it down doesn't look like one guy's out in left centre field. The best way to describe it... it's almost like the fashion runway where you show your collection.

The second facet, which is the most interesting one, is we all, the five people in the kitchen, we do an appetizer, main course, and dessert for 100 people, start to finish, no advance preparation. You have five hours for preparation, and after you do that, you serve the food to the 100 people. It's just like a restaurant situation. So you have to be able to cook as well to win. Sometimes the cold food no one tastes, but the hot food the judges taste, they maybe take the 5th plate, they maybe take the 16th plate, they maybe take the 90th plate, and they'll try those three plates. And they'll take one plate with a picture and make sure it's consistent the whole way. So that's tough. It's great pressure.

To get back here, do you see a certain kind of style or way that you're cooking now?

I want to try and go back 10 years, I'd like to go back 20 years, back to when I got my apprenticeship. Take the same food as that, and this is what I'm really working on, especially Café Victoria right now, and in the rest of the hotel, do two things, two components. A dish, whether it's a piece of chicken and a piece of shrimp, one sauce, one potato, that's it. And forget about the hoopla, make a nice curry, a chicken breast of curry, with a piece of pork, rice, and that's it. And make sure it's the best.

That's quite different from the hotel's menu right now. For example, what would you say is one of the signature things right now on your menu in Chiaro's?

Possibly the Lobster Marrakesh. It's a signature thing, but it's a very good thing because all it really is is a lobster with a sweet and sour sauce, which is a creamy sauce but with honey and lemons. There's a lot of acidity, a lot of citrus, with a little bit of vegetables. But you can taste the sauce, you can taste the fish, and you can taste the veg. And the three components go well together, and that's what I want to try and do even more. Just think of this... poached salmon, asparagus spears, boiled potatoes, Hollandaise sauce. You tell that to anyone in the world who's been in a restaurant, they already understand the tastes... the flavours, and to cook that, to cook it well...

The thing is, if you're going to do something half-assed, forget it. Be consistent. I read something in an article in a magazine, and the chef said that nine out of 10 times a sauce, a pre-made sauce in the bain-marie, is better than a fresh sauce made à la carte, and that's true. And why is it true? Because that sauce in the bain-marie is consistent, whether it's consistently bad or consistently good, but the sauce that's made out à la carte, unless you're a professional, someone who really knows what they're doing, it'll be a disaster. And I think the same thing. If you can't make fresh french fries that are perfect, use the best thing you can get. I don't think anyone's going to cry because you used frozen french fries. I'll be very honest with you, we used to make french fries for the whole hotel, fresh, and you know how many complaints I got? From the fine dining, even from next door in the café, "Oh, can't we have the frozen ones we get at McDonald's?" Why am I going to make my own french fries if that's what they're asking for? Forget it. But then some people come in and say, "Can we have fresh french fries?" I say, "No problem." So I want to try an experiment. Again, go back and do the fresh french fries, nice and small, and if we can't get them, if there's too much sugar in the potatoes, too much water in the potatoes, if we have a problem with the potatoes, we go and use frozen, whether it's McCain's or Cavendish or York's, or Joe Blow's french fries. It doesn't make any difference, and make sure we do them well.

You mentioned the sugar and water content of potatoes. Do you do a lot of product testing?

Yeah, big time, because it varies too much. We've been testing peaches lately. Some of the peaches you get are terrible, disgusting. So we say, okay, if we don't have peaches we can use, we'll use cherries.

Do you have a special place or time for working out ideas?

Sitting in the car, in the shower, anywhere. Sometimes it just comes. And I mean, I'm even there driving on the highway for names of things. I just think all the time. For me, food is 24 hours a day. Most of my friends are in the food business. I see myself at 40 and still so interested in food. Sometimes, people lose the passion for food? That scares me because I've seen a lot of people who have gone before me and they get 50, 55 and they really don't care any more. They get burnt out. And I think that's where you have to be smart, to do it well, or to change what you're doing.

I look at teaching. I'd love to go teaching. I'd love to go teaching! I think I know a lot. I could give a lot. And I think I could put my point across, hopefully, to the students. I think that's something else, you know? Maybe I'm not a chef in a big fancy town, and I don't have all the fancy restaurants, and the hoopla, the silverware and the china. But, it doesn't make any difference. The chef in the hospital, he has as much to offer as I have. And I think it's just that appreciation. So, Wayne Gretzky can't play hockey in the NHL until he's 65. He has to say, there's a time you have to pack it in because of certain reasons, and I'm going to do something else.

At the same time, earlier you were talking about sometimes it's really pretty tough.

I must admit, I still love what I do. I still enjoy what I do. I feel, maybe, the corporate thing is a bit of a pain in the ass at times. But I have been to so many places. I've eaten in the best restaurants. Food, to me, is an interest, it's a hobby, it's a way of life. I've been able to eat in the best restaurants in the world. I've stayed in the best hotels in the world. I've met kings and queens. I've met all these people. And then you have one personal opinion of the person. You understand, it's not what you see in the paper.

There are maybe one or two things, that, yeah, you think, oh, maybe I should have done that. But, you know, shoulda woulda coulda. The next 10 years will probably be more interesting. You change, or your philosophy has changed or your life changes.

I look at myself. When I came here I was 29. Now, I'm almost 40. I've had five general manager changes. I've had five assistant manager changes. So many different things happen to cooks. Sometimes something gets stuck in that cog and it stops, and you have to change. That's what I'm looking forward to.

You talked about this wonderful background and training you had in Scotland. Most North Americans say food in Britain is bad. What is that background and is it different from North American cooking? There is a history in Britain.

There's definitely a history. Whether it's a good history or a bad history, there's always history. I think the food in Britain has taken leaps and bounds. I think there's an interest there. There's a raw talent there. There's product that no one's ever developed because it wasn't important.

I look at Scotland— all the big hotels had French chefs. They all came. Escoffier, for instance, Carême and all those guys; they all came to Britain to make it big. There was so much product there. There was a lot of stuff that's never been turned. People wanted a certain thing. If you look at Scotland, for instance, food was there to feed the body so you could work. It wasn't there just to be gourmet. I think most places are the same, you know. The farmers, whether you go back to Spain or you go to North America, the farmers in the field— down in Kitchener, the Mennonites— the reason in the end they ate well was to sustain the body. People think, this is what we need, and that's what we do.

Things have changed. People've travelled. They've seen different things.

Cooks have seen different things. Cooking has become much more fashionable. People have more interest. People have become much more knowledgeable. So when a cook from, say, Scotland or London or somewhere else travels, they sort of say, well, we could do that. Now there's more Michelin-starred restaurants per capita in Britain than there are in France. That tells you something.

I've had a look at cooking in Britain, versus here in Canada, and it's the same thing. At the end of the day, if they're not interested— I don't care if it's Paul Bocuse's son or whoever— if the person is not interested they ain't gonna make it. If they don't have the love and the dedication, in this business, they ain't gonna make it. Maybe your father's name or your mother's name will open a few doors, but eventually those doors, they'll stop being open. When you do get through those doors, and your heart's not in it, it's not going to happen.

Is there a difference in attitudes and what is in fashion between Britain and North American?

I think, yes, definitely. The Britain that I see now is much more fine. It's what we were doing here maybe 10, 12 years ago. It's more like upscale brasserie, bistro-type food. A little bit fusion, but nothing major. But a lot of people are making a lot of cash and a lot of PR to use ethnic food. You know, it's like using black pudding cooking. It's like using whole new Yorkshire pudding stuffed with things. There's a lot of stuff there that's just been the basic stuff. You know, it's like pancakes have been in North America. Pancakes are pancakes are pancakes, but then you put blueberries and then you put strawberries in them. You put smoked meat in them. You put smoked salmon, anything, and it becomes a crêpe, it becomes a French crêpe, that thing. And that's what's happened, there's been all that stuff there and now it's, like, wow, we can do this as well.

I don't think the cooks are any better in the UK than they are here. I think where they may be luckier, at this present time, there's a lot more people who've got more experience over there as far as history and knowledge. But I will take any of my cooks here. Any one. And would take on anyone over there. And maybe we'd have to change the menu and do this and that, because

I know what their weaknesses are. I can go beat them. The Canadian National Team can go and compete in Scotland and take on the Scottish and take on the English and the Welsh and the Germans and whoever all is there, the South Africans and, whoever, and beat them. We're doing something right.

But I think here the problem is the companies, large companies like McDonald's or Denny's. It's quick. It's easy. They need something fast. Fast food. Whereas, over there, it's a little bit different, fast food could be fish and chips but it's much more healthy than fish and chips or something over here. But people here are maybe a lot more demanding now. They want some quality stuff. It's like Ace bread. They don't want airy bread. They want something with some substance. And the reason people know more is there are many more magazines. There's always that information. It's on television. So they go into your restaurant and they want a venison chop. "I've seen that on TV..." and they'll try the venison chop. So that's the evolution.

But I think you need to tell people over here. You put beef bourgignon on the menu or you put coq au vin on the menu— they don't know what the hell it is.

So has that been the kind of a challenge that you're looking at now?

Yeah. Fifteen years ago at Four Seasons Yorkville was the first time I'd ever seen lamb shank served— a guy called André Daguin from France, Hotel de France— and everyone said, oh, that's not bad, this taste, but how d'you have this big thing with the bone? Five years later, 10 years later, it's the biggest fashionable thing in bloody North America! You start saying, what's wrong here? But that's how long it took. Now people love that. Why? Because it's tasty. It's juicy. It's succulent. As long as it's got some seasoning and salt and pepper in it, it's a great dish to eat. That's the sort of thing I see being able to do more. You can't go in leaps and bounds, but I want to go back and do things like a piece of sole meunière, make sure the pan's nice and warm. Sear the fish on both sides. Cook it nice and properly, it's golden. You take a look, just, you don't need a lot of butter, only a little butter, some almonds, some lemon juice, and *puht!* over the top, and that's it. And serve a potato that's not falling apart— that's not undercooked, that's not overcooked, that doesn't have parsley that's been lying there for five hours and dried out. That's what I want to try with my guys here.

For a chef to be successful, it's the success of cooking: salt and pepper, making sure you design menus that the staff can do, at their level. And then the secret of the chef is you can do a menu that's at the staff's level but you have to be able to put a few tricks here and there that people will say, "Wow." No different than you would do a menu that's even more complicated and they still say "Wow." But that "wow" has to be the same "wow." And it's like, "Well, that's a good idea. I never thought of that." But it's so bloody simple, it's silly. And that's show business.

John Higgins

John Higgins is a realistic Scot, born and trained in and near Glasgow, including an apprenticeship at the Michelin starred restaurant of the Central Hotel. Arriving in Canada, he worked at the Four Seasons hotels in Toronto and Washington, DC. He returned to Toronto, working for the Sutton Place Hotel, before achieving his goal, at age 29, of becoming Chef de Cuisine at the King Edward Hotel. Higgins has won many international and national awards, but is particularly proud of a Mouton Cadet Menu competition award he won in 1987. He has been voted Chef of the Year by the Escoffier Chefs' Society of Toronto for his outstanding contribution to the profession, and was the winner of the Master Foods Chefs' Olympic Challenge in 1992.

John Higgins

John Higgins'
PUMPKINSEED CRUSTED LAMB RACK AND FRICASSE OF ESCARGOT,
POTATO LEEK CAKE, CHANTERELLES, HERBED VEGETABLES AND
PEPPERED PASTRY RING [for four]

INGREDIENTS

LAMB RACK
2 x 400 g lamb racks, 2nd bone
removed
5 ml grape seed oil
5 g black peppercorn, crushed
10 g garlic, chopped
5 g fresh thyme
30 ml grape seed oil
30 g grain mustard
30 g toasted pumpkinseeds
to taste, salt and pepper

MIREPOIX
10 g onions, chopped
10 g carrots, sliced
20 g celery, diced

SAUCE
10 g canola oil
100 ml red wine
200 ml lamb jus
20 g butter

ESCARGOTS CREAM
10 g butter
12 each escargots
15 g shallots, chopped
10 g garlic, chopped
60 ml white wine
30 ml chicken stock
100 ml cream
5 g parsley, chopped

WOODLAND MUSHROOMS
60 g chanterelles
30 ml white wine
5 g butter
5 g shallots, chopped

POTATO LEEK CAKE
20 g butter
100 g leeks, julienned
400 g potatoes, peeled
20 g shallots, chopped
200 ml milk
30 g butter
15 g garlic, chopped
60 g Gruyere cheese, grated

HERBED VEGETABLES
10 g butter
20 g brown sugar
5 g fresh shallots, chopped
70 g golden turnip, cut into tear drop
70 g golden squash, cut into tear
drop
2 petit pan squash, cut in half
60 ml chicken stock

VEGETABLES
10 g butter
12 asparagus spears, cleaned
4 baby broccoli flowers
8 baby onions, cleaned and braised
5 g sugar
2 g fresh parsley, chopped
to taste, salt and pepper

PEPPERED PASTRY RING
125 ml water
240 g flour
240 g butter
pinch salt
pinch cream of tartar
7 ml lemon juice

METHOD
LAMB RACK

1. Rub the racks with grape seed oil, peppercorns, chopped garlic and thyme. Marinate for 20 minutes.

2. Season and sear well in a hot pan with the grape seed oil. Place in a moderate oven and cook until pink. Lift out and keep pan for sauce.

3. Spread the racks with the mustard and dust with the pumpkinseeds. Glaze under a salamander.

LAMB JUS

1. Pour off excess fat from the pan used to roast the lamb. Add the carrot, onion and celery and cook for 5 minutes. Pour off excess fat.

2. De-glaze the pan with the vinegar, add the wine and reduce by one-third. Add the lamb jus. Simmer for 5 minutes.

3. Strain through a fine sieve and reduce in a pot to approximately 200 ml. Adjust the seasoning and add butter to Monté au Beurre.

ESCARGOT CREAM

1. Place the butter in a hot pan. Add the shallots, garlic and escargots. Sweat out, then add the wine and chicken stock. Season with salt and pepper and reduce by two-thirds.

2. Lift out the escargots, add the cream, then continue to reduce to 100 ml. Place mixture in a blender and blend until smooth.

3. Place the sauce in a pot and add the escargots back. Bring to a boil. Season and add butter.

WOODLAND MUSHROOMS

1. Place the butter in a hot pan. Add shallots and chanterelles. Cook until the shallots are translucent.

2. Add the wine. Season to taste and serve.

POTATO LEEK CAKE

1. Place butter in a hot pan. Add the leek and shallots and cook until soft. Let cool.

2. Slice the potatoes thinly.

3. Mix the milk, eggs and cheese, reserving 15 g of cheese.

4. Mix in the potatoes and season.

5. Line the dish with silicon paper. Rub the baking dish with garlic and butter.

6. Alternate layers of potato and sautéed leeks.

7. Sprinkle with cheese and bake in a moderate 350 F oven for 1 hour.

8. Let cool, then refrigerate overnight. Remove from pan the next day and cut into wedges. Reheat on a baking dish and serve.

HERBED VEGETABLES

1. Melt the butter and brown sugar in a hot pan, add the shallots and sauté.
2. Add the root vegetables and the chicken stock, then season.
3. Place a lid on the pan and cook until tender and crisp.
4. Dust with fresh chopped parsley and peppercorn.

VEGETABLES

1. Place the butter in a hot pan, add the broccoli and sauté. Add the asparagus spears, onions and sugar. Sauté together and season.

PEPPERED PASTRY RING

1. Sieve the flour onto a slab and form into a well.
2. Add the water, salt, and lemon juice and mix into a smooth dough.
3. Allow to rest 10 minutes.
4. Soften butter to similar consistency as dough.
5. Pin out paste into a square, leaving it twice as thick in the centre.
6. Place the butter in the centre of the paste and envelope with the paste.
7. Pin out the paste into an oblong shape keeping the sides straight and the corners rectangular.
8. Give two half turns. Repeat this operation, pinning to the open ends. Allow to rest 15 to 20 minutes.
9. Repeat the above operation until the paste has six half turns.
10. Roll out the dough to 3 mm thickness. Brush with egg wash and dust with peppercorns. Use a 5-inch circle cutter to cut a pastry ring, then place a 4 1/2-inch cutter on top of the 5-inch circle and remove the centre pastry (leaving a tire-rim shape). Place on a baking sheet and bake at 375 F until golden brown.

PRESENTATION

1. Place the pastry ring on the plate. Arrange the potato at the top followed by the asparagus and herbed vegetables.
2. Slice the lamb and arrange to the right of the circle.
3. Add the parsley to the escargots. Season and pour the escargot cream first, followed by the dark sauce.

Jamie Kennedy

There's no question that the opening of Scaramouche with its young critically acclaimed chefs Jamie Kennedy and Michael Stadtländer heralded a new and axial phase in not only Toronto but Canadian culinary history. From the excitement of those times, Toronto gastronomy has grown and chefs continue to make news year after year. Through this all, Jamie Kennedy has continued on, a steady given of Toronto dining, and after many more accolades, he remains a soft-spoken chef whose quiet but unswerving pride instills a drive to challenge himself without loud fanfare. Though I'd met him briefly years ago, I really got to know him in the summer of 1998 as part of a group of food writers and chefs invited by the Trade Commission of Spain on a gastronomy trip to Spain. On his last day there [he returned a few days before the rest of us], in Barcelona, the two of us spent an afternoon wandering around the famed La Boquería Market and food shops as he sought out gifts for family and his chefs. Enroute back to our hotel in preparation for dinner, we couldn't resist stopping to share some fabulous Catalunyan tapas and cava, Catalunya's superb sparkling wine. Talking with him, I saw how ecstatic he became at the opportunity to not be the working chef, but a willing customer to good food in a ritual without pretence but of palpable tradition and love. It made him profoundly comfortable, at ease with life. He wasn't cooking, but seemed to generously transmit that spirit to me and our tasting of Catalunya. A couple of months later, he invited our group for a lavish lunch [as John Higgins would do as well], to rekindle the spirit of our discovery of Spain, by sharing his wise culinary expression of what real food and conviviality is.

Several days later, I was looking across at Jamie again. A flash of Barcelona's Ramblas, clinking our flutes of cava, seemed to float in that space between us. We began.

Jamie Kennedy

Well, we've been talking about Spain and it's been about two months since we've been back from our trip. What are your general reflections about that trip now that you're back in Toronto?

It's not so much recipe ideas— I think there's always a danger in transferring an idea from one location to another and expecting it to have the same glow— because a lot of what is appreciated in any one area is more than simply the food, the meal. It's everything— the ambience of the room— and there are certain subliminal things that happen when you're dining in a place that's preparing food from that part of the world. There's always that intrinsic relationship which takes place without really being that obvious. It just kind of feels good— under the surface. And then, when you transplant that to a different context, or a different location, often it doesn't work the same way. Something's missing, but you can't identify what it is. It's unconscious.

So I don't ever try to take away actual ideas for food. It's more like the spirit I take away with me. And the spirit of the people in Spain— something for which I feel a great affinity— doesn't really exist here. I felt really comfortable with the hospitality we received there— speaking with the chefs, all the restaurants we went to— it was reaffirming for me. It was reaffirming in the sense that there is this passion that I share— it's so natural.

More natural than your experience here?

Yeah. The profession of cook there is probably more integrated into their society. Only 30 or 40 years ago the cook was considered a domestic servant, basically, with no social ranking whatsoever. Not that I'm for that. It's kind of a residual attitude toward a server, toward an indentured servant, that has been abandoned for a long time in Spain and other European countries. There is real respect for the profession of cook. The cuisine of any given country in Europe is their tradition. It's highly respected, so the practitioners of the tradition are given due respect, where they aren't really here. There's no history, there's no tradition in that way. What's happening though, here, is that there is definitely an awakening going on in the sense of what to expect. The standards have certainly improved over the last 30 or 40 years in North America, because people have travelled and come back with expectations.

They're excited about what they've experienced somewhere else, and they want to perpetuate that in their own area. So I think there's this real search going on, a regional search for identity in cooking. Something we can call our own, terroir. You know, when you go to Spain and you drink the wine and eat the food of a certain area, there is this intrinsic relationship which happens if you're sensitive to that. Not everyone would be, but if you're a gastronome, then you are, you're tuned into it, and you feel it.

But then, average people there wouldn't consider themselves, as you call them, gastronomes.

They are a part of it. But there's a higher level of appreciation going on, without them really knowing it, compared to us.

How does that happen here if we put food onto this different level?

Well, it just has to come into society across the board, more like it exists there. For example, *everyone* goes to have tapas in Madrid, and they do a big circuit. I think the standard is very high because it must be a highly competitive business on the restaurant level. I mean, they can't be serving schlock because people wouldn't buy it. There's a huge market for it, but it's also tradition driven, and there simply isn't that demand happening here. People settle for far less quality. It'll always be a real battle here in North America. Food has always been cheap here. There, people are willing to pay extra money for the quality, because they understand that there's a difference and that there's an artisanal difference that's gone into the extra quality— someone's proudly standing behind it. They recognize that and they're willing to pay for it. But here, that relationship is not so clear. North Americans still demand artificially low prices in restaurants and at the retail level in grocery stores. It's an incredible demand on the local, provincial and federal governments to subsidize agriculture from a long time ago, a demand for totally accessible cheap food.

And it's also bred mediocrity, in terms of agriculture. The actual things being grown are not that great, as a rule. You really have to pick and choose and know who your growers are, and you really have to look on an artisanal level for high quality foods. In France and in Spain at the consumer level, the commercial level, there's still lots of variety and lots of quality.

When you think of the grower, the producer, do you think most would like to produce a certain quality, but are forced to produce what they produce? Or are they really after this level of mediocrity anyway?

I think some of them are— definitely. I think that's how agriculture was defined for them by their fathers and others before them and that's how they do it. We are poised for a niche opening up in the quality area and the people who are producers or growers who recognize that and have some business acumen, can really do something. There's definitely room, because there's nothing wrong with the land or climate— we have access to seed varieties and breeds of livestock that would approach what the standards are in Spain or in France. It's simply not done because people, up until now, have not been willing to pay the extra dollar. But now, people are. I think it's changing, slowly. It just needs to be explored and developed a little bit more.

You're not unfamiliar with Spain or the Iberian peninsula?

My parents live in Portugal so I go there pretty regularly. The first time I was in Spain was about 20 years ago, in 1978. I had already finished my apprenticeship at that point. I was already cooking, and it struck me when I was there. What was supposed to be a five-day visit to Sevilla turned into three weeks, just like that. Just because it felt so comfortable.

It wasn't specifically the food?

No. The vibe in the city— the energy, the people. To me, they embrace life. I've always felt this affinity with the culture there. Before we had that trip in June, a year before that, I had a visit from the Trade Commission that sponsored this visit, and they brought in olive oil producers, wine producers and cheese— all products alimentaire from Spain— and I had a chance to work with a Spanish chef. Again, it was like rekindling this feeling. When our trip came into the offing, I was like, wow, this is great— a sign from the gods.

I should go there! Going on the trip made me even think of relocating there at some point, though I doubt if I ever really will— after building up my own place and niche here— it'd be tough turning your back on something like that... But I think, as I get older, I'll put less emphasis on gruelling it out every day and more emphasis on travelling.

When you travel is there something very specific— for your own— creating, making your food?

No. When I travel it's for my general... life, my curiosity. It's not specific to my profession at all. I'm interested in all aspects of culture when I visit a place. But I really haven't done a lot of travelling since I did that two-year stint abroad, and that was right before Toronto. I worked in Switzerland, then I came back to Toronto in 1980, and I've been here ever since, with one or two trips that were work-related in that 20 year span. The rest of the time it's been kwoooooh... nose to the grindstone... here. So, I'm interested in opening up the side of me that likes to travel.

That first stint being abroad but also working, experiencing another culture, what kind of effect did that have?

Well, I think it immediately differentiates you from being simply a tourist, because you have a connection to local society. Then you become aware of what it's like being a citizen of that place, because you're paying taxes there and understanding how the whole social structure works. And you get into the rhythm because you're working in that place and socializing in the same town. When you get into the rhythm of the place, depending on the kind of person you are— if you want to assimilate more— the circle of friends grows. You try to make friends with people who speak the language there— you don't hang around with too many English-speaking people. Not because you don't want to, but because you're curious about this new environment and you want to assimilate as much of it and learn as much of it as you can, language included. That was already a very strong thing with me— abroad. I was REALLY curious about languages. I REALLY tried to learn the language there. When you're a tourist, you're on the periphery, and people have you labelled. They know you're a tourist and relate to you in a different way. But if you're showing that you're trying to integrate yourself, it opens up many other doors and worlds. And that's what I found— I really valued that— the ability of my trade to put me in that position. So, in a sense, I probably came back too soon— I should have stayed there longer.

Do you regret that?

Sometimes I do, yeah. Sometimes I wish I'd just stayed. I was in the door, working in Europe, and once you start in Europe— as long as you're doing your job and you're doing an okay job— people would be quite open to hiring you. Chefs talk to other chefs— oh, I've got this guy. He's Canadian and he's pretty good... and boom, you've got a job. It's that easy. But if you're trying to get a job from Canada, having seen these potential employers, it's almost impossible. You have to be extremely lucky or have incredible connections.

You talked earlier about the relationship between a chef and the culture in other countries and here. But you come from very Canadian roots. Was it just that experience in Europe that brought you to this place with a certain grounding, or something in your family background?

I guess my upbringing was normal in a sense— typical Canadian— whatever that is. My parents both are extremely culture oriented. They appreciate the arts, they're liberal-minded— had always exposed us kids...

How many?

Three kids— and encouraged us to appreciate culture in all its forms. So maybe that was definitely an open invitation to expand on that. I had no idea it would take on the form of cooking as a ticket.

What were you eating, tasting?

You see, that was the thing. Nothing crazy— pretty ordinary stuff in the suburbs in Don Mills. My mom wasn't into cooking, really, she just had to prepare food for a family, right? So she did that— I guess later, after I started to feel some interest in cooking, the family— my parents both really started to get into it.

When was it you started showing this interest?

I was 14 or so— 13 or 14. Restaurants always fascinated me. Being taken out to a restaurant, ordering food and having it arrive, was SO different from what I was being served at home— not that it was better or worse, but it was different. And just the whole theatre aspect of it. Everything about it fascinated me. I was in awe of the people who worked in these places. It was magical, an attraction, definitely.

In high school I became the president of the culinary club, which didn't exist... [we laugh] Me and a girl... We just cooked at each other's houses. It was an excuse, really, to do something and drink wine. Part of it was that we drank wine. So very early on I realized the significance of the food and wine.

One of my parents' friends would visit us and would always bring wine, good wine, and drink wine all weekend, and they'd pour it for me. That was another thing about my parents, they didn't have a puritanical approach to alcohol... it wasn't, heyyyyy... let's get pissed, but always in moderation— hey, taste this... this is this and this is that. Always. And as kids we felt lucky and quite honoured in a way. We felt really good about that— young teenagers being allowed to drink wine. I had an early introduction to fine wines. I've always loved the fine things in life, having that as part of my character as well as needing to express myself creatively. And the two kind of— fine food, fine dining as a creative outlet and as a vocation— make sense to me when I think about that, in retrospect.

So when did the decision of the vocation happen?

It happened when I was 17. It was an apprenticeship I agreed to do in a kitchen, full-time, with one chef. In those days— it's not so stringent any more— but then, when you signed up, it was like you were indentured to this one chef and it was looked upon in that way. Before you signed, you were about to enter a contractual arrangement with a chef. It was at the Windsor Arms Hotel, and I took that possibility home and mentioned it to my parents and, once again, I have to credit my parents. They probably felt they wanted me to go to university and at least have the university experience for all the reasons, you know. But they had the common sense to see that this was something that really attracted me and they also knew me and that having finished high school, I was still pretty young, and it wouldn't do me any harm at all to defer entering university for a couple of years, to do something else that might teach me something else— a different discipline— which it did. And I never stopped. I kept going with it because I had an affinity for it and I was able to develop my skills and parlay them into an opportunity like Scaramouche eventually.

I was offered the job while I was over in Europe. That was a huge turning point for me. That was relatively early on to be offered a chef's position— at age 22, to be considered for a chef's job was unheard of. I wasn't sure I was ready for it, but at the same time, I was challenged by it. And I felt that I should go for it. I knew that Toronto was still in its infancy as far as fine dining went, and you know, in essence, the model was the three-star Michelin restaurant in France. There wasn't anything like that in Toronto. There were good restaurants, but none that were doing Nouvelle Cuisine, like, this renaissance in cooking. Again, you know, as is the same with fusion, it's all in how it's practised. The practitioner's the total difference to me. Someone who does Nouvelle Cuisine well and someone who's just playing with ingredients and throwing them together in a haphazard way without any discipline behind it, not really knowing how the chords are, how the chord changes will...

What were you thinking, just coming back, because you had had that training when it was an important time in European cuisine, and coming back and knowing the context in Canada— the Canadian ingredients, the Canadian attitudes...

Yeah, it's funny, because at that point we were not thinking regional Canada at all. We were thinking French cuisine, and we started buying direct from Rungis Market in Paris. That's how we handled that. We were buying foie gras, Dover sole, fresh mushrooms— all kinds of ingredients that you would find in Paul Bocuse's place.

Trying to recreate it?

Yeah. And Michael had had an experience in Germany before coming to Canada where he was into the Neue Deutsche cuisine, which was like a movement going on in Germany, a German renaissance in cooking away from the stodgy, potato and pork combination of dishes, to a much lighter expression of regionality, that was being practised by this man Vincent Klink, at a restaurant near Stuttgart. So he had his great experience there, and Michael is an amazing cook. He's such a natural, and for him to have the ability to do whatever basically he wanted to in his own country under the auspices of this chef, whose sister Michael was soon married to for a time. But Klink recognized Michael's innate skills and let him run with it. So he brought that fresh experience with him into that whole creation at Scaramouche.

We really had quite a thing going there. There was a real lot of energy connected together and we started off doing that kind of thing— just trying to recreate the European three-star experience at Scaramouche, but then it started to change, because we began to recognize the importance of what was being produced around here, and that process took another five or six years to really amount to anything, and what it amounted to was really Knives and Forks [a Toronto organization bridging chefs and organic food producers].

The thinking behind Knives and Forks was never really parochial in the sense of being strictly organic; it was a quest for quality in ingredients. That's all it was. And the desire to make direct contact with local farmers so that we could start this dialogue of a niche market with growers who were like-minded and who were trying to offer something of higher quality than what we were so tired of— broccoli from California— things that just didn't have any taste— because you get so involved working with food that your taste becomes more heightened, your whole palate becomes more discerning, and you start to recognize that there is this mediocrity in the ingredients that are being grown here, right? So, naturally, we started to search for better ingredients, and ended up establishing ties with organic producers. They seemed to be the ones who were using the heritage seed varieties, like pre-chemical intervention seed. They were growing them again because these seeds had a resilience to pests that chemical-intervention seed stocks simply didn't have. That resilience had been genetically phased out so farmers would have to rely on chemical fertilizers. And it was basically a sham— a total post-World War Two sham— to use up wartime chemicals in another way. It was just really disgusting when you think about it.

You and Michael had been influenced while you were in Europe...

It all made sense to us... totally. It was like doctrine. [laughs] It was the new religion and European chefs were the prophets. So, I guess there was a turning point in Scaramouche where all that was being practised. And it became too big a canvas for Michael and I to paint on because the room was huge and the demands on us became more economics-based. The first couple of years Scaramouche didn't make a penny and we lost money. It was the dream of the Yolles [brothers Burle and Morden], and their patience; they believed in what we were doing they backed us up 100%.

Is that uncommon?

Very uncommon. But I was starting to feel that if I stayed around there much longer, things would change in a way that I didn't want them to. So my reaction was to go into a very small arrangement where I had my own catering company. The only assets I had were my skill. I cooked in people's homes and I used all their kitchens and all their overhead— gas and [laughs] electricity. I just made meals. So I'd show up at nine in the morning and present a dinner for 12 at the end of the day and I'd go home totally exhausted. I did that for two years.

The one drawback for me was that it was very isolating. I wasn't connected with my peers at all. I was just doing this thing on my own— it was very internal... To cook for a party of 12 it would take me three days because of the planning, and then the shopping and then the arriving and then the cooking and doing it. And it's so layered, right? Fine dining is extremely layered. The final plate presentation is simple, but what's behind that? There's a lot more to it than meets the eye... A couple of years later, I opened Palmerston, which again was another springboard into a very rich day-to-day practising life of cooking. Those years I was really trying to find my own style, my own identity. It was necessary to come to grips with who I was as a cook, and Palmerston was where I began to formulate that and find my own way. That's when I really started to get into the regionality quest and it's still what I do, but it's connected at the basic level with classical French cooking, because that's what my training was.

So many of my colleagues trained in classical French cooking simply because it's structured... I don't know what to compare it to in another trade, but guys like Escoffier, for example, took the time to write down postulates and theorems— "this is the way you approach this"— and he had names for everything. Most of the names are not in common use any more but certainly the disciplined approach to cooking was the building block. People were assigned to doing different things in the workplace— those are the models I use to this day in how the kitchen runs.

For instance, the menu I have, I limit myself to the seasons and as many local ingredients as possible. It's incredible how many different things are local to here that are some of the linchpins of French and Italian gastronomy.

So there are two things here: you're Canadian and going very much towards the regional and local, and yet out of the French. Is there something fundamentally Canadian you're working out of?

I don't think about that consciously, but I think that it would emerge in the finished product. What I do think about is reconciling the different influences in Toronto, like cultural and ethnic influences, like in the marketplace. I mean, you can't help but be exposed to several Asian cultures in Toronto, Indian, South American— from just about everywhere in the world— because Toronto is such a multi-ethnic place. You can't help but be influenced, and you are sort of working at a disadvantage there, because there's so much you have to wade through in order to find a thread that's not too complicated, that reflects who you are. And still you have these strong needs that you want your work to exhibit. And so you kind of draw your ground rules and hope that what you're doing is a synthesis of these things.

Jamie Kennedy

Say, compared to Spain, where if you're from Barcelona then you have to look at the Catalan cooking tradition and you can choose to be a practitioner of that, and a very good one, or a mediocre one, or not at all, or you go the route of what's his name... [Ferrán Adriá of El Bulli] He's a freak [laughs] because he's chosen to blow himself right off the map. I have nothing bad really to say about him except I just think this guy's like, wow, unbridled.

These Catalan people know the food is from there— they know the taste already. For us, it's wonderful because it's a new experience and we get launched into these cultures. But here, is there such a thing as a Canadian palate that develops and grows— or does it get confused?

I think that more times than not it is confused. I think a lot of places out there, chefs do get confused, like just, what is that? What I'm trying to do is not get confused. The older I get, the more simple I'm becoming. Not conservative, but I look for two or three things on the plate to work that are harmonious. I'm not asking for any more from a plate of food.

Harmonious in what way?

Taste. For example, tomatoes and basil, which is obvious, but there are less obvious ones.

How about the assembly and composition of the caribou, and the chanterelle soup you made for our Spanish trip group?

There you have caribou and it's marinated in berries caribou would eat that they would find in the tundra. So there's a harmony there. I marinate the caribou in juniper and blueberry, and the sauce is made from the bones of the caribou plus the marinade, and it's a distillate of all that. My cooking is like a distillation process, extracting the essential flavours of everything in it. Then, I put a couple together— with the caribou you had a cross-cultural thing. I brought spaetzle— but gave it a distinctly Canadian twist by supplanting some of the flour element with wild rice flour. So that's having fun— but not in a way that's frou-frou. It's very logical. It's almost hip, but it's not, hey, look at me. It's not that at all. It's just there. It's there for you to find if you're looking in the right way, right? You can really see a lot of what kind of cook I am from that dish— from the things I'm describing— caribou, wild rice— it's Canadian, not just... Spaetzle, for example, in German culture would be paired with venison, quite easily, and because we're in Canada, I put wild rice flour into it.

Then, in the same dish, you have the bacon— which you know the French use: pearl onions, bacon, mushrooms— that trinity of ingredients which happens a lot in French country cooking. Bourgeois— so I introduce that as a bow to French culture. But when you have it all together, it becomes this... which, I'm satisfied, is an expression of what I'm doing.

Chanterelles' essence? It's like this time of year. Chanterelles are now. What's inside the ravioli? Celery root, squash, beans— everything that's earthy. Those are the kinds of things that work for me in that dish.

Yet you maintain a certain lightness.

Yeah. And when you look at it in terms of the whole menu, start with foie gras— very rich, with walnuts— nice— and the wine— Indian Summer Riesling from Niagara— you know, the grapes on the plate— very fall looking, and the tastes are all harmonious.

And then the next course is very light in comparison. And then the next course, the red meat is positioned properly, you know it's that part of the meal. I could have gone on, but it was lunch and I cut it short and just put the dessert there, which has chocolate— but the berries were last year's in rum, so the flavours are all macerated together.

Where does all that happen— the thinking process— or your feeling process? Do you actually set time aside to go in the kitchen?

Oh, you can do it anywhere, Gerry. You have to put everything else out and think harmony. It's become easier for me to do that because... Immediately I say, okay, where are we in the year— the seasons— what do I have available to me now? And there are certain ground rules that that has to pass before I give it my internal stamp of approval. And so that'll just sir up ideas and things will come together. And I'll say, I like that; I don't like that. Finally, something will emerge and I'll say, okay, I like that, and I'll write it up, and I have the further challenge of coming and sitting down as well as going back and cooking. It takes quite a lot of planning... And I wanted to present this whole Spanish tapas part of it as well— a quite separate and distinct sit-down dining experience. This was kind of like, the part at the bar [we had begun with drinks at the bar]— here we are again— we're in Toronto but in Spain. This is for you, José-Luis [Deputy Trade Commissioner José-Luis Atristain]. But at the same time, I wanted to show you guys what I was all about. You see, that's me talking... to prepare a meal. And it's theatre, too, how you choreograph— it's all very exciting to me. I mean everybody around here, if you asked them about that day— I was so excited— because it gave me a lot of joy.

It's rare that you get to share the meal and the company and prepare the meal. It's usually one or the other, right? You're either dining as part of the group, or you're cooking and not really part of it— the dining experience with the company, to be able to do both, is wonderful.

How do you get a sense of that in a normal situation, that sense of feeling the relationship with people in the dining room. Is it hard?

Oh, wow... sometimes, yeah. It depends on the kind of place you have, right? And what level— at lunch it's a bit more general. You're not really aware of who the people are necessarily. If you do know who they are then you might try to cater to them. When I say cater to them, I mean understand them, and maybe even suggest a menu because you know who they are and what they might like. However, at dinner it's a different story. Palmerston was small enough— you sort of get a sense of who's coming to your place.

Palmerston really taught me a lot of business lessons. Even though I had a lot of notice in the papers for the work I was doing, the business basically collapsed at the end of the '80s. So I had to ask... what happened there? It was a combination of things, but, basically, it was inexperience in running that sort of non-compromising expressionist food place. And something weird happened when I closed it. I moved into the space so I didn't have the run of an apartment any more, so I was saving some money, and I decided to open up sort of a catering operation. People would come there and I'd do private parties on demand and I sort of became known for that and I ran it like that for about a year. And in that year I made more money than I ever had before. So I said, well, the food's still the same, I'm still presenting the same menus, but I had a much better grip on what my other costs were— in terms of the labour— in terms of the overhead. So in that year I was able to pay down all my debts, whereas I never operated in the black as Palmerston, ever.

You worked at the Skydome after, but then re-opened Palmerston...

I went back to Palmerston with a new partner, who was a much better businessman than I was, and we had a really good two-year run. And I lowered the prices. The prices were lower at Palmerston than they had ever been— spanning eight years. And we started playing to full houses again every night. But the difference was that the partner was a veteran of the business and knew how to save money— saving a few dollars so that we could make a few more dollars. This was essential and I started to think about that. You just have to be smart about how you operate and you can still be successful creatively. And having been partners with Marcel Rethoré at Palmerston showed me that that was possible— and wonderful. And having another example in the city... a single operator chef in a small restaurant in Susur Lee. He did incredibly well, both artistically and expressing himself non-compromisingly, and he made money. He was an inspiration to me, for sure.

Are there other chefs you looked up to?

Well, my chef— I don't really follow him now— but the man who taught me the basics of cooking— I'll always have respect for because he was damned good. Ulrig Herzig was the executive chef at the Prince Hotel— he still is, I think, and we don't talk to each other. He didn't really believe in my taking that leap to Scaramouche— after having been only five years in the profession. For him that made no sense at all. He thought I was quite cheeky for doing that. He basically said, it's not going to work. Well, I guess he didn't really know me all that well. Once I get a bone in my mouth I don't let go. I really am quite tenacious.

Jamie Kennedy

People like André Soltner at Lutèce in New York. When we were scouting restaurants in New York to gain inspirational ideas for Scaramouche. This is what a broad thinker Mordy was already, at that time, because he valued taking a trip to New York for research and development ideas. He spent money where other people might have thought it superfluous, excessive. As a result we had an encounter with Soltner in New York one day just before lunch. We kept him an hour and a half longer than he should have been— he didn't show one sign of anxiety of needing to get back to the kitchen and seeing his own restaurant into operation— he was so— I don't want to use the word polite because he wasn't just being polite, but he realized this was something that we were embarking upon and he wanted to make sure he gave us the time that we required of him. I think he felt that he had this obligation to us to answer all the questions we had. He didn't try to kick us out of there, so he was very inspirational. He said some great things— some encouraging things.

Any foods that really excite, inspire you? Where the ideas really come—

Well, yeah. Things like seafood, which are so beautiful in their own skin and don't require a lot of external working and when you cook them they give lots of flavour. Clams, for example. I love clams. I love oysters. I love making things like oyster stew. Really simple little things. I think I love the oceans— fish and shellfish— and vegetables— nothing like fresh vegetables— beautiful. Really good vegetables you don't do much with. Again it's the quest— simple. I think the restraint you show as a cook is a mark of wisdom in cooking and confidence in cooking. Sometimes I think earlier on in your career you have to apply— you have to do something with potato— where the wisdom might be to leave it alone as much as possible— manipulate it somewhat to bring it up to level where it will be appreciated more. It's something you have to develop. It's like impressionist painters who can capture movement with just a very simple line— you know, it speaks volumes.

Do you think a customer understands this?

They'll get it if it's executed properly in your eyes— how you envisioned it.

But if it falls short? That's when they'll dis you and say, what's this? What is this? Nothing. I'm paying $24 for this... whereas if it had been cooked a little bit longer or the presentation had been— whatever— I'm talking about the degrees— tiny little things that make huge differences in how people perceive what they're about to eat. That's what I try to drive home to all the cooks here— the details— no matter what— you have to pay attention to these little things. Like a salad— that the leaves are entirely dry— or the vinaigrette is not going to stick.

Has there ever been one evening when you think— oh, that was perfect?

No. I think there's always something— but we're in a profession where every day we have to meet certain professional standards— somehow satisfy the sort of contractual agreement we have— providing the meal for the customer who's paying for it. So there's certain level you have to keep, and if you're worth your salt and you're doing it all the time it's 100%. But then some days are extra inspiring for whatever reason. It could be the freshness of certain ingredients. You have a dish you created that was really— everything about it you just loved, and the rhythm of the kitchen that night— everybody's clicking. The choreography of an evening is never the same— there's an incredible number of permutations.

And I'll say, isn't that great? We did 75 covers and...

Does the staff know before you say it?

Oh, yeah— everybody knows it— sure. But then when you say it— it's reaffirming. And they feel good about what they've done.

How about the performance itself, of yourself and the kitchen?

The focus is on the experience of dining. Dining includes the eating, the drinking, the service, the ambience, the company that you keep. All those things converge and then one single element can feed the others. For example, if we're aware that the group is predisposed to having a good time, for instance, if they arrive in a good frame of mind, they're knowledgeable gastronomically, they don't have restrictions of any kind in terms of what they're eating, so they're an appreciative audience, then we're already in a better space, as cooks, in the kitchen. Now, if we have our mise en place together, you know, and we have this good feeling going into the preparation of the dining experience for these people, and we're getting feedback constantly as it's happening that this is a good thing, then it just helps to feed us and makes us better. So we rise above.

Usually, it's just being professional and hitting a certain quality as an indication of success or failure. If you don't hit it, you know you haven't hit it. But if you do hit it then you're satisfied, but it's not like you're having an orgasm or that kind of thing; it's being professional.

And, as you grow older and wiser in a profession, what matters to you— what makes you feel okay at the end of the day is— you've done your best that day. You can go for a certain level and then, as I say, the events or the atmosphere of the event that you happen to be a part of, if it hits a high, then you know, you're lucky enough to be there at that time and provide an experience... But otherwise, you're just there. You're there every day and you're plugging away and hitting a certain level.

And you convey to your staff when there is a "high"?

Yes. I absolutely do. The reason I do affirm what we just achieved is to tell them that that is a highlight of cooking for a living. When you experience a day like that, that's a real highlight, and it's not something that happens by chance. It happens very much by perseverance.

It's not a matter of luck that you happen to be there when it happens. It's a matter of working towards something and having it finally happen. It's like working towards anything and achieving it.

I know you've been thinking about maybe another restaurant or smaller place...

Professionally, that's my next goal. I'm not in any great hurry, but I'm looking for a spot that has a square room— that isn't a long narrow room, you know— that has some space. I think that's important. It's integral to the dining experience to be in a space that's pleasant to be in. There are long narrow rooms, which are the norm in Toronto, that just don't cut it... That's how they make me feel, anyway. There are very few exceptions, and when you're in a room that is an exception, you notice. You notice right away. Wow, this room is square, the ceilings aren't so low. There's something about it.

It inspires you?

Yeah. And so I think, probably, the thing about the next step is that I can do it on my own terms. I can. It will happen very organically, I think, when it's supposed to happen.

You've talked about the conflict and the struggle of doing, achieving a kind of cooking, and compromise... So do you have any regrets?

No. Because, you know, nothing I've ever embarked on in business has been a tragedy. So you can sort of draw on it as a positive experience along the road to learning more about how to operate a business and where your niche is and where you stand in the industry. If you decide, okay, I want to be in the hospitality industry, where you fit in is very important because you'll only be honestly pursuing, you'll only resonate, if you're happy in what you do. And it can be, you know, slinging hamburgers— which, you know, is another part that attracts me— not slinging hamburgers— but doing something for a great number of people on a very small scale in terms of the depth of the operation. If you offer 10 different dishes, you know, the quality of preparation of every single one of those dishes is extremely complicated and it's time-consuming. It's your whole day's work. Easily.

Daryle Nagata, at the Waterfront Centre in Vancouver, said, at one point, that in Switzerland early on, he was walking along this road and he realized that things were really moving well for him there, but that his personal life sucked. He said he had to start to put both of them together. Can you talk a little bit about that?

I haven't talked at all so far about integrating private life with professional life, but the private side is always a huge factor in any decision making. I'm not in any great hurry to find that perfect little restaurant. A large measure of taking my time with it is because of my family. That, if I am, in a sense, writing myself out of the script here in order to free myself up to be able to leave these people, all my mangers and support staff here, in full confidence, to manage it, with less and less dependence on me being present. I'm also setting myself up to have more freedom to make decisions based on my family life, like, what are my kids doing today? Is my son going to be in a softball game tonight? Being able to say, yeah, I can go to that game. I can do this. Especially because the kids are at an age now where I know that if I close my eyes and open them again it's going to be 10 years later and they'll be out of the house and I will have missed out on a very important part of their development. And I don't want to. Up until now, the demands on my professional life have been so great. It's always work first and everything else second. And now it's come to the point where... it's really coming from inside me. It's not an external thing... not my wife saying, you know, you have to spend more time at home. It's not that. I want to.

How did this change happen?

I had one marriage go on the rocks. I don't really think it was really to do so much with time spent at work, but I'm very interested in not letting that happen again, and, just like anything, relationships need to be nurtured. They can't be nurtured if you aren't spending time with your spouse or your children, and I don't want that to happen.

When this is kind of thing is happening to you, you still have to go in and cook...

I think at that time the work was, in a way, like a drug, to escape. Because I would just plunge myself into work and just shut everything else out. Especially during service. Service. Your whole world is just about that service, getting through that service, a dinner service.

It was a time that I was so focused at work that I also became more

practised and more immersed in the details of how to work in the kitchen. In other words, I was honing my cooking skills to a point that was unusual.
So, it was like this cliché, getting the positive out of a terrible situation?

Yeah.

Was it worth that cost?

In terms of my professional ability and depth and experience, yes, it was worth it. I think, as you grow older and become more wise, you sort of look back on these parts, or these chapters, in your life, and you go, well, you've always said to yourself and to others that the relationship didn't break up because of working too much. That it was more a fundamental difference of opinion to do with the two parties involved. Well, you know, to grow older, it's like, you know, yeah, that can be. But it could also have been different if I had spent more time, if I had worked on the relationship more, if I had invested more in the relationship, made that a priority rather than pursuing the career. So that's what I mean when I say that I don't want that to happen again. That things have to be more in balance in my life.

Any foods out of that period, I'm talking about dishes or an individual thing, throwing this up in the air, resonate with that time?

No. I think, probably, if I look back on the menus that I was doing during that time, that blue period, or whatever you want to call it, when I was struggling with my break up and was coming to grips with being a successful restaurateur, is that I made it really hard on myself. But I think I was, in a sense, almost punishing myself, you know?

It's weird. I'd just pour it on. If we had six or seven main course dishes, then each one of those dishes was composed as an individual dish that had nothing to do with anything else on the menu. So, if you're picking up a party of four and they've ordered four different main courses, there could be as many as 32 different cooking applications going on to produce those four plates. And you're talking myself and one other person to do this. And then it's the next table right after that and then the next table after that. And this is going on for three or four hours and you have to do it within a certain time period to satisfy the cadence of the meal— and I would pour it on, you know. Make it even more difficult. So, that defines that period. It was wildly experimental. I was exploring the combinations, possibilities— it was a very creative time.

We just had some roast beef here— something pretty traditional, Canadian. Can you speak a bit on that?

It's funny. During the Spanish trip, I was intrigued. The spirit of the people surrounding the traditions of food is so natural. I find, as North Americans, we're not tradition bound in any sense, so we're looking all the time. Or we're not comfortable in our own skin, in several respects to do with food culture. And there it's a natural. People from Galicia will say, this is how you prepare this, and that's it. This is what we eat, and this is what we drink, and it's beautiful, it's wonderful, and it's so easy for them. On the other hand, those same people are less adaptable themselves; they're less accepting of other cuisines. Whereas North Americans are more appreciative of beauty in other cultures, I think...

For chefs, or people who would be chefs, who are starting out— what kind of things would you tell them, to gain a perspective on this profession?

Well, you know, if you're talking about pursuing it the way I pursued it from an expressionistic platform in a fine dining establishment. This restaurant serves regional Ontario cuisine, modern Ontario cuisine... If you're the kind of cook who really is in it for the art and being an artist and expressive in the cooking, then I think the trick is, you know, that there is no trick but to experiment. What happens is that if you're on that kind of quest, at the beginning you experiment with lots of different colours and textures and things going on on the plate, because you're turned on by a lot of different influences, and you want to make them all happen on every plate that you do. So, at the beginning, it's kind of muddled. You know, it's your stuff. The stuff's coming out kind of muddled. It's like a painter experimenting with colour and texture and imagery and then, as you gain more experience and more confidence, you're using fewer colours, but the colours are better. You're using fewer textures, but the textures are better. There are better marriages happening on the canvas, or the plate. It's like you're distilling your knowledge into a less cluttered look, but the end product is much more meaningful and beautiful. So that's sort of the process. That comes with time and you just have to have patience. That's what I found, anyway, only the last five years, and I've been doing it for 25 years now. I can really say that I'm beginning to recognize myself and what my niche is... and it gets further and further refined as I go on. That's why I'm so excited about the new little restaurant I'm going to do because I'm going to approach that enterprise with a lot more confidence than, say, I approached Palmerston, where I was wildly experimental and just cutting my teeth, really.

Longevity in this field also has a lot to do with balance and not succumbing to alcoholism or drug abuse or broken marriages, you know, as much as you can avoid them. Because that starts to affect your morale and your ability to function. So if you're going to be at it for a number of years, then you have to take care of yourself. You have to get enough sleep. You have to exercise. You have to, basically, be healthy in mind and body because, you know, it takes its toll. It's a crazy business, the hours are brutal, and you can easily want to escape. It happens to a lot of people. There are a lot of brilliant, brilliant, brilliant cooks that just, in the long run, can't cope with the hours and the stress. So, in order to protect yourself from that you really have to take care of yourself. Which is a real challenge, sometimes, to come back. Back to the centre.

Jamie Kennedy

Jamie Kennedy apprenticed in cooking at the Windsor Arms Hotel in the 1970s, after finishing the Advanced Cook course at George Brown College in Toronto. He went on to become a journeyman cook in Europe, coming back to Toronto to partner with Michael Stadtländer in Scaramouche. Caterer, partner and chef at Palmerston Restaurant, member of the Chef de Cuisine Founder's Club are all part of Kennedy's history. He was also a prime mover in the establishment of Knives and Forks, an alliance of organic growers and chefs, and is author of the *Jamie Kennedy Cookbook* (Oxford University Press, 1985). Kennedy is currently owner and Executive Chef at Jamie Kennedy at the ROM in Toronto.

Jamie Kennedy's
POACHED TROUT WITH AROMATIC HERB PASTE [for six]

INGREDIENTS
6 filets of rainbow trout (arctic char or salmon are also nice)
4 medium-sized shallots
coarse ground black pepper
salt
2 oz (60 ml) white wine vinegar
1 bunch chives
1 bunch chervil

FOR COURT BOUILLON
2 litres water
3 oz (90 ml) white wine vinegar
1 medium-sized Spanish onion
1 carrot
1 celery root or three stalks of celery
1 bunch dill
salt
coarse ground black pepper
1 lemon
1 bay leaf

PREPARATION FOR COOKING
When you purchase the trout, it either comes whole or filleted. This recipe calls for filleted trout. Even if you purchase the trout filleted, there are still tiny bones which you might want to remove. You can feel them embedded right in the filet if you run your finger up and down the length of the filet. To remove them use a pair of needle-nosed pliers.
Bring the water to a boil. Peel the onion, cut it in half and slice the halves thinly. Scrub the carrot and celery and slice them both thinly on the bias. Season with salt, coarse black pepper, bay leaf and white wine vinegar. Add all the vegetables to the water. Boil vigorously for 5 minutes. This is the Court Bouillon. For the aromatic paste, chop the shallots into brunoise. Place them in a bowl and add coarse ground black pepper, finely diced shallots and chervil. Pour the vinegar on top and mix to paste consistency.

COOKING
Place the Court Bouillon on the stove and bring up to simmering point. Poach the trout filets for approximately 3 minutes. Decorate the perimeter of six warmed plates with slices of the Court Bouillon vegetables. Remove the trout filets from the Court Bouillon and place them on the plates. Peel the skin back to reveal the filet beneath and place some of the herb paste on each filet. Serve warm or at room temperature.

Andrew Milne-Allan

Zucca Trattoria, Toronto, Ontario

I first met Andrew Milne-Allan over 15 years ago when I was waitering part-time at a bistro and he was working as chef after he and another of Toronto's most gifted chefs, Greg Couillard, had sold their legendary Parrot on Queen Street West in Toronto. Not only his talents, but his knowledge and exacting standards immediately became obvious to me. Already working as a food writer, I learned a lot from him then as I would down the years as we became friends, both of us living in the now hip Little Italy district on College Street when it was relatively peaceful. We had many opportunities to discuss food over an espresso or when I had the chance to eat meals at his home. We are both products of the same generation, his wife, Gianna, a poet like I am, and I have seen how he, while not Italian, pioneered with peerless quality much of the Italian food style which now is done with far less savour on College and elsewhere in Toronto. His use, for example, of legumes, raisins, saffron and lemon in pasta or other dishes keeps me a dedicated student of his unrelenting quest for Italy's true culinary legacy to which he respectfully adds his own careful nuance. Having gained prominence during the same period as Jamie Kennedy, he remains a chef the writers have trailed down the years. Although his latest restaurant is located in North Toronto, he continues to live in the College Street area where we sometimes meet. It was an obvious choice to talk with him at home.

It was early fall with just enough radiant warmth left in the morning sunshine to sit with espresso in his backyard, a quiet time before he'd head off to do some marketing for Zucca and before the College Street crowds would start heating up the brisk autumn air.

When people come in and are impressed by the food and the menu— are they surprised to see that you're not Italian?

Yeah, that's a standard response, but it comes up less these days— and they say, what's a New Zealander doing in Toronto cooking Italian? The easiest response is, I married into an Italian family— and that ends the discussion. [laughs] It depends how much time I have on my hands.

But that's not where it came from?

I think it really evolved. I remember in New Zealand being with people who dreamed of leaving New Zealand, of seeing the world, and I'm not quite sure we were caught with the bug of the Mediterranean— because that's what it was. When you live in New Zealand, you feel like you've just arrived on the earth in a way, and the Mediterranean seemed like history and a sense of time and civilization, everything that, in New Zealand, we seemed to have felt we didn't have. Which is ignorant, but relatively speaking it was true. I had contemporaries who felt, similarly, that we wanted to get in touch with something that had a lot more history to it. We were all interested in food, I maybe a little more than others, but we were attracted to the cuisine of the Mediterranean. I was in my 20s.

So were you already involved in food then?

In a sort of, semi-professional way. It was one of those things that evolved. I was going to university and art school and I washed dishes, like most people, to support yourself, and I happened to get into a restaurant that was serious about food, one of the leading restaurants in the city at the time, and I suppose that coincided with my own growing interest in food. Later, in another city, I again worked to put myself through school at a kind of funky Italian trattoria style place run by Australians, in what we would think of these days as very unsophisticated, but in those days was the happening thing.

It was steaks done in different marinades and spaghetti done in meat sauce, tomato sauce and mushroom sauce— all ladled out of huge vats, which sounds disgusting, but for the time it was fresh food. Overcooked pasta, of course— terrible stuff. [laughs] But that's probably all we knew— it was done in a funky environment with lots of antiques or pseudo antiques.

So did it twig your interest?

Yeah, but it was really just a restaurant that I worked at that was close to the school. By that time I was reading and, like a lot of people at the time, inspired by people like Elizabeth David— who was like a goddess to us. I say us because there were three or four friends at the time— and we would have dinner parties, that kind of thing. We were foodies way back then...

Was it a minority?

It was, because New Zealand cuisine was pretty primitive, mostly hotel food that favoured kind of pretentious French imitation. And that's why this Italian place, called Tony's, impressed me. It was run by these brash Australian lads [laughs]— no more Italian than I was. They were entrepreneurs and they were out to make money and it was a busy little place. In fact, four or five Tony's had sprung up all over Auckland by the time I left.

What kind of art did you study?

[Laughs] Well, yeah, that's the question. [laughs] What kind of art? That's why I got out of art. I couldn't decide. I was doing photography and sculpture, and... I think I got out of it because I decided I wasn't good enough at it. There were plenty of photographs being taken, plenty of art being made. I'd leave it to the people more talented than I was.

Not everybody goes into food— what was growing up like— was there food in the family?

There was in the basic sense. My mother was a good cook. My father was a good gardener, as far as vegetables were concerned— a wonderful gardener, period— and she was a wonderful cook— very plain. My father was very conservative in his tastes, so she didn't cook anything out of the ordinary, but what she did, she did very well. More and more these days when I'm older I realize— fresh flavours are what I remember about growing up— the taste of vegetables, the taste of dishes— it was very clean, very simple, and I think I must have inherited that.

So you think about that?

Oh, all the time— the smell of fava beans, say, and I'll be right back in the garden.

I was saying to Gianna the other day that he would know all the varieties of the vegetables that he would be growing. It wasn't just potatoes, it wouldn't be just tomatoes— but it would be the different varieties— the different times they would mature. It was fairly common— he wasn't eccentric in any any way— he was just like other men of his generation— they were into gardening and they did it in a purely organic way in those days— because there was the compost bin and the chicken run with its manure and that's the way they gardened.

I can go to the organic gardeners now at Knives and Forks and I think of these people, and that's basically what my father did before large scale commercial insecticides and chemical fertilisers became more popular in the '50s and later— they were using blood and bone [laughs] which is organic.

So I never thought about it at the time— that we were a food-oriented family— but we were, I suppose— my mother was always concerned about the quality of things—

We bought very little produce. Everything was fresh out of the garden. We did buy meat, bread and stuff like that, but the garden is almost year-round in New Zealand, and I don't remember my mother doing much preserving or pickling. It was just using what was seasonal. I still use a lot of Swiss chard, which I remember very strongly from growing up in the garden— silver beet, we called it in New Zealand.

That's very Mediterranean, too...

It is, [laughs] it turns out to be... and fava beans— but of course, we called them broad beans in New Zealand. It was only when I got into Italian food...

These things have begun to get a bit trendy...

They have... yeah, they have. Sometimes I feel like everything's caught up to me— I'm just an old fogey. [laughter] Which is funny because we used to be talked about as the young chefs— but I realize I'm no longer one of those. [laughs]

How important were family meals?

Family meals were important and regular, but that's something in me. I embraced my Italian connection— because the culture I come from is much more reserved and uptight...

So you think there's no sense of celebration in your culture?

Not really— except that good food on the table with healthy appetites would always give you a little celebrating. We always ate well, and my mother always provided— but maybe that's what I was looking for. Maybe I didn't know it at the time, but that's part of what I've been looking for— that sense of celebration— pleasure that comes with friends sitting around the table which has always been one of the most important things about restaurant life to me— even if I'm not sitting down myself.

I think that sometimes the concept of the chef as artist gets in the way of that. People think of a chef as putting on a performance— that's a very popular concept, but it's not something I embrace before anything else.

How did this former art student from New Zealand, who'd been reading Elizabeth David, end up cooking in Canada?

I came to Toronto in '73, and things were pretty quiet, gastronomically... I was with somebody who was connected to the university in Kingston and we ended up in Toronto because, there again, we were looking for the bright lights and the big city, and Kingston certainly wasn't it. [laughs] By that time I'd decided art was not a fulfilling thing for me and cooking was something that I enjoyed and was reasonably good at... it was something to pay the rent, and seemed quite a logical thing to do. Quite by chance, I walked into David Cohlmeyer's Beggar's Banquet— he must have had a sign on the door saying

"Cook Wanted"— and the rest is history. It's funny— I could have walked into some other place and things wouldn't have turned out the right way.

How important was that part of your background?

I wasn't vegetarian at the time...

But the attitude that he brought? Or was it just somewhere you worked?

In a way, yes, sure, because he was doing a round-the-world tour. When I joined Beggar's Banquet, every night was a different menu— a set menu, three course— I don't think there was even a choice. He would do Peruvian, one night and Mongolian the next and African, and he really was all over the map. It was obviously a totally unique concept to Toronto.

What did you think of it?

Great— it was fun. As things developed, I was less impressed with the concept because it was superficial— he was doing his research out of books— which is fine— but, like I said, in a week we'd do seven different countries and we might not come back to that country for two or three weeks. For him it was more a showcase for vegetarian food. His idea, I think, was that most cuisines in the world had dishes that could be adapted to a vegetarian diet. He would often take meat dishes and just remove the meat. We used to joke a little bit that it would always be eggplant, so we'd have cases of eggplant. There were things about his concept that I grew a little disenchanted with, but basically I enjoyed the freedom of it and the imagination of it. I found, as time went on, that I would want to know more about a fewer number of cuisines, than a very little about a huge number.

So did Mediterranean cuisine begin poking its head...

Yeah, it did. Also because people responded more to it. They might enjoy individual dishes from Peru or wherever it might be— Sweden, perhaps—

but I don't think they could respond to it in the same way people respond to Mediterranean cuisines. And it did coincide with my feelings about those countries— and so I took over more and more of the research aspect of it. I think he relied on me to come up with the menus and refine the menus, and I found that I would develop the dishes in a different direction than what he had originally started out with... Certainly by the time he suggested that Greg Couillard and I buy the restaurant— I was already moving it in a different direction, focusing more on Mediterranean food and trying to do dishes that weren't just meat substitutes, but actually existed as classic dishes...

We kept it as Beggar's Banquet for six months, I think, before we changed the name, but we definitely moved it in a different direction. We got rid of the uncomfortable wooden benches... [laughter] That was a ritual, that.

I was learning more about different cuisines, and I was reducing the number all the time to ones I felt most comfortable with— Southern French Provençal, Italian, North African Moroccan food, Greek; I was narrowing it down all the time— Spanish— but of course, people enjoy Italian food and you realize those were the cuisines that were most popular— that's the business aspect.

Do you think people's tastes in Toronto were changing at the time— and were you going along with it?

In those days, we thought of ourselves as terrorist chefs, actually. We were joking around, of course, but we did have that feeling that there was nobody else in the city doing quite like what we were doing on Queen Street. And when I say we, I don't mean just the Parrot. There was a feeling down there— everybody was a bit of an outlaw in the lifestyle...

We'd have artists show their work, and even work in the restaurant and we'd go and listen and hang out in the different bars...

It must have been exciting—

Yeah. We were young and stupid, and all exploring things ourselves at the time. One of the reasons I decided to call it a day was that I felt like I didn't know everything even though people thought you did. I wanted to continue to develop and learn more and mostly I've had to do it on my own, which involves reading and travelling rather than going to school. Oh, I've taken the odd class, but...

You and Greg Couillard went in very clearly different directions—

Yes, you're right. He went in a spice direction, I suppose you could say, and I went in an Italian direction. I think I always felt a natural affinity for the cuisine. These days, I sense that it does come from how my taste buds developed as a kid. Of course, we didn't have strong flavourings in New Zealand foods at all. My mother, I think, even rarely used garlic because my father didn't like it. So it was very plain, very plain cuisine. The cleanness and freshness of the flavours are what's still relevant to Italian cuisine, or especially about me.

I met my wife Gianna during the Parrot years, and that brought me in contact with real Italian people— the Italian family and the whole bit.

It was great. It really was another world, because up to that point in Toronto I'd known Queen Street, and Queen Street was full of dysfunctional people with no families. We used to joke that we were a bunch of orphans. Of course, we all had families. We hadn't exactly disowned them, but we had made the decision to lead our own lifestyles and for some people it did mean disowning, and leaving them up in North Bay or Scarborough or wherever it was. Meeting Gianna meant coming into contact with a culture that was intensely family oriented, a big change for me and a big enrichment for me. I cooked Italian cuisine as well— in fact better, than a lot of them— but I felt I was enriched by knowing the people and knowing the origins of some of the dishes.

I could have come across dishes I'd enjoyed and learned how to cook either through travelling or more often than not my own reading— but with her family you get the feeling of the history of those dishes in the sense that they'd learned it from their mothers and their grandmothers and that was how they knew about it. They didn't know it from books. They knew about it because that was the way they always cooked it— that's one of the characteristics of Italian cooking— they cook it one way on this side of the mountain and totally different on the other side. I was made more aware of that aspect of it. How dishes are learned, passed on.

Does that give you a feeling for it that enables you to grow in your cooking as opposed to learning from books?

It gives me a respect for how a dish has evolved, or why it has evolved, or why it hasn't evolved, why it's stayed the same— a kind of rationale for it— and that's really important for me.

A dish of baccalà— cod— that Gianna's family always cooked with tomato and raisins and onions— it turns out that it's a classic Roman dish. I've found it in Roman cookbooks and that's where her family's from— the south of Rome— Ceprano— which is obviously influenced by Roman cooking, and that's the way they cook baccalà— in a stew. They cook it also in salad, boiled, with parsley, garlic and oil. For her and her family, that's the way they cook it, and they're not necessarily interested in some flight of fancy that some other cook from some other country might do. That gave me an insight into Italian cuisine, and I always found it interesting. I'm less interested in just creating, although obviously every cook does that when they cook a dish. I like the idea of things that work, things that have sense to them— and they have sense because people have cooked it that way because they liked the combination of flavours. They don't want to add anything more to it; that, to them, is perfect.

When a chef cooks, you say a chef is already creating— what do you mean?

They're creating because they're adding a few extra onions or they're cooking it a little bit longer or a little bit less. They're creating in that sense. I think there's a whole other approach to cooking which says, let's take a whole lot of exotic ingredients and see what we come up with. That will be labelled creative, but I'm more interested in why classic dishes taste good and why they have stayed the same through generations. I think you need to understand that before you can add or subtract, and once you understand that I think it's perfectly fine to go through that process. Maybe you're working on the same theme, but your ingredients are slightly different— you've got the same combination of tastes in mind that work, and then maybe something similar will work. I diverge from classic Italian dishes when I'm following that kind of precept.

When you travel— to New Zealand, to Italy— how important is it to what you're talking about?

It's very important... Travelling to Italy— means going with Gianna, which means I'm meeting more Italians eating at their homes, and understanding a little more each time... We always shop in markets and end up cooking.

And you research in books as well?

Mostly with some sort of personality to them. It's often a kind of reference to see how a dish is different from region to region or cookbook to cookbook, to get an understanding of the dish itself. I try to find books that have history attached to them, but I don't research in any academic way. I try to find books in Italian...

How do those influences come together for you— putting together a menu— putting together a dish?

Well, first and foremost, in people eating it, people enjoying it, rather than a show-stopping dish. I always favour simplicity over fireworks, I guess. I like to put together a menu that has a progression— I think that's one of the beauties of Italian dining.

But do you sit down somewhere, at some point, and think about it, or does it evolve?

I'm always thinking about it. Dishes will come to me in the car, driving, or at the market, or tasting something that I've cooked and liking it and thinking it would go well with something else. It's not a fixed process. I change the menu at Zucca about four times a year, so there are periods of more intense menu formation.

We have a small menu. You can only put a certain number of things on a menu at a small restaurant, so it's always more a process of elimination, plus having a sample of different types of tastes or different ingredients so you don't have too much overlap and people don't have a really hard time deciding. I feel I have a really good menu if that's the case. There are dishes of enough variety so that you can make a nice progression in a meal.

I always like to have a few difficult dishes on a menu and I try to avoid too easy choices. I like to challenge people, challenge their idea of Italian cuisine, which is fairly narrow even now.

Really?

There's been an explosion of pasta places in the last few years, which has widened the choice of restaurants, but there are so many that are similar. I think that's meant that people are less adventurous than they used to be. I'm always struck by their lack of adventure, so I usually end up with even more difficult dishes— putting some sort of hook in there that will entice them into ordering it. People need to order things. The food needs to move off the shelves, as they say.

There's a huge number of restaurants, but I don't think the understanding of the public has expanded in the same way. Most of these pizza and pasta places have opened with the idea of making money, which is a great thing— [laughs] I'd like to make more myself— but unfortunately everybody has identified pizza and pasta as a great way to make money because the overhead is low. Challenging people is the last thing on their minds, so I don't think it's necessarily done a great service to Toronto dining.

Isn't there a dilemma— wanting to hook the people, be not quite so challenging, but still decent quality— and you make a profit?

There is a dilemma— because people will still ask us for fettuccine Alfredo.

But there's nothing wrong with that, in a sense.

No, there's nothing wrong with it, except, not only is it boring to cook those dishes, really— but it shows you that the people aren't thinking about what they're eating. They don't really care that they're eating the same thing they've always eaten, which, when I think about it, is a bit of a contradiction— because it's how Italians get by— just give me a good plate of pasta! [laughing] But I think people who enjoy fettuccine Alfredo have had their taste buds removed at some point— so it's not the same thing, exactly.

I would like to present Italian food that's not as common. It's not that what I'm doing is particularly original, because Italian cuisine is incredibly varied. I'm just picking from a few of those traditions and a few of those dishes and presenting them on one menu and trying to show people that this is an Italian dish. There's a reason why these flavours are together, and it's not as strange as it may sound. People are very conservative in Toronto in their eating— there are dishes that they will eat in a high-priced restaurant that they won't eat in a medium- or low-priced one. Context is everything in Toronto and also what they're told by the critics about what they should enjoy.

The media have a big responsibility, too, and sometimes I don't think that they fulfil it. They encourage the idea of what's hot this month or this week, and people flock to those places. You do have a small percentage of dedicated diners who don't follow the critics, but that's a small minority.

Do you feel uncomfortable that, as in poetry or art, you're cooking for a certain small number of people?

I do feel uncomfortable with that, because what I like to do is present food which is good to eat and tasty first and foremost. I don't think I like to rely on presentation or environment— although I do think we have a nice environment at Zucca. I think our food relies on what's on the plate, the taste on the plate and the contentment that comes from eating a nice plate of pasta or grilled quail or whatever it may be. That's been my main goal, to get my fulfilment from other people's enjoyment.

I remember eating here at your home one New Year's Eve— a plate of pasta with shrimp, mussels, a bit of tomatoes, chili peppers, parsley, garlic and olive oil. I distinctly remember the separation of flavours— the

parsley, for instance— cooked to an exact point... now, you can get that dish all over, but how you work those ingredients is very important to you...

I'm very precise and careful about how ingredients are combined to end with a particular result. I guess I drive my cooks crazy like that— add it now or add it 10 seconds from now or... [laughs] especially in pasta cookery, which is so fast and immediate and relies for its success on a few steps executed well and at the right time. So the line between success and failure is a fine one: when you add ingredients, what ingredients, and how much of each.

In a restaurant environment you have to produce food on time with a certain amount of time, so you're refining those techniques. Maybe you switch the order around because it's easier to expedite whatever without sacrificing flavour and quality. You're always thinking about those production-line things. Restaurant food is all constructed from what is called mise-en-place— ingredients all around you, part of it prepared, part of it raw— all a matter of timing, for sure. Flavour's everything for me, which is the same for a home cook, too.

Certainly Italian food relies on that separation of flavours with a minimum number of ingredients, so there's a challenge for me. On one hand, there's a desire to create an interesting dish, but you also have to sell it. I suppose it's like writing a song: you have to have a hook. I think it's because you're dealing in large part with jaded appetites or dulled taste buds, or people who are programmed to respond to certain stimuli. It sounds cynical, but it's true, because when you're cooking Italian food, ethnic cuisine, in Toronto, you're not necessarily cooking Italian cuisine for Italians or Japanese food if you're Japanese; you're cooking for a dining public in Toronto which is multicultural— which tends to be WASP and Jewish with a smattering of other nationalities thrown in.

So that does affect the way you cook?

Yes. There are dishes which are quite austere, quite severe, quite plain, but to an Italian palate— it could be slices of fine salami on a plate, or cheese or pasta with nothing but oil and wonderful cheese. Things like that are wonderful to eat, but enticing people to order it in a restaurant and pay money for it is sometimes a challenge— though not for people who have a background in that cuisine, or are sophisticated enough to appreciate it. It may sound a bit patronizing but people need a jolt from what they're reading on the menu— oh, that sounds great. [laughs]

I tried to avoid flowery— I suppose that the part of the restaurant business that thrills me the least is that need to entice people. I always thought I'd be in the business of just providing food for people who love to come in with their friends and put their elbows on the table and enjoy it— just as long as I provided food that was tasty in a nice environment. I thought that was quite unique because there are so many restaurants where that's not the case.

I see so many places where I haven't had good experiences, doing very well. So it's a little bit demoralizing sometimes to think you have to conform to certain models to be successful. I suppose, going back to the Parrot days, that thought never entered our heads, because we seemed to be unique and were foolish and didn't really think about our future. Right up to Trattoria Giancarlo, doing what we liked doing was enough— but mind you, that was the '80s. I suppose things for restaurants were easier, in a sense, because the economy was flush; things are harder now because the economy's a bit rough and there are more restaurants.

But the popular belief is that the food scene is fabulous here...

There's always the struggle of operating a restaurant in a highly competitive market and that may be just an economic factor of the times.

Somebody recently stormed out of the restaurant saying I've lost my touch [laughs], but generally we have great word of mouth; we get a lot of repeat business and that's quite flattering.

What kind of things have gone wrong?

People do send food back and say, I don't like it, I don't like swordfish, and they may have ordered a swordfish pasta. People are always confounding me with that kind of thing, sending back a dessert and saying I didn't know it had eggs in it; it's a flan or a custard and you wonder what goes through people's minds when they're eating out. Especially when you know the quality, generally speaking, is uneven out there in the restaurant world. So why they're complaining about that particular dish— you know, there's no accounting for taste. People will send back pasta which is undercooked or overcooked according to their taste or— we have a lot a trouble with Pecorino cheese— too salty— which is part of its charm. Some people are not used to flavours like that— or olives— "they're salty." Sometimes they want the dish, but don't want the ingredients... [laughs]

There must be certain nights when things are going great and you feel, god, it's going well.

Nights when you get really good customers and they order well— they maybe order the slightly more offbeat dishes and drink good wines, and you know you're in the presence of diners— those nights are great. Also, when the timing's good and you get the food out on time and you feel you've done each plate as well as you can do it.

There are also times when somebody on the staff doesn't do something exactly the way you want it, but in order to fix it you have to slow down the whole machine and sometimes things go out less than perfect. I won't say the customer won't notice. Sometimes the customer does notice, but you have to move the food along. People won't wait for their food. Even cooking pasta to order, people are surprised that they have to wait 10 minutes, which seems outrageous to me— because that's the case. In most places, the pasta is pre-cooked. There are a few places where they cook it to order— but they're in the minority.

So people already have that expectation.

Yes, of instant food, and because they taste it in other restaurants so many times, that's the way they're accustomed to it— a little overcooked. We cook it to order, although we have gone through times of pre-cooking it because of the pressure of business.

Do you have an ideal of the situation you'd like to be in cooking in Toronto?

I'm not sure it would be in Toronto. I think it's a fantasy restaurant by the sea [sighs] with a patio— those are elements in my ideal restaurant— overlooking the sea. That's more in the fantasy realm, I suppose, because I grew up with it so much a part of me in New Zealand— the connection to the sea. But I also think patio dining is part of the Italian feeling— al fresco— sitting around with friends in a nice environment— that's still the ideal for me— creating a place where people enjoy themselves. I suppose I'm known for things I do, to a certain extent, but sometimes I think I don't have enough of an ego. I don't think that's an essential ingredient for me— the publicity—

Do you think an ego is important in a chef?

Yeah. Obviously, you want things done the way you like it, the way you enjoy it, the way you want it presented; that's an element of ego for sure. But I'm happy not to be known personally by a large number of people— it's never been part of my style. If they're enjoying my food and I hear about it afterwards, I'm just as happy.

People say, we've followed you, we used to eat at the Parrot— that's a great satisfaction... just when you're despairing of reaching people who have a certain amount of integrity in following their own taste— rather than just what's trendy.

Do you despair of that sometimes?

Oh, sure, yeah, on slow nights or slow months. You see other places doing well, not that I begrudge them, but for questionable food, I think— and Toronto is trend mad. There's no doubt about that.

Something keeps you going.

I enjoy cooking. I enjoy restaurants. That's the drug that keeps me going. I do enjoy doing it, though physically it keeps getting harder and harder. [laughs] I have 20-year-old cooks who complain about things I'm complaining about— aches and pains— and I think, well, they have quite a future in store for them— at 20. Legs are a big problem with cooks— standing on your feet all day long, twisting and turning and jumping around like crazy— most of them have bad legs— arms— tendonitis is a common thing— I've had it in both arms, lifting heavy pots and pans...

So it's not just this glory thing? [laughter]

Well, it is, maybe, if you're successful enough to have a big enough restaurant to do less of the hands-on cooking. That's a goal that I've always tried to work towards. Obviously I'll have to do it in the next restaurant. To be more relaxed about it— and to have it more of a family operation. I think that's been my greatest regret or disappointment— is that Gianna is not involved, which means our family life is pretty fractured, which is not ideal at all. The best times for me were the summers at Giancarlo when she would work there— and she's very good at it. She's great with customers and on the floor. But I don't know that's a realistic— because she has other interests and is not necessarily business-oriented. I envy families that can do it— and I think often that's a key to success— to have a family operation where more than one person is involved in it.

That's more the European model— maybe in Montreal and Quebec it's more common. Restaurant lifestyle is really hard on families.

It would be nice to have an easier lifestyle— more family time, social time, too— friends...

So, to look at your fantasy place by the sea again, you must carry memories of all the seafood in New Zealand?

Strangely enough, no. White people in New Zealand weren't exposed to fish beyond fish and chips hardly at all. There was a fish store in the village, the suburb where we lived, where I'd go to as a kid— my mother would send me and we'd get filets of terakahi, which is like a snapper, and she'd cook it up using a white cream sauce or bread it and fry it— very simple English-style cooking. But generally speaking, considering the incredible seafood in New Zealand, we didn't eat that at all— the Maoris did. That's one thing that's developed in New Zealand cuisine. I think it's booming, like, in Australia— maybe to a slightly lesser extent. It's developing a lot. Because the wine industry has gone crazy in the last decade, so there's some great wine— and whenever there's great wine produced it generally goes hand in hand. So maybe in the future going back and being part of that— if I can extract Gianna and her family from this environment.

Is there any pull?

There is a strong pull on my part, but it'd be hard for her, with her job and career and family, to start out again. She keeps saying she was an immigrant once and that's enough. Maybe for a period of time... it would be nice to see if I could fit in again, which might be difficult. I've become too much of a Canadian.

Is there anything of home cooking from there that's a comfort food when you're feeling low— to take you back?

Well, things I grew up on, like scones and pikelets— they're a kind of little savoury pancake you put butter, sugar and jam on— I used to make scones with Gia [his daughter] when she was little or put dates or blueberries in them— it's an English thing. It was just something we survived on in university, I think— midnight scone production. [laughs] But it's not something I crave. There's nothing I crave. I'm perfectly comfortable in an Italian environment now— eating in an Italian way. I grew up on butter— I use very little butter now. Half a pound of butter will sit in the fridge for six months— at home, anyway. I've changed in that regard.

That's a pretty fundamental change.

When I go back, my sister always chides me I've given up the ways— because they still slather on the butter— or margarine now— because they're heart conscious— but the same concept. Whipped cream with a dessert after every meal— pudding— the kind of thing I grew up with— pudding after a meal. We'd never have an appetizer— but a main course which is usually meat of some kind, and a pudding. That was dinner, which is completely different from the way I eat now. I love antipasto— the appetizer is one of my favourite parts of a meal— and then slowly easing into it with a little pasta and then some simple meat or fish— I just feel very comfortable with the Italian way of eating. I think it's a very sane way and a civilized way to eat. You can stretch out the meal, the time you spend at the table. The pleasures of the table are not necessarily the opulence of the food, but rather just the simple progression of a meal, which means you can spend more time at the table in conversation and there's always something happening— move onto the next course. I spend more time producing it than eating it. It's very common in Italian restaurants here to just eat a plate of pasta and then share a dessert— which is closer to what I was describing— the English style of eating. Have a main course which is just an excuse to have dessert. [laughs] But you still get people who eat well.

I guess people fewer people are prepared to spend time— they're on their way somewhere else. One of the keys to the pizza-pasta operation is turnover— get 'em in get 'em out— you can't do that if they're lingering over multi-courses. But it can be condensed. It's proper to have an appetizer— just a simple little slice of something— or something a little more involved. I think we should approach it in that kind of way— preparing yourself for what's to come, enjoying it in smaller amounts rather than just the one plate. So I guess that's the ideal clientele— which means they're getting maximum enjoyment out of the restaurant and their company.

What are your current projects?

The season's about to change so I'm about to work on the fall menu. The summer menu's just about done its dash. I'm starting to think about fall items— wild mushrooms, maybe more stewy things, braised dishes, richer sauces, more meat sauces, maybe.

I always like to do new stuff— even of it's just changing an approach slightly. There again, there's limited space on the menu and you have different slots to put things in. And I always do some dishes that I've done before, maybe from last fall or the fall before.

I always like doing meat ragu— and I might vary the meat or seasoning slightly— with a little pasta, stuffed pasta, pappardelle— or that kind of noodle. Maybe warm appetizers. Right now we're doing a lot of raw stuff— salads, even raw vegetable accompaniments with main dishes, which fit into my idea of summer eating, but it's getting harder to justify in October. So it's about time I changed it. We get more into stuffed pastas, different, richer sauces, like pasta stuffed with squash for example— zucca [pumpkin]— it's something we do at this time of year, with a simple butter and sage sauce. Pasta with a ragout of chicken livers and chicken gizzards. They're cleaned and chopped up and sautéed with things like porcini mushrooms, herbs, a little tomato and broth— it's a simmered sauce. It takes a little time to prepare— it's finished with a little of the sautéed liver which is passed with the sauce— I think I did it last year for the first time in a little while, and I was surprised that people responded to it. So chicken giblets are something they have in their memory from when they were kids and their mother cooked so-called poor foods. It's done in a lot of places, but it's popular in places like Emilia-Romagna, and Tuscany.

Are you partial to any particular regional food?

Yeah, I'm fond of the cuisine of Puglia, and Sicily and Liguria— with the herbs and the fish, and mushrooms. I suppose I'm less attracted to Piemonte and even Emilia-Romagna, where the food is a lot richer— more cream and butter and the flavours are a little blander, but rich. I like the kind of spicy food and simple heavily vegetable-based dishes of Puglia— fish vegetables, pasta— you can't go wrong with that.

I haven't been to Puglia— I've been to those other places but never Puglia. It's a place I'd really like to visit next time. Sicilian cuisine is really great, with a kind of Arabic influence, a sweet and sour influence, spicy. There's an endless variety of food, and so little of it is offered in Toronto, which is a shame. But then, people tend to want things they're familiar with and that's always the challenge. Do you have pasta with vegetables and tomatoes? You mean pasta primavera by any chance? Things like that— they were introduced in the '80s and have an Italian antecedent; they came out of New York, I think, and then every menu had it on it.

And then people expected certain kinds of vegetables...

Yeah, sort of crunchy... crunchy vegetables. Which is another one of my pet peeves, the whole crunchy vegetable thing. In side dishes for meat or fish, it's still quite common. It's still a style at higher end restaurants, that still put the beautiful, turned vegetables— they look beautiful, but they don't have much flavour. I tend to overcook mine, by those standards, I guess. A lot of vegetables don't give up their flavour until cooked to a certain point. You take a green bean and cook it crunchy— there's texture, but it doesn't have a nice bean flavour, it doesn't have that real essence of bean until you've cooked it for at least five minutes, depending on the bean. It's true of a lot of vegetables. Swiss chard, for example— if you undercook it, it doesn't have the same flavour at all. It has that beautiful sweet earthy flavour when you cook it until it's tender. Tender is a word I keep using with my cooks. You'd be amazed how difficult it is cooking vegetables sometimes on a regular basis every day. You'd think they'd get it down quickly but, actually getting to taste the beanness or chardness takes them a while to appreciate—

That's really important to you.

Absolutely. Because I enjoy the flavour so much. I think it goes back to memories from being a kid— the sweet flavour of fresh vegetables— and I suppose most cooks have been brought up and trained for that undercooked taste— and I think that's a hangover from the '80s and Nouvelle Cuisine or wherever exactly it came from. Every restaurant was doing it— that style of cooking.

But I guess people think of health reasons...

Yeah, but if I want raw vegetables I'll ask for dip. [laughs] I say to the cooks quite often, when they're cooking pasta and vegetables, you don't want the vegetables to be more al dente than the pasta. The dish is about the pasta and not the vegetables— they play a secondary role. If they're crunchier than the pasta it throws the whole balance of the dish off.

What do you mean about the balance?

In the case of the pasta and the vegetables— when you're taking the trouble to cook quality pasta to the right length of time until it's al dente and it has a nice texture, everything has to be subservient to that— it enhances the pasta but you're still eating pasta. So if you've got a dish with crunchy vegetables that have a starch accompaniment, it reverses things.

I think it's all about different textures and combinations, as well as flavour. It's a hard thing to get across sometimes. Mainly, people are not so used to examining the taste of things quite so minutely, and I always like to examine why a dish works, why I enjoy the flavours. Often when I'm thinking about a dish, it needs something else— another texture or another flavour to complete the triangle. Three does seem to be a magical number— I don't usually like to go beyond three. If you go beyond three, you're into a different style of dish. I did this dish the other night— Swordfish carpaccio— it was on a bed of sorrel leaves and it had a spicy pepper purée— hot cherry peppers and sweet mixed together— and it had romano beans. I thought it had a nice balance— soft flesh of the raw fish and the unctuous pepper and the crunch of the bean and the sharp flavour of the sorrel cutting through it all. Any more flavours than that— one of my cooks put cherry tomatoes on the outside, and I said, no, that's not it... it's more about reducing it. How few ingredients can you get away with to make a dish successful? What can you take away? For example, the cherry tomato is there to look pretty? Why are you putting it there? I argue myself out of ingredients. Does it need another one or can you do without that to make it balanced? Balance is important. You don't want something that's too sharp. The sorrel, by itself, is quite sharp, but when it's combined with a creamy unctuous flavour plus a kind of pop of a romano bean and a floury texture— by themselves, they're not quite satisfactory, but you put them all together...

That must be interesting because, say, with Sicilian cuisine, the balance...

Yeah, they're even more baroque. They put more ingredients than three, usually, but they always try to end up with harmony: the sweet and the sharp and the sour and... the classic dish with sardines... pasta with sardines and fennel and pine nuts and raisins and saffron and onions and anchovies— a huge number of ingredients.

When you're dealing with that, how do you work it out to what you like?

I don't touch that! I just enjoy the harmony of it. You can reduce it. I do pasta with monkfish and tomato and saffron. And that's just reducing it down to fish simmered in tomato sauce, a little fish broth and saffron. But just a vague memory of that dish with the sardines. And if I have fennel, I put fennel in, too. It still works, because it still has that harmony to it, but it doesn't have the sweet of the raisins; the richness of the fish and saffron and fennel bounce off each other.

North Americans are crazy about pasta with seafood— the more seafood the better— the more grilled shrimp, the better.

A dish like that does depend on the variety of seafood, in a way, for its success. But there again, if you're going to have too much seafood, you're missing the pasta. You might as well have it without the pasta, and have the pasta separately, using the sauce or the broth. Yeah, there's a grilled shrimp mentality out there. [laughs] I don't care what it costs, just grill me some shrimp and put it on top...

Andrew Milne-Allan

Andrew Milne-Allan was born in Wellington, New Zealand, and finished both a BA and a fine arts diploma before coming to Canada. Presently chef and co-owner of Zucca Trattoria in Toronto, Milne-Allan has been breaking new ground in Toronto cuisine since the 1970s, from the Beggars' Banquet to Trattoria Giancarlo to the Bar Italia and Dooney's Café, among others.

Andrew Milne-Allan's
BACCALA ARROSTITA al POMODORO, LIMONE e PNGRATTATO [SALT COD ROASTED WITH TOMATO, LEMON, AND BREADCRUMBS] [for six]

This simple baked fish recipe has its origins in both Greece and the heel region of Italy's boot, Apulia. The layering of ingredients is characteristic of both cuisines and serves to keep the fish moist and allows for a slower cooking to develop flavours. The home salting of the cod duplicates the process of the traditional BACCALA or SALT COD but in a much accelerated version. The result, for our threatened but still noble and tasty second national fish, is some of the firm texture of the original but with a lighter and fresher taste.

Andrew Milne-Allan

INGREDIENTS
3-4 lb of fresh cod filet in 1 piece
1 lb coarse sea salt or pickling salt
3-4 large salad tomatoes
2-3 garlic cloves sliced thinly
1 large lemon, washed
dried oregano
extra virgin olive oil

—

1/2 c coarse home made breadcrumbs
1 anchovy filet, minced
1 garlic clove, minced
1 tbsp extra virgin olive oil

COOKING
1. Spread half the salt on the bottom of a shallow dish. Lay the piece of cod on top, skin side down, and cover with the rest of the salt. Cover with plastic wrap and refrigerate over night (approximately 15 hours). The next day rinse off the salt and leave in a container of fresh water for 6-8 hours, changing the water frequently. After 6 hours taste a small piece of fish. If it's still a little salty, keep under very slowly running water for another hour or two.
2. Preheat oven to 375 F.
3. Peel the tomatoes. Cut in half, turn cut side down and slice thinly. Cut the lemons lengthwise into quarters and slice crosswise thinly. Reserve lemon and tomato slices together in a bowl.
4. Make the breadcrumb topping. In a small pan, sauté the garlic and anchovy gently together in the olive oil. Add the breadcrumbs and mix well with a wooden spoon. Continue to cook, stirring often until lightly toasted. Reserve.
5. Drain and dry the fish on paper towels. Cut into serving portions (approximately 6 ounces each) removing the skin and any bones.
6. Choose a shallow oven dish big enough to hold all the fish without crowding. Rub a little olive oil over the bottom of the pan. Spread with a layer of sliced tomatoes just enough for several under each portion of fish. Salt. Add lemon slices, 3-4 for each portion. Scatter with garlic slivers. Place the cod on top of the lemon and tomato. Arrange overlapping slices of tomato then lemon on top of each piece of fish. Salt lightly. Sprinkle oregano over all. Dribble olive oil generously over each filet and any tomato/lemon juice that accumulated in the bowl.
7. Bake in preheated oven for about 25 minutes. Baste frequently, spooning juices over the fish. In the last five minutes of cooking time, sprinkle the crumb mixture abundantly over each filet. When the milky "sap" first appears on the surface of the fish it will be cooked.
8. Carefully remove each filet to warmed serving dishes. Scrape the pan to loosen any browned bits and pour the juices around each portion.

Serve with olive oil and roasted potatoes.

Anne Desjardins

L'Eau à la Bouche, Ste-Adele, Quebec

In the last several years, the name of Anne Desjardins and L'Eau à la Bouche, the hotel-restaurant, she and husband sommelier Pierre Audette operate in Ste-Adele in the Laurentians north of Montreal, has spread well beyond Quebec and even Canada. Profiled in *The New York Times Magazine, Gourmet* and publications in France, has brought vistors from the US, France, Japan and elsewhere who make a special trek to sample the artistry from one of the pillars of contemporary cuisine québécoise. Decades ago, for me, like many Canadians who'd never been to Europe, the Laurentians were as close as I'd got, where onion soup, cretons, pâté and cosy crêperies converted from barn-board cabins were formative introductions to "cuisine." Thirty years after my first stay in Ste-Adele, and during that quasi-holiday tranquility between Christmas and New Year's in 1998, cuisine was again to define a Laurentian visit. I was joined by a friend as dining partner, and we arrived at L'Eau in late afternoon, snow just beginning to fall upon ski hills which had yet to see very much. That evening, we leisurely ate our way through a remarkable understated subtle cuisine. Although elegant, the restaurant, converted from a wood, stone and brick house built by a craftsman from Germany in the '40s, maintains a soothing homey charm beneath its low ceilings, surprising for sophisticated food of this kind. Thus coddled in candlelight, we ate while outside the window by our table, the snow had continued its gentle descent. It was Laurentian winter as we all might imagine.

The next norning, the sun brilliant upon the snow-covered mountains, Anne came for our talk, already in her chef's whites. Her round face relaxed and immediately welcoming, she began telling me that this was not the world she and Pierre had once thought they'd explore. Her voice took on a vivacious exuberance, bringing a soft gleam to her eyes.

We are both geographers; we studied at the university, and finished in about '76. It was not in my mind to become a chef, not at all. I love to cook, I love

Anne Desjardins

to entertain, and I did that a lot in my family because my father was a businessman and we entertained for him; we cooked for the family and guests. We travelled a lot, and went to great restaurants in great hotels in various parts of the world with my father. And I never suspected, when I was dining in France at 16 or 20 years of age, that one day I might be doing the same thing. I was just there, enjoying what life had to offer. But I loved to cook, even when I was young, at my grandmother's place... I think she was the one who gave me my first touch of cooking, because she had a very acute palate. She had a house in the country, in Ste-Rose near Montreal, near the river.

We went there in summer, and she would be having guests for dinner... In June, she'd pick fresh strawberries, and wash them with the stem still on. I remember, because it was like a little flash, you know? "Grandmother, why do you keep the stem on the strawberries when you wash them?" "Well, Anne, it's because otherwise, water would come into the strawberries and lessen the taste and make it bitter." For each guest, she picked the stem out and then made little plates for each convive; she made whipped cream. It had to be the best for her guests. She wanted to cook the nicest things. When we came in the house and it smelled of cooking, I'd ask, "What is it, Grand-mother?" And she would say, "Guess." She wanted us to guess from the smell: was it a turkey cooking, was it roast beef, was it ham? She was always cooking very large pieces of meat, because there were always friends, family, guests...

I remember those little sequences of smell and of always caring for the best products. But, of course, it was not that sophisticated at that time. Fifty years ago, people were not cooking the way we do.

So what kind of food would you be eating then? What would her specialities be?

Roasting meat, the smell of roasting meat, that's something that has almost disappeared. You came in the house and you smelled roasting chicken or roast beef or pork or even fish... mussels have a beautiful smell. I think the smell is something that appeals first. It gets in your mind; you don't see it; it will be good. Then, the appearance of the food, its freshness, the abundance. I don't like to work with foods that do not seem to have freshness.

So this way of thinking came from your grandmother's table?

Yes, maybe. But also, when the idea of opening a restaurant came to me in '79, I had gone to different restaurants and knew what a customer wants. I had the enormous luck to have a father who had taken us everywhere to dinner when we were very young and immature; we were adolescents.

How old would you have been when going to top-rated restaurants?

Between 13 and 25.

Were there certain good restaurants in Montreal where you grew up?

Yes, but the best were mostly in France, and some in New York. And of course, when we travelled to Hawaii, we went to Hilton Hotels and things like that— with high standards; not necessarily great food, but with all the trimmings and great service. Part of the experience of a restaurant and a hotel is the caring, the hospitality, the welcoming, how the table is set, how you feel when you are welcomed. It's a lot of details. Sometimes people will say, you go to that restaurant, it's supposed to be the best in the world, and then you wait— you wait to receive the menu— you wait— you wait to receive your plate— and then, when you look at your plate, it doesn't seem as nice as you expected when you read the menu, and even the taste disappoints... It was not only what the cook did, but also many details that would make you feel happy, that you had a nice evening, that, really, you enjoyed it. And part of it was, I would say, the humanity... It's those kinds of things that I thought were important, so when I opened the restaurant, it was important for me that the setting was welcoming, and I put a lot of effort and time into that, and after that, the produce, the food.

At first it was more like a bistro. I had no ambition of becoming a great chef. I opened a small restaurant; I was not known; I didn't do that to be known one day, it was only a way to earn my living. Because at that time there was not a lot of work for geographers if you didn't teach at school or university, and I didn't like that. I started teaching at university, but I felt that people at universities were very much inside an ivory tower, very centred on their research, and that there was a lot of competition between the qualified professors. I didn't like that. I felt that it was quite disconnected from the real world, from everything I liked. Even now, in my profession, I don't like it when there is a lot of competition. I've got to that level, and I still don't compete. For me, it's, well, you do the competition, I don't. I just continue to do it my way.

But cooking at this level does have an ivory tower aspect... and then you talk about your relationship with the customers. Many people say, oh, I can't go somewhere like this, because my palate, I just like to eat my hamburgers...

Yes, that's true. It's a strange thing, you know, because when I opened, I really only wanted to have a good restaurant. I just call it a "restaurant"; it was not a gastronomic restaurant, fine dining; it was nothing like that. The first sign was right near the restaurant, because the hotel was not built at that time, and it just said, "Restaurant." In my mind, a restaurant is a place you go when you're hungry. It doesn't say "Bar," it says "Restaurant"; so, you see that and you say, well, I'm hungry. Why don't I go there?

So, when I first opened, in '79, we called it "L'Eau à la Bouche." "L'eau à la bouche" in French is nicer than it is in English. In English, it's like "mouth-watering," it's not extremely appealing; but in French, it has many many many meanings. "L'eau à la bouche" really means something that is appealing, and when you think of something that gives you "l'eau à la bouche," it's pleasant, with a good, nice feeling, not in English, but in French. We were a bit intellectual, I suppose. We were young.

So, what kind of food did you offer?

It's strange to say that today, since it's been almost 20 years, but I was like a pioneer without knowing it at the time. I was just cooking fresh food, and, at that time, in all North America, most people were serving frozen food, processed food, General Foods, Kraft Food, from all those mega, gigantic food industries that control almost the whole world, from the farming to the processing to the selling, and they infiltrate everywhere. I didn't want to serve that produce. And, not doing that was being different. Because when you went to hospitality school and studied how to manage a restaurant or operate a kitchen or become a chef, you learned how to work with processed food, not how to do it with the real thing, but with the false thing— as in, how to cut the tiniest tomatoes to get more money from your tomato, not how to get more taste from your tomato.

For me, this is very important, because in North America, it was profit. You look at food as future profit. Not profit for the pleasure of the customer, but profit for the pocket of the owner. And it was all over North America... people were telling me I would go bankrupt, that I didn't operate the right way.

In the first season of '79, I just bought the freshest I could get, and it was very difficult at that time to maintain a supply of fresh free-range chickens. You had to argue and battle with your local purveyor, to have fresh fish, to have fresh vegetables— just to ask for fresh broccoli... I served fresh broccoli in my restaurant. Everything they wanted to sell was canned or frozen, or big, large carrots or cabbage or potatoes. It was— how can I say it?— dull. And when there was gastronomy, as in Montreal's fancy restaurants, it was false gastronomy. They'd say it was gastronomy because they'd add a lot of béchamel and a lot of garlic if it was a French chef, but, in fact, it was not fresh food. It was just arranged so that it would seem better to the customer, but it wasn't really.

While this was happening in Montreal and North America, you were travelling to France?

Yes, and at that time in France, the revolution had come, because chefs like Michel Guérard, or Paul Bocuse or Pierre Troisgros or Charles Barrier were the first generation of chef-owners, and that is what makes the difference. For a long time the chefs were employees, so the owners were people who wanted to make money. And then one day, the talented chefs became owners, and they decided to do the cooking they liked.

So you saw this when you were travelling?

Yes. I saw that when I travelled and I tasted it. And then in '81, '82, when the restaurant was only two or three years old, I realized that I knew nothing. Maybe I had a good palate, maybe I could cook a bit of chicken, a supreme of chicken, maybe I could do a few things, but I knew nothing.

So, where did you learn even those simple things? You weren't in school at that time?

No, but since I had always cooked with my grandmother and my family, it seemed easy for me— I don't know. And maybe the other part of the business, of being a chef, is organization. Maybe it was in me and I didn't know it at the time. Now I know how important organization is, but at that time I was just organized because that's the way I am: you decide to do this first, that second, and then you do this, and I did that right from the beginning: I want to go there, so how many steps do I have to take to get there? And if I want to go further, and it takes more hands to help, what do we do? We hired someone. It was very simple for me to go from one point to another point. I wanted to have this, so I went and got it. If I want to have fresher products, I go to my purveyor, and I say, I know that place is farming that kind of vegetables. I want it. They might say, well, you will be the only one... and I would tell them, I will buy the whole case, don't be afraid; buy it for me when you are downtown; I'll buy it all. I had friends, restaurateurs— at that time there were a few of us who wanted to do things differently— in a better way, we thought— and sometimes we split the case of fresh food, and then our purveyor took confidence in what we said, and he began to offer it to other restaurateurs, saying, well, Anne Desjardins from L'Eau à la Bouche is buying that, if you want to share it with her... and they often said, well, she's buying that, why not me? So then it spread a bit, and over the years it became easier for us to get the food we wanted to have.

Buying is very important, and the other part is learning. I realized that I did not know enough. When you go to university, there is one thing you learn: you learn how to learn. You might forget everything you have learned, but you learn how to learn. So, what I knew was that I had a problem. I wanted to go further, and I needed to know more in order to do that.

**Was there something, during this time, a vision that said, I love this, I
really want this...? How did this happen?**

The first year, when we bought that house, wishing to live upstairs and have
a small restaurant downstairs, we had only 44 seats, and we had to hire a chef.
I was not supposed to work there. Never. I was to hire a chef. We didn't have
the money to do this; we didn't even have one customer. We were opening!
We were wishing, but we knew nothing. So, what I did was say, well, for
the first month I will cook, and we will see what happens. You see how foolish
you can be when you're young? I was 28 years old. I said, well, I know how
to cook! And we don't know, maybe we'll only have five customers the first
night! So we did the menu— I still have my first menu, written by Pierre,
because at that time we still wanted homemade things. I had my little herb
garden; even at that time, I wanted to copy what my grandmother had done.
She had had an herb garden, so I wanted to have my herb garden. Six months
before, I had a little rehearsal with friends at home. I invited 15 of my friends;
I said, come at different hours, I had set little tables, I had made a little menu.
I started with two choices: first course, two choices, main course, two
choices... one was chicken, and the other one was a pasta dish, and the first
course choices were a soup and a special salad. One dessert was fruit, and one
was my favourite of my grandmother's cakes. It went well, and we liked the
idea; we were having fun, you know? We were not taking ourselves seriously,
and if it went wrong, the house was still very pretty and could be sold to
become what it was before.

At that time I had my first son— maybe you met him last night at the
reception. And he was, at that time, five years old, and I wanted to stay home
with him. In my mind, cooking downstairs and living upstairs was the perfect
combination, and we just made a try at it. I liked it very much. I liked the
heat, as we say in French. I like it. It was a challenge, you know, and I like
challenges. And I just wanted to get better.

So, we were working very hard, but it was interesting, and Pierre was
getting interested in wine-tasting, and I realized that I had to search, to learn
more, because I knew a bit, but not much. So I began to buy magazines and
books, and read everything and try things. And then, the Seminar for Chefs,

in the south of France, accepted me. One chef came each day to teach his ways to other chefs, like me, ordinary people becoming chefs, or future chefs who wanted to learn more, and what I realized when I took those courses was that the idea behind my opening of the restaurant, they were actualizing it. They came with their menus, they explained the way they worked the menus, and, most important, they were very proud of their products and produce, of the freshness, of the best. It always came up in the discussion... It was really the process of buying the best and never compromising on the best. So when I came back here after that, I decided I would never, never lower my standards.

Because here in North America, people in the industry will say, well, customers don't know the difference. The word everywhere at hospitality school was, *The customer doesn't care. It doesn't make any difference.* And it was not true, for me, because I was once a customer, and I did know the difference; if I did, many others would, too. Why would my customers be stupid? Why would my customers not see the difference between fresh fish and frozen fish? Or real butter sauce and fake chicken sauce? They would not tell the difference? So I decided always to go and pursue the freshest, the best, the best way to cook, the best way to buy, and it was the customers who made the difference.

So that was the first part of my learning, really having a strong conviction about freshness. I don't like short-cutting in cooking. If there is a way to do something, it's the way to do it. If you take a short-cut, it will lessen the taste. If it's a short-cut that is just chemistry, I mean, you may want to make your hollandaise old-style and things like that, it's okay, but you can also do exactly the same thing in the blender because the heat of the butter will create exactly the same emulsion as in the old way. That's not a short-cut; it's just a different way to work with the chemistry of the ingredients. But I would never buy a powder to make that sauce— that's what I mean by short-cut, buying processed products.

Or a commercial stock?

Yes, yes, that's it. I would never compromise on stock. The things that I've told you so far are from the first part of L'Eau à la Bouche— before the trends.

Because of course, in France there was Nouvelle Cuisine, but it hadn't arrived yet in North America, and Nouvelle Cuisine, even here, in Quebec, was perceived by customers and by the industry as something unappealing. Small portions and al dente vegetables, uncooked foods and things like that, were considered just a way to give less to the customer. And at the end of the '80s, the trendy food came from California cuisine— Italian trends, and Oriental ones, and whole American ones, and some French. This was called "cuisine fusion," or fusion cuisine. It became like a play for chefs, to pick extra virgin oil, sun-dried tomatoes, soya, any kind of new thing from different cultures, and to match them together and to experiment. Experimenting in cuisine is a very good thing, but it takes a lot of talent. The problem with trendy things or experiments in cuisine is often that the chef does not go out enough to eat in other restaurants. They don't go to restaurants and have fun— ask for a nice dinner, take pleasure in it, make their own judgement and say, gee, I like that; that's a good recipe. I like that, it gives me ideas. No, it's just chefs in their own kitchens, and they like to pick and choose new products. Everything now is globalized: products and produce. You can have everything, every-thing, fresh or sun-dried... and then they just mix things, take this and do what imagination or dexterity empowers them to do. And they don't go and sit and have gastronomic experiences enough; I mean, pure pleasure in eating, with friends around the table having pleasure in eating, and laughing, and drinking a good glass of wine, and then rethinking all of this and saying, oh, gee, that was great...

And does this come just from the restaurants, or also at at home?

Of course it can come at home, also. You are at the homes of friends, and they cook... A very good friend of mine, and my own sister and brother-in-law are wonderful cooks, and the mother of my brother-in-law was... now, she's very aged... but she had one of the finest palates I know. She could identify everything you put in a dish, and she knew how to mix things... that's the secret of the good chef. The real truth is the taste; it is the pleasure. A good chef is someone who wants to share pleasure. What do you do at home, or when you receive your friends? You want to have fun with them, to share pleasure; so in your mind you go and shop for the best, not the worst; you go, oh, that will be good! And then you try to make your best recipe— you cook it, you sit, you chat, you have a nice evening— and in that, there was, I suppose, I hope, gastronomic experience.

Then, if you are at a restaurant, the same thing can happen; you choose to go to a nice restaurant, you know you will have pleasure, you love that dish, you come back for that dish, you love it when the chef really gives you pleasure; and everyone at the table says, mmmmm, that's delicious! Many chefs today don't go out as often as they should. They work, they work, they work, they pick and choose products and produce, they assemble, but there is no wish to share pleasure, only to create something stunning or trendy. But it will come back, you know, because that's a trend, and after a trend is over, when everything settles down, the right thing comes out.

What part has technique in all of this?

There is originality, creativity, and also technique... Cooking is something you have to understand from inside... it's chemical, it's physical, what happens— so technique can be chemical. It can also be a physical reaction, when you cut your vegetables, or you slice your meat, the way it changes the taste; or you dice in small pieces or in larger ones, or very large ones; this will change the way it feels in the palate. So, those are all technique; and it's something you have to have inside you. Some people will never learn it, because it's a lot of detail, it's a lot of organization, even when you are chopping and cutting.

When I'm thinking of a new recipe, it's like three-way thinking: of the technique, of the time it will take to work it, to transform it, the kind of dexterity it will take. Does this require a very high level of skill, and is everybody in my kitchen able to do this, or only me and my second? How will it stand? How long does it take? Does it take all day to make only a little? Then, it's a waste of time; it's not a good idea to do something like that. So everything, when you see it in a menu like mine, is thought out: the time it takes, the dexterity, the technique. Also, the edibility of the products, the produce, the freshness I can get: is it the best, is it what I want to serve to the customer? And then, how long after the waiter comes with the order, how long after it's all settled, does it take to give the food to the customer the way I had imagined it? Is it worth it? The time it took to do this, when we eat it, is it worth it? That's why I say that it is many things...

For example, let's make it very concrete. The foie gras, how did you come to compose all this?

That's one of my simplest ones; it's not one of my most sophisticated, because the sophistication is in the product, in the foie gras. It's very often like this. The more sophisticated the produce, the less sophisticated the technique, because the main thing is the quality of the foie gras.

That's important for a chef to understand, no?

Yes, absolutely. But also, in the case of the produce for the foie gras, I want to have the best, and foie gras is fat— it has a fatty taste, a very agreeable one, but still— so I always try to do a very lean sauce with a bit of acidity, and a bit of fruity taste. Of course, the area is full of apple orchards, and I work a lot with the farmers of this area. I am on a board, for my region, that consults with the Quebec Ministry of Agriculture. For me, it's very important, because I want to serve the best, so I want to encourage my farmers to do well, because they need encouragement and they need to know what we need to have to serve to our customers.

In Toronto they have the Knives and Forks organization, and in BC, Farm Folk/City Folk.

In Quebec, we have La Corporation de la Cuisine Régionale, it's for chefs and producers, it's like a round table where chefs, distributors, farmers, and people from the agricultural ministry try to work together. I'm very strong on that; I think we have to be part of the chain.

I could talk to you for hours about sauce, because sauces are the true essence... With home cooking, sometimes you will do a great dish, but too often the sauce doesn't have finish, long presence in the mouth. That's because, in the restaurant, you reduce your own stock, and you take the fat off and you reduce it again, and then you add a little bit of chives and maybe some garlic, and then you pour in some alcohol— it was apple cider with the foie gras— and you reduce the sauce again, and then you pour the broth again. When you reduce it, it gets a clarity, and these stages are important in the creation of that different taste. You take those steps when you do it; then, in the mouth and on the palate, it will be the same thing, step by step. If you just poured those ingredients all together it would never taste the same. That's chemistry. I cannot explain it any other way, because it's pure chemistry. And, why do I put the bit of lettuce with the foie gras? It's because I like the crunchiness and the wateriness of the lettuce, that balances... the sauce will balance, but the crunchiness and the little watery taste will also balance, with the foie gras.

That was the green.

Grown just nearby. And I will have a little chip of apple. That's, I would say, the fantasy.

You have to have some fantasy sometimes.

It's like a signature. It's not something essential to the dish. It's just a fantasy, and when you taste it, it's amusing.

That's another step, no?

It's another step, yes. In a dish, you compose the central aspects— you choose your meat and the trimming, and how it will be and what will the important taste in it be. That's the structure. Then, you have to visualize it. How will it look? Because a dish always has to have three qualities: it has to be very good; it has to be visually appealing; and, it has to be not too complicated. When there is over-complication, you miss what should be the first thing, the taste; that's what you should reach, the best taste. The appeal is in the eyesight, but taste is more important and is the sense of the dish that will linger. For me, a dish should be like this.

How many different taste elements can you have in the finished dish?

I would prefer to have at least three different levels of taste. There is— oh, it tastes like meat— and then, oh, there is a little fruity flavour— and then oh, my God! I think there is that kind of spice in it, maybe cardamom... but I don't describe my dishes in such detail on the menu. My menu is quite simple.

In a very French style, I see.

I don't like to write everything down; I think there has to be surprise when you receive the dish. Also, when you write everything down, maybe someone will choose from the menu because he likes that item, but not for the main thing. For me, now, after 20 years, it's still really in my heart.

You said a minimum of three levels of taste. Do you think you can go much beyond that?

Oh, yes, but not everybody can... You have flavour, and then you also have texture, and the more you tantalize the customer, the more he will love it, even plain roast beef...

I remember going to my grandmother's: you have the smell of roast beef, and we would take a little chunk of the outside cut. There is the crunchiness, and that side is more salty, or she would put mustard on it, and then it was more tangy and still juicy because it had just come out of the oven. That gave us lots of pleasure; we were young and knew nothing about palate or taste, really; just pure pleasure. I like this, I think that it should be natural.

We are talking about this and analyzing as if it was something very strange, but pleasure is something that comes from ourselves. I hope my customers do not dissect my food the way we've been doing; I want them to just have pleasure taking a spoon or a fork of a dish and saying, well, yes, that's nice, and, oh, yes, there's that! That's what I wish. That they have a good glass of wine, and my sommelier has made a good suggestion that works with the meal, and that the customer says, yes, oh, my God, that dish with that wine, and then he has nice people to serve him. For me, that's restorative.

Anne Desjardins

You've travelled a lot, both to learn cooking and as an adolescent.

Yes, I was very young, and sometimes the chefs did not impress me, but most of them were good communicators, like André Daguin, who is a master of foie gras. I took several courses on foie gras, and foie gras in Strasbourg is traditional. And there was another chef who came from Burgundy and taught us a way to cook foie gras— they were all different.

I came back from Europe to my own kitchen with these different ways of cooking foie gras. I don't know why it comes out the way I do it. From all the questions you asked, I realize there is a part I cannot explain, because it's not all technicalities... I think it's a passion. I live for cooking, I read about cooking, I still take courses. Last year, I took Italian and I went to a cooking school in Italy, to learn. We never stop learning, and that's why it's still a passion, because with so many products and so many different ways to do it, how can there be an end to the taste? How can you say one day, well, that's enough, I've tasted everything, I know what is the best? How can you do that? You will never achieve that, you know? Because when I go to a nice restaurant, I still get emotional when the chef does something...

I had a taste in Jean-Georges in New York last year— it was scallops with— strange to me— grape and caper sauce. I saw that, and I just wondered, what will it be like, grape and caper? But it was perfect, because Jean-Georges is one of the great creative chefs in the world, one of a new generation with new ideas and ways of doing things. It's always exciting when you go and you taste and you come back to your kitchen. Of course, you don't copy what you have tasted; that's not the idea. What you want is to be inspired and to go further in your own thinking. Two years ago, a chef from Nantes came to l'Ecole Hôtelière— we have a hospitality school, a very interesting one here [in Ste-Adele]— and it was quite traditional. There was a small, little recipe— it was a spicy caramel that accompanied a warm salad with a cheese crouton. I didn't really like everything he did with that, but I remembered the idea of spicy caramel, and I connected it with the honey-wine that we have a lot of in the Laurentian area— there are many honey farmers in the area— and I came back and worked with the honey and the honey-wine mead to adjust the spice to my taste. You always find a new thing to work with. That's why we are not bored. After 20 years in the same trade, many people will say, for instance, I'm 48; I'd like to do something else. Not me. I still want to be in my kitchen.

Well, you're talking about passion, of course. Do you think that's a natural thing for people, or can it be learned? Did you see it in other chefs when you were travelling?

Yes, but some chefs disconnect. I saw chefs acting like businessmen, too. If a chef is only a businessman, if he gets so wealthy that he can hire as many cooks as he wants, then you can lose... You have to be in your kitchen to see each part of the dish you prepare, so that you can show the other cooks... you cannot simply say, you do this, you do that; you have to adjust the taste with the whole brigade so that they can get the taste you want.

How important for you is your relationship with the brigade, the team?

Powerful, it's powerful. It's a love thing, but also it's a business thing. It's not your children, it's not part of your family, it's people you hire, you pay them. A chef alone in a restaurant is nothing; he needs a brigade, he needs people, and it takes so long to form a good brigade. I'm very lucky. My second has been with me for 10 years, my pastry chef 12 years. He is also a good cook.

How do you know, when somebody comes who wants to work for you, that this is going to be a person you can work with?

Sometimes it's the way they come and say why they would like to be part of your team. I let them talk a bit about food, and their ideas about food. That's important. They have to be very meticulous and precise people. There are people who will never learn. You show them and they still always put it in the wrong place. Food is not plastic. It doesn't come in a square thing. The chef says, you do this with a dish, but maybe one week that mango or apple is not the right size, and you have to have judgement. A cook needs good judgement, and to be able to adjust. Food is food, it's organic, natural; it doesn't always come in the same shapes or the same size. You have to adjust your cooking time, you have to adjust your method of slicing... you have to use your head, that's what I say. Sometimes people will say, you told me to do this! Yes, well, last week it was that shape, but now it's smaller. But when you have to repeat this too often, that means that the person doesn't understand that she has to adjust all the time. That's the difficult part; you have to work with people who will be low-paid. That's terrible, terrible. It's such specialized work, the kind of cooking we do, and the pay is too low. We pay a plumber $40 an hour to repair plumbing, and we pay only $15, $20, $10 to cook. I'm talking about the worker in the brigade, who has to do the thing right, and it's specialized, and it requires memory, organization, concentration, and also judgement, and you want to pay that person $10? I don't think it's right. I don't know how to change it, because I have to pay salaries that are part of my budget, and I cannot be overpriced; this is something I have to work with. But it reminds me of art. Most artists are not well-paid, and it's a bit like this.

In the brigade, how many men and how many women do you have and does that make a difference?

We are a brigade of nine cooks and two occasional cooks, and usually, one-third of the brigade consists of women.

A woman is usually quicker to work with a finishing touch at first. It's much easier to teach them how to garnish a dish and how to fit things; that comes quite easily for a woman. It may take longer with a man, but it can get to be the same after they have learned. With a woman, well, one of my assistants for four years is now pregnant, so she will leave for a year. That's something that is difficult in the brigade. That's why there are not so many woman chefs.

What happens in a restaurant kitchen is that women do not want to be in the kitchen so much. The chef-owner, that's completely different. It's my business, I live upstairs, I make my own choices. When you are talking about women in cuisine who are not owners, you will find a lot of women, but not with much responsibility, because of maternity. When you have a team and you say, my second will be a woman, most of the time a woman will want to have time with their family, or, if they don't, they will wish one day to have a family, so they will ask you for a leave of absence, maybe for a year or something like that. And it cannot be.

It cannot be?

Well, it can be, you have to work it all over with a new member of the brigade. And very large brigades, like at big hotels, CP Hotel, the big chains, I suppose it is not a problem, because there are maybe 40...

But you don't see that many women chefs in the very top positions. Do you think there is discrimination, or is it a question of maternity?

Absolutely! Many people say it's discrimination. Maybe a man will say, well, because she's a woman, but in his mind it's not because she's a woman, it's: because she is a woman, she will have children; she will then maybe one day ask to have a leave of absence, and be more with her family and her children, you see what I mean?

So, is there any solution for this dilemma?

If you are a cook in a cafeteria or a hospital, or a family restaurant, or McDonald's, or any kind of very ordinary restaurant, I don't think that there is a problem. But if you have a special restaurant, a gastronomic restaurant, then there is a signature when you go to that restaurant; there is a certain style. When people come to my place, most of the time they know that they are coming to Anne Desjardins' place; if I'm not there for a year, will it still be Anne Desjardins' place? The signature will become that of the person who replaced me. It cannot remain exactly the same. I can take a vacation of maybe two weeks and there are no problems; nothing will change in two weeks, maybe even in a month— but a year of absence, I'm sure that would make a huge difference, because it's a signature dish. Maybe it would be best; maybe the other who has replaced me would even do better; but if I have a second who is a a woman, and she leaves me, then how many years will it take me to coach another person to be a second and to be as good? That's why it's not discrimination; no, I don't think it's discrimination, it's just that women bear the children.

Anne Desjardins

You talked about the creativity and the art of it, and of course the freshness of the food... Are there other things? Music, books, other things does that influence you in your food?

Yes, I think we're part, and I'm part, of the world; I am part of the Era. I feel very strongly that I belong to this century, to this end of the century; I feel very right. I know very exactly where I am, and how I want to be. When you're a beginner, this is something you want to achieve— I know now what I want to do in the kitchen. Many articles were written about me, and that amazed me, because I never looked for publicity. I never wanted to be a celebrity. I just wanted to have a good restaurant with good customers. I just wanted to serve good food. I still want to have a restaurant where people take pleasure when they come, and when they pay, they say, maybe it was expensive, but it was worth it, and we had pleasure, and we will come again, or we will tell people to come. That's what I want; I want to share good things. I try to transform things, for my friends, my customers, everyone...

I cannot understand a waiter snubbing a customer. It reverses the roles. We are honoured to have customers, and it should never be the other way around. It should never be that the customer feels it is an honour to be allowed into the restaurant. We are honoured; we feel respect for the customer, for anyone who chooses to come to my restaurant. He may be a jet-setter, or he may be one who broke his little piggy bank to come for the dinner of the year and have pleasure. For me, this is very important. I think that food is like this: food should be democratic, like sex. Sex is democratic. Everybody can have sex; it's a pleasure, and everybody can have it. Of course, it depends on your own intellectuality to enjoy it in different ways— food should be like this.

I'm don't like competition; I don't think I'm the best, and I don't want to be the best. I just want to do my best, to do what I think is best. I believe that it will be good and people will have fun, or take pleasure in it. That's my purpose.

Of course, to have customers in your restaurant, you have to be rated. I'm not against that, but I don't want to search for the trendiest thing or to be the plus à la mode.

Your vision is also that you are somebody in this century. What does that mean in terms what you want to do and see in the evolution of cuisine in Quebec and Canada?

Everywhere in North America, talented chefs will discover their own roots more and more. In France, I saw a cheese factory where they've made the same kind of cheese since the 12th century— that's tradition. You go to a restaurant and you eat, and it's not the way of the grandmother, but the way that the old, old, old, old, old grandmother did it. That's tradition, and people in Europe have a very strong feelings about tradition. Most of the people know exactly the taste of a traditional dish, and sometimes it is very well made. They are good traditions.

It's very difficult for a chef in Europe to change recipes and to evolve. Some of the wittiest ones do it. And in North America, except for the Amerindian, traditions go back maybe three, or three and a half centuries, and people came here to be free. Because they suffered religious war in Europe, or came from very poor families, they were the petites dernières de la famille, and nothing was left for them, so they went to North America for freedom and prosperity. They came to a country that was like virgin land, and their main purpose was not to keep traditions; all they wanted was liberty. And so those people, my ancestors, my great-grandmothers and great-grandfathers, were astonished to see the abundance of game and fish here, because in France you could not hunt; only lords and gentry could hunt. You were killed if you were caught poaching, but here you could hunt as you wanted and fish and eat as much as you wanted. They had freedom, and they ate plenty; they were not thinking about tradition, let me tell you that, absolutely. I think what forged the mentality that we feel even today. It took a few centuries for an authentic North American cuisine to emerge, in BC, in central Canada, in Quebec, in California, in Texas, in New England, New York... Manhattan is quite a special thing, because most of New York is dominated by French chefs. But these cuisines emerged without barriers and with liberty of ideas, and that's why it was so easy for fusion cuisine to emerge in North America... That's my theory.

It's strange that, at the end of the century, so many chefs and cooks popped up, really popped up, from so many places with so many ideas. I was a pioneer in cuisine and products, discovering, going to our roots and then coming back to what we have here. Trends come and go. People will say, that I like and I'll keep, and that fancy they will simply discard, because people are like this.

But you also spoke of globalization. Is there a danger that we will lose this evolution in the future?

We should not be afraid of the future. There will always be intelligent chefs, and there will always be opportunistic ones and lazy ones, but the best ones will always survive and go further. There are always periods of time when you fuse things and you try things, people experiment. The best ones do the best, and the ordinary do strange things nobody wants to remember, but what will come out of this, I think, will be the best, because the other things just fade.

If you go to any city the size of Montreal, or Toronto, all over North America— except maybe in the centre of the United States, which is really traditional— you will find many kinds of restaurants. Sometimes, it's the first generation of immigration that opens a restaurant that gives ideas to others, because it's based on that freedom again. People do not feel obliged to stick to one kind of meal when they want to please themselves. And that's the beauty of it, you see? Because afterwards, it will go further. Tradition is good; we have to take what is good from it. But I don't see tradition only for tradition's sake as the best thing to go after in cooking.

It sounds also as if some of your studies as a geographer are all part of the philosophy.

Yes, maybe. I've travelled since I was very very young, and for me, it's still a passion, travelling. Really, I'm a Quebecker. I was raised and born in Quebec. My family is totally Québécois, but I feel at ease with everybody in the world. There is not a place in the world where I felt like, well, where am I? Who are all those people? There is always an explanation for the way people live, how they cook. I always go into grocery stores, and I look at the way they cook, how their stoves are made. I'm always curious; it's part of their history, or their geography. I find that very very interesting. I don't want to reproduce the things I observe, necessarily, but I keep the taste in mind. You say, yes, I tasted that, and it was very good, and then maybe you can add it to your own cuisine, in a different way. But it won't be in a Thai way, but in a...

The same way as the chef from Nantes.

Yes. And I think that the future of cuisine in North America will be like this. Even the most traditional French chef who comes here changes. They pop over here from France with their tradition, and they just... change. They accept things they never would have if they'd stayed there. We have a different way of thinking in North America, and I don't think it's bad, really.

If you were going to a big family gathering, what would the food be like? What would make your mouth water?

I like to have a big roast. If I could transform my restaurant, I'd like to add a rotisserie. I really would like to have a big fire. So that when people came in they would see quails, or other kinds of meat, roasting.

So, if all your relatives were getting together...

It'd be at our house, usually; at my house or my sister's house, and usually we have a big roast. It could be beef, or veal, or turkey, or quails or, sometimes, different things. Maybe a large salmon. Because when the family is together, we need a big piece of meat or fish, to visualize, and to share together. I wouldn't do small portions; I think that it would break communication at a family gathering. Everyone shares; everyone gets a piece of everything, including a lot of dessert for the sweet tooth.

Usually, the one who is at home does all the work. In some families, different people will do this or that, but we don't do that in our family. Food is sharing, sharing good things, good memories. If it's a more homey reunion, we might have a beef pot, something more humble, but we would still be sharing the same pot. It's the smell and the look of it. And of course, the cooking: the taste of roast meat, and the juice that comes from it— the sauce made from that has an inimitable taste. You cannot replicate that, not even in a restaurant... And for vegetables, we'd have, maybe, mashed potatoes— that's the best— or a big casserole au gratin— you know, things like that. Quite traditional fare, I would say, quite traditional.

Anne Desjardins

In December of 1979, a young couple graduated in geography at the Quebec University in Montreal. Anne Desjardins and Pierre Audette found and transformed a little house in Ste-Adele, deciding to make a small, bistro-style restaurant where they would serve simple meals cooked with a lot of passion. L'Institut du tourisme et de l'hôtellerie in Montreal, l'école hôtelière des Laurentides in Ste-Adele, and the Foundation Auguste Escoffier in Cannes, with seminars of Chefs for Chefs made it possible for the young couple to go further. In June of 1987, with the help of Anne's father, a small inn was added to the restaurant. As the years went by, Anne became an ambassador of fine québécoise cuisine, representing Canada and Quebec in Paris, Albi, Toronto, and New York. She has also appeared on television shows, radio, and at gastronomic events, and has received a multiplicity of accolades and many awards, including *Table de Prestige* du Québec, the Grand Prix du Tourisme Québec, and Number One (Montreal region) in *Gourmet Magazine*'s America's Top Tables.

Anne Desjardins

Anne Desjardins'
NORDIC TROUT FILET ROASTED ON ITS SKIN, MÉLI-MÉLO OF ROOT
VEGETABLES, EXTRA VIRGIN OLIVE OIL, SAGE AND GINGER
EMULSION [for four]

INGREDIENTS
4 x trout filets
a few drops of olive oil
salt for taste
1 carrot (cut country-style or julienne)
1 parsnip
1 turnip
1 leek
150 ml white wine
75 ml water
1 tsp fresh chopped ginger
6 branches sage, chopped
74 ml olive oil and 75 ml 35% cream
1 tbsp lemon juice

METHOD
    1. Prepare and cut your vegetables.
    2. Simultaneously, start the cooking of the trout and the vegetables.
    3. For the trout, in a pan put the olive oil, heat at medium temperature and place the filet skin side down and cook only on that side until the flesh becomes opaque, not more. Then reserve warm.
    4. For the vegetables, in a small saucepan pour the white wine and water, add the vegetables and 30 ml of olive oil, the chopped ginger and the chopped sage. Cook slowly until the liquid has almost evaporated. (The vegetables will then be cooked.)
    5. At service time, put the méli-mélo of vegetables nicely in the plate and place the trout filet on it. Reheat briskly at the same time the 75 ml of olive oil, the 75 ml of cream 35%, the chopped sage and ginger as well as the lemon juice. Taste and salt, pour onto the trout. Decorate with a fresh leaf of sage.

    The trick for this recipe for a perfectly cooked fish is to take the fish out of the pan as soon as a white liquid appears.

Nicolas Jongleux

Jongleux Café, Montreal, Quebec

One reason I moved to Montreal at the beginning of the 1990s was that after regular visits and a year living in France during the '80s learning about French cuisine, my palate had irrevocably changed. I was elated to find acceptably prepared bavette, duck confit, salmon with sorrel and cakes less than six inches tall, with little expedition. But what was virtually impossible to find, I came quickly to know, was the more finished innovative contemporary cooking of France I was familiar with. And then, I discovered Nicolas Jongleux, who had recently arrived at Le Cintra. The clear clean flavours of meats, fish, fruits and vegetables of highest standard are never hidden in his cooking, where nutrient-rich juices are extracted through exacting technique. His kitchen between services was spartan, much as I remember the kitchen of the illustrious Alain Passard on a visit to Arpège in Paris. Writing about Nicolas back then, I remember chatting with him one afternoon and thinking what of the philosophy of the current La Grande Classique he could bring to translate into Quebec. Since then, he has moved about to various restaurants, never unfortunately, having found his niche; critics and diners, even from New York have followed. And I have, even after moving from Montreal, always traced his movements, curious to watch his evolution as he became more at ease in Quebec, its terroir, its seasons. We met in the handsome bar of the restaurant Opus II in the Westin Hotel, where he worked briefly, on that most elegant stretch of Sherbrooke.

He was obviously excited, on the verge of opening his new bistro, a home of his own where he could finally fulfil his vision. That vision and his creation will always be indelibly marked by his rare background with some of France's master chefs. I wanted to hear as much how that shaped Nicolas, as of his latest venture.

I began at the age of 14 in a patisserie, Chez Monsieur Bouchard in Dijon— I'm originally from Dijon in Burgundy— in a very very traditional patisserie,

Nicolas Jongleux

classical— and I worked there until the age of 17. Then, I went to train in cooking in a one-star Michelin, with a young Burgundian chef named Joel Perrault, who was self-taught in cooking. He did fabulous things, superb. I stayed for two years at his place. It was truly for me the most difficult period, because he was very hard to work for, it was still the mentality of the old chefs, very hard with the cooks, the method of learning and a completely different culture— than perhaps Montreal, where it's more "cool" more trendy, just like in Toronto where the chefs are "cooler" with the staff— in terms of the staff learning the work. In France, the discipline...

Tell me the story of when— you made the decision to be a chef.

I began to do patisserie because I was at school and my days off I needed to make a little bit of money. I did dishes in a patisserie when I was 13 years old, and I'd help out a little, putting the cakes into the display cases, arranging things and all that. I began to think it was really interesting. I wanted to have a manual profession. At the start, I was not taken by this profession at all, at all, at all. I told myself I'd get into graphic arts because I could draw really well, or high fashion— I wanted to do something very very manual. I wasn't much for things like woodwork— but something very artistic.

When I was in the patisserie, I was really a kid— and saw the pastry chef who was there. I began at 4:00 in the morning. I'd do nine kilometres by bike to get to work. I arrived and he was baking the croissants and I remember smelling the odour of the croissants outside the boutique— and smelled the viennoiseries and it was really a very amazing odour. The croissants were baked in a huge oven and all kinds of viennoiseries were baked— pain au lait, pain aux raisins, and this style of work was superb. It was that period when the patisseries were still the big big patisseries and there was an incredible style of work— with one person who only worked the oven, one person who did the cakes, one person who did the small cakes, one person who did the ice creams. Each person had his own department like that. I remember that the person at the oven had to use the oven as often as possible because the oven cost a lot to operate. That's why he put things in without cease. He began at 4:00 in the morning until 7:00 or 8:00. It was a huge electric oven with this fiery hot stone. They fired the oven to 300 or 400 degrees in the morning—

began with all the viennoiseries, then the genoise [cakes], the biscuits, it was all thought out— at the end of the day the temperature had come down scarcely 100 degrees— that was for the meringues— and I had the chance at 13 to see all this... I'd taste it all— I found it all so ingenious. The huge pyramid cakes— superb— and it was so creative... I was really attracted by that and I asked if they needed an apprentice because I thought he was looking for someone. So, I was the only apprentice they had and the first they had. That's how I began. I signed an apprentice contract, because it's a special training and school is obligatory until you're 16. So I did one week in the patisserie and one week at school, but in specialist restaurant training at school. There were general studies like mathematics, history, along with that...

So, I had already decided at 13 years of age that my profession would be as a pastry chef. I never changed. I was hooked— above all by pastry. I came into cuisine after that because I went out with my diploma when I was very young— I had training in pastry, chocolate, ice cream, confectionery— at the age of 17 years. Once I had my diploma, I was too young to do my military service— because the military service is obligatory at 18 years. So, I did not have a lot of choice— to work in pastry or to get more training.

I lived in a village called Marsannay La Cote— which is the beginning of the Cotes des Nuits in Burgundy. And just next to Marsannay La Cote— I didn't know cuisine at all— didn't know top level restaurants at all— there were just two restaurants. One was a Novotel— there's no gastronomy in that— and the other was a one-star Michelin and rated 17 [of 20] in *Gault-Millau* [along with the *Michelin Guide*, France's most influential food and travel guide]— Chef of the Year. But I had no idea it had a Michelin star.

I arrived and introduced myself. He was very interested because I had pastry training. We were 12 apprentices to try out— and two of us were kept and you signed for two years' training with him. It was three weeks at the employer, one week at school. But at his place I did two years and a half— it was the hardest of my life— on the level of training it was killing, killing, killing.

He was a young chef, and he had a lot of pressure, and he put a lot of pressure on the people around him— above all on his apprentices... I remember that there wasn't a break in the afternoon. The afternoon when we went for a break— he'd call us and we'd go down and there were the terrines, the foie gras— and after he'd make us come into his office and ask questions about the recipes: give me the recipe for 12 persons— for that and that and that and what you do... It was total hell. But we finished those two years as the best regional apprentices. Then I ended up at Alain Chapel's and the apprentice with me ended up as chef at Guy Savoy's.

So, you see that it was murderous training, but the young that he trained— they all broke through— after, when I left— and said I had worked at Joel Perrault at Marsannay La Cote Les Gourmets— it was like *pshhhuhh*... the door opened like that. You were in the hardest establishment in France.

Do you think that's important in the beginning...?

I think it's important to have a good foundation, I think it's important to learn good things at the beginning. It's important to learn a very difficult way and go through a good establishment at the start to follow through to the major establishments.

I stayed two years, then I left for Luxembourg— and worked with Jean David Daudet, former chef of Marc Meneau, of Alain Senderens, and of Chiberta. It was also hell to work with him. We were 12 in the kitchen— and I did all the stations and did all styles of cuisine— different cooking methods— it was really really exciting. I stayed for a year and a half— a very creative menu but above all accented towards birds and poultry. It was a restaurant which existed on the principle— it was in the Ardennes region— that all the products came from the farm. The birds came from the area, all the vegetables— there were five gardeners who collected all the vegetables for us— the herbs... we learned to work with that— truly regional products, a very very creative kitchen.

When I left him, he sent me to Marc Meneau in St. Père Sous Vezelay. Then at the last minute when we met, he told me— I have a problem because you haven't done your military service. I can't take you. Well, I was very disappointed to not be able to go into a three-star Michelin, for me it was like the best...

But he sent me to Brittany to a two-star Michelin-rated Relais Chateaux and I worked for a chef at an establishment which is very very well-known in France which is really at the top level— Chateau Locguénolé— many chefs are trained at that establishment.

I saw all the chefs down there— Michel Guérard, I saw Joel Robuchon there. We got back two Michelin stars in six months and Chef of the Year in six months in *Gault-Millau*. This chef, Denis LeCadre, is one of the very very grand chefs in France. He did his apprenticeship at Charles Barrier in Tours— Charles Barrier was the master for Joel Robuchon's apprenticeship. He worked at Napoule. He worked also at Maximin's. He worked as chef at Marc Menau's. Very, very, very creative... a very fish-based, very creative cuisine. So, I had the chance to work then, with Denis LeCadre for a year and a half. When I left, I sort of left everybody; I went to do my military service.

Not long after your military service, you were able to interest Alain Chapel. What happened?

When I went to Alain Chapel's, I had a four-hour interview. Why do you want to work here? What's your motivation? Why do you cook? What pleases you in cooking? The way I thought... he had all the choice of cooks at his place since everybody wanted to work for him. He just wanted the best, wanted the top chefs, cooks. I was the only chef there who had not been at a three-star Michelin. I had just been at a two-star. All the chefs who were there— there was one who came from Joel Robuchon— another from Guérard's— who came from everywhere, everywhere, everywhere.

That's the strength that's in that establishment— to work with all those chefs de partie who had learned in their different establishments, so you think your ideas, you change your ways of thinking, you create totally different things. That's what's amazing. For me what's the most important when I think of Alain Chapel's, it's the fact that I was a pastry chef. If I hadn't been, he wouldn't have taken me. He didn't take me just for cuisine, but because I had pastry training. I worked in pastry at Alain Chapel's.

It was truly a super place, a revelation of cuisine because— I think if you go to France and you talk to many chefs, and ask who's the greatest chef— all would say to you, Alain Chapel. Alain Ducasse worked at Chapel...

I can't explain what goes on in that establishment, it's incredible. The red berry fruits come only from the Vallée Turenne because it's the best red berries in the world. The apricots only come from the Ardèche. The lamb only comes from the Pyrenees. The veal comes from the mountainsides at Mirande. The cheese, the comté comes whole from the Juras, the lobster, the St. Pierre [fish], all the cold seafish comes directly from Brittany, a gentleman sent them directly to us. All the small vegetables came from the garden producers St-Etienne. Alain Chapel didn't put much importance on journalists. He wasn't all that concerned with media. He put an enormous importance on his suppliers. For him the suppliers were everything, everything.

Each year he created a meal, a meal of the year with the best suppliers of Alain Chapel and the best winemakers. It was 100 persons and we closed the restaurant and the meal began at noon and ended at 7:00 in the evening. It was a gastronomic meal— it was incredible! Each producer brought his best product, each winemaker brought his best wine— among the winemakers, there was— Monsieur Ramonet in Puligny-Montrachet, there was Trapet [Domaine Trapet in Gevrey-Chamberlin], you had people like Chauvenet. All the top, the top the top. I worked with ortolans [small gamebird of luxury cuisine], the woodcocks, the snipe, the thrush. We did a menu of birds— seven different birds— all done differently. It was incredible, incredible, incredible.

For dessert, I remember it was a pain d'épices [spice loaf] served with a chocolate base— crème anglaise, chocolate, melted butter, moulded with a spice loaf dipped in old rum and finished with acacia honey. And with a jam of macerated fruit... all was worked. The pre-dessert was a huge meringue not too cooked so that you could pierce the interior, to put very cold vanilla ice cream inside, so you cut that— with all that ice cream on the inside. It was tops. For him it was the consecration of the meal. It had to be the best meal of the year. For me— to work in a place like that— how can I explain that?...

I left Alain Chapel after his death; he passed away in 1990.

Before your move to Montreal...

I arrived chez Georges Blanc when I was 25, as chef de partie. I stayed for six months at the meat station... and then he sent me to his bistro. I was in charge of his bistro for four months and then he called me back and he promoted me to be his second.

I stayed three and a half years at his place. And for me it was a revelation because to go through an establishment like that... A three-star is a three-star... It's in Europe, it's completely different. A huge brigade. It's 40 cooks, to work for a master chef in France.

Following that I came to Montreal. I knew someone who knew someone who was looking for a chef in Montreal. It was an opportunity to come to Montreal for me and then— I arrived in '93 and the standard of the cuisine, it wasn't truly superb, there weren't many restaurants— Toqué! wasn't yet open, James MacGuire as well... on St. Laurent there was only Luna at the time. There was nothing in restaurants.

Ah, so it was that year we met...

Yes, it was I believe in '93 that you did the review in *enRoute*... '93, '94. I had arrived in Montreal in that year.

There was a great demand for food in Montreal but there wasn't a real need of gastronomy in Montreal. There is gastronomy in Montreal, but I think for the people who go to restaurants, it's not the first thing they're looking for. They're looking for the atmosphere, the ambience, the decor... if the food can go along with that, the better.

I don't know about the rest of Canada, but in Montreal it's begun to get a lot better because there are many micro-bakeries which have opened since '93 a lot of micro-breweries which have opened, and you find a lot of small organic vegetable producers now that there weren't before. You find a lot more products also; since '93, the restaurants that open are a lot more first-class, a lot more progressive, they're a lot more exacting, do things a lot more professionally.

But you were moving quickly, at a young age? You already had the experience to move into top establishments— pretty different from here...

Well, quickly— I was working 20 years in restaurants, so I don't know if that's so quick. Well, sure, when you've done two years in an establishment directly as an apprentice in a Michelin-starred place, you're a lot more shaped than any young person who works in an institute or who works in hospitality school, even privately. You don't have the same shaping at all. On the level of experience, through an apprenticeship, you have a lot more strengths when you've worked at an establishment out in the world, on the condition you also find a good establishment. I had the luck to fall upon a very good establishment.

It was very difficult, it's sure. But for me it was something very revealing because it permitted me to persevere. In France you have a lot of young people who want to get into a good establishment but it's not easy at all. To get into a grand establishment like that you have to look more abstractly at your salary and hours because you don't earn much money and you do a lot of hours. And you don't have a life, eh? You work from 8:00 in the morning, you'd finish at 3:00. You begin at 5:00 and you finish at 11:00. You don't have anybody in all of North America who works like this. Same in the United States, it's a double brigade: a day shift brigade and an evening shift brigade.

The sole advantage is that the establishment is more stable because there's always the same brigade, but I don't think it's better. At a certain point you're burnt out, you can't think about other things. It's the way France operates, it's the way this kind of establishment operates— to work 17 hours a day— I don't know if it's the best way to learn, but that's the way I learned.

Let's say as I'd been doing interesting work, above all a training in pastry, thus, all the bosses who hired me at Georges Blanc and Chapel were interested because I was a pastry chef but I had a chef's training. For them it's always good to have someone who's a pastry chef but has a vision in the kitchen because he does completely different desserts than someone who just does pastry. I can say that that's what truly opened doors for me.

So, that's it— that's the direction. Afterwards in Montreal, it was Le Cintra and La Cigale to work in a bistro... to open that bistro on St. Denis which for me was superb.

You then went back to the Le Cintra location and were successful at Les Caprices de Nicolas but decided to let that go. You've been temporarily working at Opus II for Westin Hotels and Ferreira Café before planning your own venture, Jongleux Café.

The Westin Mont-Royal approached me to work here— M. Fasel who was the director-general of the hotel asked me to come to take over the restaurant— for me it was very good because it wasn't to do gastronomy in a restaurant dining room, but also to look after 300 rooms, to look after room service, also to look after the breakfasts every morning— for me it was the first time to do this— it was the first establishment that asked me to do a lot of management. Young chefs, after they start in the métier— they have to, at some point, go through a management course for the business end. Because to cook and be at the top, it has to be profitable, too. Look at all the three-star Michelins— 80% of the personnel are trainees. Because you can't pay 40 cooks— at Georges Blanc— each year, I would say there were 18 or 20 directly from Japan on training at Georges Blanc— paid by Japan to be at Georges Blanc. If he didn't have these training staff, he wouldn't be able to do what he does. That's the difference with North America.

So I did eight months and then decided to go to one of the restaurants in Montreal which to me currently is the most successful— it's the Ferreira Café— the restaurant which does the most covers. It's Portuguese "bistro" cuisine, authentic— with a real ambience. I wanted to see what it was— what the difference was to do volume— because we did 200 covers— I wanted to get out of 40, 35 covers— to see if I was capable of doing quality for 200 persons. We were 12 cooks— so I saw that yes, we could do good things, but it was difficult to do the highest level with big crowds— it's very difficult, very difficult.

You're now planning your own bistro... like the bistros you find in France— like Michel Rostang— his Bistro à Coté— traditional bistro food but of top quality which has been trendy in France these days?

Yes, in the same spirit as the Bistro à Cote. In Paris there are a lot of bistros— but I'm not doing a bistro where you go to eat andouillettes, boeuf aux carrottes— I am going to do very creative dishes— bistro, but very creative. In fact, bistro can be pejorative— bistro is in the price, the prices of the wine list, the structure of the service and all that— but the cuisine I think will be something very creative. Classic at the base, but progressive. I would say that in North American cuisine there isn't really a base.

Nicolas Jongleux

What do you mean by base?

There's isn't really a culinary history— a history of cuisine— in Montreal, or likewise in North America. It's really done, created by the chefs who come from everywhere— Greek, Italian, Chinese, Japanese— who are transplants in Montreal. Because there's a francophone aspect— perhaps the people are a little more free in gastronomy than perhaps in Ontario— thus it evolves a little faster— in that since there's no base, it allows one to do more what one wants. For example, in France, it's not possible to do what one wants. Because always there are the old establishments which are next to you and you have to stay classical, it's difficult to evolve— the people like to see the familiar on the plate— to have refined things but it remains in a classical base. You have very few chefs in France who are very very progressive.

It's difficult for young cooks in France to stay in France because there's not much choice but to stay in the grand establishments and take the position of chef, or to leave to open one's own restaurant— but it's hard to open a restaurant— it's easier here— whether in Montreal, Vancouver or Toronto, or New York— you find money more easily and the people are more prepared for new creations— and more prepared to finance the young who have an open spirit— who want to do something.

But, at the same time, if the young want to set up, there has to be a basis in cuisine, a basis of a restaurateur, notions of management— a lot of notions to set up. You can't set up with just the cuisine. It's not possible.

You speak of the basis— techniques, practice— you come from France, from Dijon— so you're really uprooted— do you feel at ease, or not at ease here?

It's true that one adapts to the country where one lives, to the culture, one adapts and all that— but one can't ever forget where one's been— the difference one can see with France is that the population is already a lot more evolved, the pool of good restaurants is also a lot more evolved too, the pool of small producers, market producers, small butchers who are going to have a particular care to choose products.

In North America— the products from small market producers— organic products— are all new. Twenty years before, there was no raw milk cheese here, you didn't find the small market producers, you didn't find organic vegetables, you didn't find very refined products. People didn't eat sweetbreads, people hardly ate fish— then— people like Normand [Laprise] and me, Paul Pelletier, Daniel Vézina— I'd say the young generation of cooks who represent, perhaps, work a bit differently— perhaps we're not precursors— there were people before us— let's say we represent the new wave of chef-restaurateurs. I think people are more prepared now to accept more refined and creative things— much more— good food than 20 years before.

Because people travel, Quebec's more open— now there's more media influence— there're more culinary institutions also because before in Quebec there was just the ITHQ that taught people cooking. It's like a totally new profession. I think that gradually, Montreal will take its place as a gastronomical city...

There are already products— there aren't perhaps as many products as you can get in France— that's for certain— it's very difficult to find top level products in Montreal— it's very expensive— but you find it— I find it— farm-chicken, I can bring in salmon from Vancouver, mushrooms from Ontario, raw milk cheese from France, organic berries, small organic vegetables...

You've been involved in working with local producers...

Since 1993 I've been looking ceaselessly for new producers... I've organized a lot of things. Through the hotel, I organized, I think the Third Cuisine Canada at the Westin in Montreal— which was a meeting between chefs and Canadian producers who produce very special things. And so, above all— several Montreal chefs— you encourage people like that.

People like M. Daignault, for example, the biggest producer of true organic vegetables in Montreal now sells in the US— like certain vegetables you don't at all find in New York. Now that Normand [Laprise] is a consultant in New York, he took Quebec products with him. You see that there's a big market for Canadian organic vegetables— these kinds of people we encourage to do things completely differently— violet mini-endives— all kinds of small salad leaves— tastoy, mizuna, de l'arroche, pourpier gras, Japanese crosnes, white asparagus— we phoned France to have seeds— which we planted here to have the vegetables. People have been doing organic vegetables for 20 or 30 years— but it was big organic potatoes, or big organic carrots— not very refined things— and they sold all the production to the United States. They have seen we are going to have enough restaurants to begin to make enough of a small production to begin to live. But the survival of gastronomy in Montreal is going to be in the fact there there's going to be a multitude of small products like this which are going to create a completely different style of cuisine.

I think all the grand chefs who are in Montreal— we're all contacted at some point to go to the United States. We're not interested, because in Quebec, in a style of work, a style which is ours, we're at home, we do what we want.

We compare Montreal's restaurants with the top tables in New York when you look at the magazines— the top— Anne Desjardins, Toqué!— we're compared among North America's top tables. We do something really different, something in cuisine which is ours in Quebec, and ours in Canada. We have a pool which is very francophone— we have a lot of French here, a big Asiatic culture like in Vancouver, a culture which has come from those countries—

I like to do a cuisine with a French basis, but I like to work with Indian spices, I like to work with Asian products, I love Asian cuisine— it's a very very elaborated cuisine, very creative in terms of health, not especially the cuisine you find in Montreal, because the Asian cuisine in Montreal is Americanized, it's not a 100% Asian cuisine. I had the chance to go to Asia and taste Asian cuisine— which was completely different. Same with Indian cuisine. I had the chance to taste Indian cuisine in Singapore, it was really the best. Well, that showed me that North America opened up my horizons about cuisine.

So, you are more positive about North America than before?

Oh, sure, because I create menus which are a lot more creative, utilize a lot more products— if you look at a French menu, and you take the menu of several grand chefs, you have very few chefs who are going to try things like tandoori or nan— who are going to really try Indian spices, or special salads or special spices, very very few try lemon grass— they stay very very classical. That's what's completely different with North America where we have access to such products. When you're in Lyon, for example, you have access to products at the most, European and above all French. When you're in North America, the fish comes from everywhere— from the Mediterranean, from Vancouver, from the Pacific— you find all sorts of fish— pompano, perroquet— not found in France.

But you are French— do you think it's important to have that foundation— or you can just put in this, this and that...

Maybe what's different with me than other young chefs who don't have the same foundation, haven't done classical things— things you cook for hours— French cuisine isn't really a last-minute cuisine— it's a very prepared cuisine, very done— so the fact of having a North American influence with the products, with a French basis, gives a solidity at the level of cuisine.

It's to say it's not a Californian cuisine. I went to California and saw Californian cuisine— and I think the cuisine in the rest of Canada is a cuisine a bit fusionish— there's a tendency to marry, to mix, to play a bit on the plate... there are people who do this very well... I think Normand does very very good cuisine, creative... I think restaurants like Lumière, North 44 in Toronto do North American creative cuisine very well.

But I think the new generation of cooks— since there isn't a lot of focus, not a lot of basis, do a cuisine a bit fusion. In Montreal you find many many restaurants which do fusion cuisine and I don't think it's what people naturally want— because at a point it becomes very complicated— and there's no longer a point of reference. Like olive oil with sesame oil, with chiuggia beet, with a bad dry tuna— it's a cuisine a bit Asian, a cuisine a bit North American, with a bit of French cuisine— and all mixed up— it's not really something— it's difficult to create something really solid with this cuisine.

When I arrived in Montreal it struck me that the fashion was above all for things very decorated on the plate— set-up for the eye. This cuisine here is not naturally a very tasty cuisine. To a lot of cooks, the first thing of importance is the visual. They go to make a dessert, they put a lot of sugar in it and do very decorated things, but when you go to taste it, you just taste sugar, a very sweet coulis, there's not a very surprising marriage.

Or to think of the grand establishments like Blanc or we can talk about El Bulli in Spain, it's a very wholesome cuisine. It's a good product, it's always just three elements which makes the cuisine— I say, it's a product, a sauce and a garnish— there's not another thing put there. You shouldn't mix everything.

I think that in any other profession— in journalism it's the same thing— there's a professional ethic— it's the same in cuisine— you just have a professional ethic not to mix everything up together— no matter what— to have things raw on the pretext of being à la mode— I think à la mode restaurants stay for a certain time, but if you want to be solid and last a long time in North America and everywhere— you have to propose something solid, very solid.

So are you talking about an ideology?

Oh, sure— for sure you have to have it— you have to have an ideal in cuisine, you have to have a certain respect, even if you're no longer in France. When you're in France maybe you're more subject to the critics, the guides like the *Michelin Guide*, the *Gault-Millau*— which are very severe and check out your work— in North America, one's more open, they accept differences in cuisine more. But I think you have to hold onto a certain rigour in work, because you see people like Joel Robuchon, if he's opened in Japan, if he's chef of the century, if he's a three-star Michelin chef for I don't know how long and a phenomenal success, it's because he has a certain rigour in his profession, a certain discipline. Even if you work all alone— a discipline in the cooking, a discipline in the products, a discipline in the work— it's like good health, to do sports— even if you're not in your own country, you have to keep what you've learned. I think that's the only thing that works— to do good work. To have a style of what you do, to not change the orientation of this cuisine every two minutes.

But what you do— does it begin with your taste— in your throat, in your mouth— now you're here in Montreal with Indian, Asian things— what is your sense of taste?

I think from the basis of what I've learned, I know the cooking itself— the cooking of meat, the cooking of fish— well then, you know just to what point you can cook a product; I know ahead what I do is good or not good. Afterwards, to marry things, sure, it's to taste yourself— to have those around you taste it— the people you work with in the kitchen and talk with those around, and to have your regular customers taste it— see what they think, is it a good marriage? When I do a menu, it's really thought out, really worked through, so I already know how it's to be cooked, how it's going to taste before I've done it. It's true that now with maturity and age— I'm 32— you end up doing more marriages. I end up pushing the cooking further; I truly reflect on the way of combining things. You ask yourself more questions at 32 than at 17 or 18 years. At 17 or 18, you do the cuisine of others— you don't do your own cuisine, but at 32, I do my cuisine. There're always influences, influences in the cooking, influences in preparation, but truly the marriage— it's my own work.

Is there a conflict between your ideas and the tastes of your customers... you have to compromise?

Yes... the compromise... maybe people will say they want pasta on the menu... But for me it's not Chinese noodles, Italians work pasta so well... but for me, each person does his cuisine. I do a cuisine with a French basis, but evolved. I am capable of working with braised things, roasts, no matter what style of cooking, so I do a style of cuisine which is mine and I think when people come to your place, they come for a style of cuisine— Milos for Greek, Ferreira's for regional Portuguese. All the young chefs in Montreal aren't French, they're québécois, or North American, or Italian or... I'm alone in doing this style of cuisine, because I do something very different. A lot of people copy Normand Laprise to do a fusion cuisine with vertical presentation— and I'm the opposite of all that. I do... I don't much like the term classic, because when you say classic, people think of a sole with beurre blanc, or garlic butter... it's not what I do.

So how have Alain Chapel and Georges Blanc influenced your approach?

Well, Georges Blanc is above all classic... a small basis of creativity, but it remains a cuisine very terroir... Alain Chapel for me is the most creative chef. If you look a bit at the history of Alain Chapel, he had the same apprenticeship as Pierre Gagnaire— the master of Alain Chapel was the last apprentice of Escoffier— it was Alain Chapel was also a chef at Fernand Point, thus he was someone who, in '71, was the first to do a jellied pigeon à l'amie étoilé. He was the first to work with vegetable bouillon, the first to work with sweetbreads mixed with lemon verbena... the first to make cuisine classic at base but very very progressive with products.

I think my cuisine has that base a bit— it's a bourgeois cuisine— when I say bourgeois I mean there are a lot of dishes carved up in the dining room, duck for two persons, chicken for two, a pâté en croute for two, that's the part which is very very classic, but things very very progressive— it was already very progressive in '71 if you look at his menu... He proposed really incredible marriages with fish... he had a completely revolutionary sauce base. There's been nothing revolutionary since that period. When I look at chefs— even French chefs— they're greatly influenced by his style...

Like Guy Savoy, Robuchon...?

Yes! Yes... even if you look since the death of Alain Chapel in '90, a lot of Parisian chefs have been influenced by Alain Chapel. Many, many, many, many.

You find once again now in France les glaces à la confiture du lait everywhere in France. It was Alain Chapel who brought that out. It was his recipe— it was a radical recipe— you find everywhere in France right now. More or less recopied, remodelled. People say, "It was me who created..." No, it was Alain Chapel who created it. When you see the cuisine at Alain Ducasse he's just perpetuated what Alain Chapel had already begun. It's a cuisine very very classic with a whole lobster, whole piece of beef, with a small stew here, a small stew there— a cuisine in one way bourgeois but classic and very very very well made.

So, these influences on you...

Imagine... say if you work as a couturier, and you work with Jean-Paul Gaultier, who's very creative and very evolutionary, but with a basis in a house say, like Chanel... you have two styles... I can say that I worked with chefs who were very classic where I learned the basics, things well-made, and then worked for chefs who were very progressive...

I travelled, too— I was in the United States, I was in Asia... it's not only French cuisine, which for me is a grand cuisine. I was struck that there are other countries which do very very good cuisine: in India— there's a very very good cuisine— in Asia all the French chefs influenced by their trip to Japan, their trip to Tokyo— their trip to Hong Kong, the same in Singapore, the same in Thailand— it's cuisine that was refined... many French chefs in the '70s cooked vegetables with bite, they began in Asia to learn about vegetables with bite, it was in Asia that they began to have this mix of meat with consommé, to poach hens... they began to get more pure. Because for me Chinese cuisine— pure Chinese but not Cantonese, is a really pure cuisine with lots of perfume, lots of savour, but also a simple cuisine. And that's what I want to do.

I don't, of course, work only with beautiful products— truffles and foie gras— to make beautiful cuisine. You can work with simple products, be it a good pepper, be it a good squid, be it a chorizo sausage, be it salt cod— to make a very good cuisine. You don't have to work with fancy products to make excellent cuisine.

It's impossible to do bad cuisine with good produce— above all if you're more or less a good cook.

What I want to do today is the small cuisine of a bistro, I'd say not low level, but not necessarily with fancy products— with low prices, to be affordable for everybody— because I think in Montreal it's a limited, select public— we don't have the pool of population to have a Joel Robuchon in Montreal. It's impossible. People aren't capable of putting down $150 or $200 every evening in a restaurant. You can't forget that. I think that in doing something more affordable, I'll touch a larger pool of the population and then little by little I'm going to get people to go after new things, new ideas, new combinations.

How do you create a dish? At the markets...?

I don't really have a specific moment during the day. Sometimes it's in the night— I begin to sleep, I think about things, I get up, I write it down.. things which I put aside.

I thought at a certain time about a tomato consommé with the spirit of a crab with lemon grass, with things like that— things I think about one night— a recipe I put aside. I think, it's okay, maybe I'll do that, I'll leave it for months, and then one day, doing my menu, it's there in my papers— I say, well, that I find interesting— I find that the idea is good. So I take the idea or the basis of the idea to work at— that's how I create a dish. Thus I do marriages of unusual dishes, like stuffed rabbit mixed together with macaroni, finished with a carrot juice made with the liver...

Me, I'm not capable of going into the kitchen, taking the produce, working out something. When I create a menu, it's gone through a lot of reflection, but often it's very instinctive. I can be in front of a page for hours, nothing comes, really impossible combinations, I don't get anywhere— it doesn't come... and then there are times you have a feeling to cook— you get tempted to buy a few things, cook at home, oh... that'll be great... I'll get that and that... and marry that... it makes you want to do things, it gives you a feeling to create things. For me that's how it often happens. Sometimes I create a whole menu in the space of a day, a complete menu with desserts. There are influences sometimes in shops, sometimes on TV— one day I saw a Chinese dish, a hen with black skin cooked in a bouillon with lots of mushrooms and steamed for hours. It was very interesting. I'll take that basic idea, but I don't create an Asian dish— from the Asian idea I'll do a French dish. Perhaps I'll take a beef shoulder and cook it in a consommé, I don't know... with lemon verbena or lemon grass or with mushrooms, with enoki mushrooms or perhaps shiitake, we'll take it from that sauce, maybe I'll poach my beef and serve it alongside... I don't know... I imagine a purée of cauliflower with noisette [brown] butter— olive oil, with perhaps a small sauce with anchovy butter, so that the customer can make his sauce on his beef shoulder and eat that with his cauliflower purée. That can produce a superb marriage.

But I really love things in two or three tones. I really like marriages— for example, we can take the meat which is done up on a plate and bring you a sauce that complements the product, and then with a vegetable— I love vegetables— and I'm always thinking about a garnish that has been very very very elaborated and thought out, to make a completely incredible marriage between the garnish and the product. There are a lot of Canadian chefs who don't place importance on the vegetables, don't place importance on the accompaniments. Often for all the dishes, the accompaniments are the same thing— they'll do something with potato and it'll be the same type of potato for all the dishes. For me, each dish has its sauce, each dish has its method, if I do a rabbit, cook a rabbit, I'll do a rabbit jus, I won't work with a veal jus or a beef jus, I am going to work a rabbit jus and maybe I'll finish the rabbit jus with a carrot jus from a juice extractor, or a cabbage jus,... but it has to be an appropriate marriage. What's important in cuisine, that all young people should keep in mind, that is fundamental, that all the chefs in the world know— if you say on your menu, *roast chicken*— au jus with thyme— you must taste the roast chicken before everything else... if the thyme flavour covers the product, it's not at all a roast chicken. The product must taste of what it is.

What I think before everything is that cooks reflect the products— it's the products before everything, the cooks are the transformers of these products who take the final recipes of all such. You must have, from the start, good products.

For me all cuisine— there's isn't a French cuisine, there isn't Chinese cuisine, there isn't Indian cuisine— there's good cuisine and bad cuisine. That's how I classify stuff. There isn't grand cuisine, there aren't grand restaurants or small restaurants. I've eaten excellent dishes in small bistros where you get dishes for $10, and I've had very bad meals at the restaurants of three-star Michelin chefs in France— we've eaten dishes which haven't always been successful, marriages which haven't been well thought out.

Cuisine isn't an exact science, it's not always successful at 100%. Sometimes you have marriages which are badly thought up, which are a bit here/there but before everything, to do good food, it's what the spirit of the cook is.

I am against cooking meat portions alone. If you take a beef filet— everybody in North America takes a filet of beef and cuts up pieces of the beef filet into portions *before* cooking. I find that ridiculous. For example, the blood of the meat— it's gone. All the sapidity of the meat, the structure of the product, has gone. I prefer to take a big piece of beef filet, for two, three, or four persons to roast at the last minute. A piece of meat for four persons, it's very quick. I can cook an entire piece of beef and cut it up in the dining room. For example, at Alain Chapel, or likewise at Georges Blanc's, if you cook a duck magret, you always cook the duck magret on the bone of the duck. Always, always, always. You are going to roast the whole duck then cut out from all the directions of the duck. In North America, the duck magret arrives already vacuum-packed; and what does the chef do? He roasts it directly, the magret in the pan. What does the duck magret do? It has no structure to hold; it shrinks, it loses its blood, it becomes dry. There's no interest.

The success of chefs all over the world, if tomorrow these chefs were talking— even if they have different origins, have different styles, not necessarily the same type of cuisine, I think they'll have the same manner of thinking when it comes to cuisine. The great Chinese chef where I ate at the Raffles Hotel in Singapore thinks like a three-star Michelin. He didn't think like a small Chinese restaurant.

You talk about thinking... but there's also passion— you talk so passionately...

Yes— it's certain you have to a passion in the profession here. When you do this for 20 years— I've just begun to really make a living, and it's been very difficult. You have to be a passionate person— you have to be passionate. At home, I have maybe 200 or 300 books on cuisine— of all sorts— it's more biographies, more old books on cuisine, books where I can dive in and relive a certain state of spirit. It's not really recipe books; it's often books on comprehensive technical practical skills. You see that from one chef to another, these skills are different, you learn different things, and you must be very open in spirit.

The precursors in France— like Michel Bras in Laguiole, people like Alain Passard in Paris, people like Pierre Gagnaire in St. Etienne, like Alain Chapel, who was also a precursor... all these people are incredible creators, with very creative menus. They're very very creative in what they do. If you look at the same time, New York chefs— Jean-Georges, I saw Jean-Georges on television the other day, he proposed a dish on Martha Stewart— a lamb filet rolled in a powder of dried orange, grapefruit and lemon— it was Pierre Gagnaire who did that— well, you say Jean-Georges— he copied Pierre Gagnaire. It was an influence— he had the same idea? I don't know. Cuisine is small... there's always the same products, very few new products, very few new things... to create a different cooking.

In North America they don't want garlic butter any more, nor sole with beurre blanc, all these French dishes which one ate and gave France a bad reputation in Quebec. In Quebec, unfortunately, French cuisine has a bad reputation because a sole with beurre blanc is superb if it's done well— but the chefs here did it in any old way.

They took out the basic nature of the cuisine which is the basis of French cuisine and thus took refuge in a Mediterranean cuisine— an accent of Mediterranean cuisine with a little Italian cuisine influenced with olive oil and all that. Thus, the people took refuge in that, but it's not only the Italians and Spanish who work with olive oil. Take all of the South of France, there's olive oil-at the same time the influence of the Arabs who were in France for 300 years— France was, at the same time, a country which has been colonized many times— a great pool of foreigners— who came to the South of France where you can find a multitude of products.

If you're in Andalusia, it's a different cuisine from the Basque country, and if you go to Normandy, it's a cuisine which is different from Brittany. And then Burgundy is different. And Lyon, that's still another thing— it's the charcuteries, the cured sausages, the tablier sapeur [traditional Lyonnaise dish of fried or grilled tripe]— I love all this cuisine. I salivate when I talk... [we laugh] Because it's ingenious. I have a desire to return to France and then eat these authentic dishes— because they're well done within the country. They're not well done outside of it.

Nicolas Jongleux

You're talking about the regional cuisine du terroir... You mentioned Alain Passard earlier. Over the years he's paid homage to his grandmother on his menu. Do you have these great memories, too?

Yeah... sure. On my mother's side we were a big family because there were 11 children and I remember my whole childhood going to spend time in an old house which was a farm because my grandparents were farmers— I recall all those dishes— those dishes which were cooked for a long time— they had the pot au feu which was cooked for hours, my grandmother made a rabbit terrine and things like that.

My mother was a very good cook and my grandmother was an excellent cook and I think it's that which influenced me, gave me a taste for this profession. At home, my mother always put importance on good products, the best products— I think it's that basis. It's sure that Alain Passard, who's self-taught, always is going to think about his mother, who perhaps has influenced his spirit, his cuisine, and all that...

When you look at all the grand chefs— as Georges Blanc who often refers to his grandmother— you have dishes which are very feminine in his establishment. In fact at his place they still do dishes from the 1900s and they still do dishes created in the past by his mother and grandmother. There were six generations of only women in the establishment. At Alain Chapel's it was the same thing. He was influenced by his parents' cuisine. Over the years, he began to have his own style, but there were always one or two dishes, the recipe of his mother Annette's blanquette de veau, or his uncle's chocolate tarte...

So with this... is there a great difference between the food from the home and in the restaurant?

Yeah, yeah.. There's a great difference because there's not the same goal. When I cook at home I don't do things that are very worked... I set the table with silver and fine china, I go look for a good bottle of wine, I go look for raw milk cheese, I go to get bread from Premier Moisson or at MacGuire's, real country bread, same white bread. For each dish I set out a different bread. I put out salted butter and a bottle of olive oil on the table, but the best olive oil, the best butter, the best cheese. Along with this I do a very classic dish—maybe a roast chicken, it could be a roast chicken with the liver inside the bird, a jus from the roast by pressing the carcass. We often eat the white meat with the jus, with olive-oil mashed potatoes, and then afterwards, I get back the leftovers on the carcass and I do a second course with mache [lamb's lettuce] greens, fresh shallots, the chicken pieces— seasoned there— and a small vinaigrette which I do with the chicken jus.

That's going to be a much more convivial cuisine— more tasty because it's done with more heart, and more convivial— you have the time to sit, time to talk with your friends. In general, when I invite people home, it's not to be in the kitchen, it's to have my evening with everybody— but often— I'm not invited by others because the people are very stressed out about inviting me over because I have a lot of friends who aren't in the restaurant business— *what shall we do that he'll like?...* I like everything, in fact. I eat every day of my life, I eat a lot of very simple things. I love cuisine, I love the profession which represents cuisine, I love what the profession of cuisine involves— it includes restaurants, hospitality, the history of china, the history of art, human relationships; it includes the relationship with customers, it includes wine, cheese, cigars... it includes many things—

This is the way in France— it's not just food or restaurants— but to talk about it as a subject of gastronomy...

You have the grand academies in France, the French academies who form a bit of the epilogues in French literature. There's also a bit at the same time in France— the old literary types, the old writers who are in love with food— who will epilogue for hours— on something they've eaten. You have many many in France which there's beginning to be here— the Confrerie [Brotherhood] of the glass of wine; the Confrerie of Cheese; the Confrerie Bordeaux; the Confreries on different products, and that's what the people are in love with: that which gives the potential to do superb things. People who are really passionate for food. And I think it's a need also.

I think that in Quebec there's a real need on the level of food which is perhaps more than the rest of Canada... That's the reason why I like to stay in Montreal... We'll be restaurateurs in Montreal— who are going to participate in the evolution of the gastronomy of Montreal. In a few years, we're going to have a completely different style of cuisine which is going to interest a lot of countries.

As chef you have these incredible experiences, but at the same time it's difficult too, there are costs— when I talk with other chefs about personal life. Is it difficult that your family is in France?

Yeah, yeah, of course it's difficult. Because I don't have anybody here. So I don't have family here— nobody, nobody, nobody. For sure, it's difficult— do you build your life here, or do you go back to your country to build your life?... My father ate in my restaurant for the first time this summer. It was a very touching moment. I hope that he can come again to see what I do, because he's had very little occasion to eat my food. It's important for me to have the family close enough and encourage me. My father thought it was great that I decided to leave France and go live in a different city and to break through. Because I arrived in Montreal with $800 in my pocket, I didn't arrive with a million dollars. I arrived not knowing anyone, and to break into the Montreal market— that wasn't easy, either, getting to know people— it was only work. It's the sixth year I'm in Montreal. I've veritably worked double time, I've worked weekends, I've worked like a madman, I haven't stopped— it makes it faster...

I think you have to take the positive things. If it comes, it comes... you have to approach things with patience...

Nicolas Jongleux

Nicolas Jongleux was born in the Burgundy region of France and took his chef's training in France. He worked in some of the most respected two- and three-star Michelin-rated restaurants before coming to Montreal. Since then, he has received critical acclaim nationally and in *The New York Times* and other American publications for his work at La Cintra, La Cigale and Les Caprices de Nicolas. He is chef and co-owner of Jongleux Café.

Nicolas Jongleux

Nicholas Jongleux's
BLINIS OF CHICKPEA FLOUR, MARINATED SALMON WITH A GOATCHEESE CAVIAR GARNISH [for four]

INGREDIENTS
100 g potato pulp
1 egg
2 egg whites
1 tbsp chickpea flour
1/2 tbsp 35% cream
fresh salmon from the Bay of Fundy, cut into 4 slices of 60 g each
1 lemon
6 tbsp olive oil
1/2 bundle fresh coriander
salt and pepper
100 g Tournevent goat cheese
1/2 bundle fresh chives
40 g caviar or lumpfish eggs
1 corn on the cob

METHOD
Peel and slice potato and boil in water. Purée the potato in food processor. Mix in the egg, egg white, flour, salt and pepper until smooth. Cook the mixture like you would a pancake.

Marinate the salmon in the olive oil with the lemon juice, chopped coriander, salt and pepper.

Cook the corn in boiling water and remove the kernels from the cob with a knife; add to the salmon mixture with the chives.

Mix caviar into the softened goat cheese.

Place the blinis pancake in the middle of a decorative dinner plate. Top with the salmon slices. (Drain excess oil from salmon first.) Garnish with a spoonful of the goat cheese/caviar mixture on top of salmon. Decorate around the dish with the leftover marinade of corn.

Normand Laprise

Toqué!, Montreal, Quebec

The signs in Montreal at the end of the '80s pointed to boulevard St. Laurent north of Laurier as the lieu for fashionable dining and drinking for the next decade. Lux, that wondrous magazine-stand-cum-candy-shop cum restaurant/bar had pioneered the move, and Citrus, with chef Normand Laprise, had every serious Montreal diner panting to its door, tongue wagging. Citrus, arguably the city's first serious French kitchen to work with eclectic often ethnic influence, eventually closed. Besides, by then, the style-brokers had decided that money was to be made further south in the heart of The Main. Then came news that Normand and another Citrus chef, Christine Lamarche, were to open a place of their own. With Lamarche in charge of the managerial end, and Normand Laprise the cooking, Toqué! opened its doors on St. Denis and ever since has been a critical, aesthetic success according to the food critics in Canada and the US. The vision and spirit of Christine and Normand are evident in service that exemplifies the best in Montreal hospitality style— a harmony of young but informed professionalism without starch, where Bombardier executives, retail workers and actors all can feel comfortable. Laprise's food is very personal, with surprising yet sensible complexities and equally stunning, controlled plating. Toqué! serves lunch only during the pre-Christmas season and in that period in 1998, I caught up with Normand one slushy evening, hot off the grill, so to speak, after two full-house services. Normand is a very expressive enthusiastic man, yet there is a always a roundness and softness to his tone— and a quietness.

We met in the small office of Toqué! where Christine joined us in the background, Normand still humming on the energy which propels his very personal cooking.

You've just done two services today— are you tired? Are you excited when you just come off working?

Not tired. Now's the big season for us, and Toqué! is very busy— for lunch and dinner it's full— it's a double service— but I think the spirit is very good, and it's fun, you know, when you make your food and you sell all the food. It's very energizing for the team— it gives a good spirit. For me, yes, I'm tired now, but not so tired that I'd say, I'd like to stop now— no, I'm okay for tomorrow to start a new day to cook.

We had a little rush tonight, a lot of tasting menus— I think 30 or 35 tasting menus, and when you sell a tasting, it's a little bit more, just for the garde-manger— minimum, just for the tasting— it's a minimum of 120 plates from the garde-manger— and from the hot station there's more and then the pastry— that's a lot of plating— a lot of work and a lot of detail.

It's very important. You know, it's possible before the service to put it all together and set it out in your fridge, and put it on the hot table, and then you serve— and you're able to get along with that. But for me, the taste is different if you cook your carrots separately, then you cook your risotto and you mix it all together after. The flavour is very important to me— the mixture of the flavour.

Are you always thinking about those kinds of mixtures when you're creating a menu?

I don't think to that end result of the plate— I just think, oh, yes, I like leeks with potatoes, with this and with this— and I take my evolution and look at what I have at the market. To see what I have available at market is the first thing— the first important thing. I try to find the maximum of fresh produce available— and with this produce, I build a menu. Sure, I don't mix everything with everything, but I just go with my feeling inside— which tells me— oh, yeah— this is good with this— and I mix and I make the plate and I finish. All the time, the plate has to be ready for six o'clock, and the cooks have to understand everything— it's not easy sometimes— but I have a good team. They understand me and have learned a lot about me— they understand what I say— they understand everything.

How many in your brigade?

I think 12 every night on the floor. I have eight cooks in the kitchen, three pastry, and me— every day, every day. And sometimes I have one person more— a commis. Thirteen, for busy days— and for 105 to 125 customers— a big brigade for a small restaurant.

Is it hard to manage a brigade like that?

Yes and no. All the people come here with the aim— they come to work at Toqué!. They're good people; I choose people to include in my brigade, and everybody here assimilates. If they don't like and are negative about the food— it's not possible to fit in with the brigade because of how everybody assimilates— but every day something goes a little wrong and this is normal. I think it's hard to ask somebody to understand everything in your mind. People would like to do well every day, but sometimes they don't understand what you're trying to say— your spirit— so you take a lot of time, and repeat it.

It's very important to be very patient. I prefer to be patient. I know I am very exigent with the cooks in the details, the tasting— everything in the last minutes becomes more impossible. That's why I like Japanese food— all the produce is pure, it tastes of the produce— they never mix it all together. For me, working this way with food is very, very important.

Before, when I started— good cooks are sometimes egotistical, and say, this is *my* food— yes, make *three* detailed points of red colour. If you put one too high, the design is too sharp— for me, it's not very important to the final result of the dish. If I put the sauce on this way, and the cook makes it another way in a rush— but the quantity is perfect and everything, and the seasoning is good— that's perfect. I prefer to accept this than to be shocked and say, *that's* not the way I like it, I want the line exactly this way— I don't put the greatest focus on the presentation. The final presentation for everything is good, it's perfect, it's okay. Lots of mizuna, a good quantity of kumquats, a good quantity of the portobella— you know, for me this is important. But if you put the portobella on the top or on the side, as long as the plate is beautiful— it's perfect.

This is a different way, I think, from a lot of chefs. But it hasn't been a

Normand Laprise

long time that I've thought like this. Before, I was stressed with everything too much— and when it was busy I was always saying, what are you doing?

I like to give control to the team. I like to have control, but I like to give a little bit— they participate with me. You know, the night I had the cipollini on the tasting menu, I put in a purée of green olives, and I put this on the plate in the way I like to have a spoon of green olives. But if you make two lines, or three lines— it doesn't matter to me. What I like is the good quantity of green olives. Sometimes I put a big line of my stuffed cipollini, and the cook likes to put two small lines instead— if it's beautiful, I feel okay with this. I don't say, I never made it like this before; I made it like this. It's too hard to ask people to make it exactly the way the thing is in your head. My head changes every hour! It's possible that at six o'clock I'd plate for you with a big splash of green onion, and at 10 o'clock it's possible for me to make three small splashes. If this is my way of cooking, I accept that it's the same thing with my cooks. But if it's too much, I'd say, oh, wow, stop! That's too much—

So there's freedom, but control.

Oh, yeah, a big control— for me this is important.

This is a big problem in the restaurant business now. You have lots of good young chefs— in North America, more and more young people— and they have lots of talent. Some young chefs come here to work at Toqué! after two years or four years at school. They have lots of good energy, but they don't have the inner control with the food. It's what I said, if you ask me why I put one spoon of green olive— my instinct is— stop— before it's too much. I go with my feeling inside. When I started to cook, I didn't have this instinct— I haven't had this feeling for a long time. It's just after cooking, cooking, cooking... and trying to understand everything. Then one day... I don't remember why this happened— when I was cooking, I had the feeling, oh, it's too much. I got the feeling *I'm sure* at this time; I sense everything is too much or not enough.

What do you look for in a chef when they come to Toqué!?

First is the spirit about food, the passion about food. I talk with him, I ask some questions. I ask him where he's from. I don't look at the CV. I never look at the CV. Basically, I like that people go to school— it's important— but for me it's when I have a meeting with the person to talk about food.

And we go into another direction, talk about something, and then come back— just to talk about food— just to see the passion he has. That's the important thing. You know, sometimes I ask the cook, why did you come to Toqué!? And he says to me, to do plate decorations. For me, that's bad. You know, he's really proud of it, but for me that's bad. I say, I don't make decorations here— here, it's cooking. Here, we're trying to make the cooking perfect. If all the vegetables, all the fish are perfectly cooked— and when I put it onto the plate, if everything is perfect, then everything is beautiful on the plate: it's easy. This is what I try to do— and when I talk to him and he says, I like to make decorations, I say, wow, okay, now we have a lot to work on.

Then I go into the kitchen to show him, and explain where the stations are, and I show him the fridge. I just show him, and I don't say, look at this, look at this... and if the person says, oh, wow, what's that? This makes an impression on me.

For me the produce is the first motivation in the kitchen.

You've just finished two services with many covers— and this has been for 10 straight days— you're tired... when you come out of the kitchen, do you get inspired— or does your mind just go?

I won't try to say today I'd like to change this— I just wait for my inspiration. Sometimes at 10 o'clock, at the end of the service, I say, oh, wow— I have that in the fridge and I have that— maybe it'll be possible to make that— and the day after that, I come back and make that thing.

But I don't have an exact time where I think up what I'm going to make today— it's possible that I might arrive at one o'clock and have no idea; nothing happens— then, I don't push it. Sometimes you really don't have a choice, but I prefer to go with the day— you can ask Christine [Lamarche, co-owner]. If you ask me for the menu one month in advance— it's too hard for me. And if I did make one for you one month in advance? The day before, everything will be changed. If I think about the produce and menu one month in advance— and one month later the produce arrives, and it's perfect, like the day I thought about it for the menu— then everything's okay. But it's not possible. For me, it's the produce that takes its place with the menu. Oh, yeah. If I think a lot about a special menu with a striped bass, and when it arrives at the market, it's not the quality I like to have, I don't buy the striped bass. I find some other thing. And if I find some other thing and it's not possible to make the same dish because the taste is different and the fish is different, I don't make this course; I change it a little bit.

Do you have a special time... sitting at home... for inspiration?

I don't write everything I make— I just make something, and tonight's over and it's finished. I like the idea of forgetting— for me, if you try to remember everything, I'm afraid about the repetition. Okay, I made this thing; now, I'd just like to forget. Will the produce permit me to make this? If I try to think too much about this— it's very hard.

It's a little bit different from the New York project [Laprise was Executive Chef at Cena for one year, during the time of this interview] I sit in my office for one day just to think. I open a book, and I see eggplant... oh, yeah, marinated eggplant— and I write, oh, well, marinated eggplant... I write a lot down on paper— and everything is everywhere. And after I have a lot of things on my sheets, I say— this is it. I might take three hours for one flash sometimes— and sometimes I take 10 minutes for one flash. Sometimes, when I'm tired, I take more time— or if I try too much to force the menu. I don't like it very much when people push me. If one day, I feel ready to make a menu, I go upstairs and I make the menu. I take one hour, three hours— four hours sometimes, but once I start, it's bang, bang, bang in 20 minutes— everything is in my head. I'll remember about something and make it later. This is good for me, and this New York project is very good...

Many other chefs who create at the last minute end up with confusion on the plate. Why do you feel confident with this approach?

I think to do this you have to like the pressure— I'm afraid I'll be dull if I write too much in advance. I like the inspiration that comes from the produce, not from books or from your head. The produce gives you the spirit to make something. You see this, you see that, you see the mushrooms and you say, wow— and in your head it goes very fast— what do I make with this? And if you don't see this, then how is a dish possible? To say, well, I like to put salmon with artichokes, yes, it's easy to think about— but to realize this now? It's another game— I prefer to see what you have in your basket and plate and work with it— for me, that's easy.

You're known for your dedication to produce and producers— where did this originate?

I'm from Kamouraska. When I was very young, my mother was very sick, and she went to the hospital for long, long years, and I lived on a farm. I had never realized that that time of my life gave me the inspiration for good food until the last few years. And you know, the milk from the grocery you find here in the Montreal market... I'm not able to drink this. I prefer to just drink water.

But milk from a farm, this is the milk I like to drink. When I was young, it was the milk I drank all the time, right from the cow— I grew up with this. And I remember the woman from the farm, and the food where I lived. They made everything from the garden, in August and September, and in October, it was a very busy time. Everything went into the jars, and she put everything into the basement. EVERYTHING. And she made bread. She never went to shop for groceries, only to buy soap. But to buy food? The minimum possible.

Before I started cooking class, if you talked to me about French food, about gastronomy... pih! I knew nothing... nothing... I'm from the country.

What did you like to eat at that time?

Mashed potatoes. Nothing complicated. The same thing if you were at home— shepherd's pie, stuffed cabbage with veal, and pork— spaghetti with sauce...

Normand Laprise

Poutine?

Yeah. Poutine.

You still like it? [laughing]

[Laughing] Yeah... some's good, some's bad.

Well, tell me how you'd make poutine.

Ohhh... it's possible. Take a good cheese, good potatoes, maybe take a good very brown chicken stock... and make good French fries and take a good cheese— say from where I'm born— Kamouraska— the curd from the farm is very good— but not raw milk cheese... I'd like Yukon gold or maybe russet potatoes.

[Speaking to Christine Lamarche] Remember at Citrus, we made a dish with potatoes and goat cheese? St. Maur [French] and slices of big russet and then I fried it, and put the cheese on the potatoes, gratineed it a little bit with a little medallion of lamb, and I made a mille feuille. And with the sauce? [laughing] It was close to a poutine. It was popular— but it was hard to make during the service— at this time Christine was working at a— station— yeah, the good cooking of the lamb and so I fried the potatoes à la minute— it was a lot of work. [to Lamarche] It was good, eh, that dish?

You said that you didn't know much about French food until you went to cooking school. But was there a certain point when you realized you were really interested in food?

I went to Quebec City to study when I was 11— secondary school and CEGEP [college]— and all the time I was going to secondary school I worked on the weekend to pay for my schooling and for travel and pocket money— I worked in a restaurant washing dishes— I started when I was 14 or 15 years old— and I liked it. I worked for a long time in a Chinese restaurant just to work in the kitchen, and I ended up being a cook's helper. I liked the feeling. Then I tried to be a busboy for a summer and I said, no, it's not for me. And I went back into the kitchen and I said, wow, I like to work in the kitchen...

What was it in the kitchen you liked?

To see the food all the time, to have the opportunity to eat, and I remember, all the time I'd make a club sandwich, you know, and I thought, wow, the bacon— every detail for me was very important. I'd make it as last minute as possible. I liked to make a good club sandwich, and if I made it too much in advance or if I cut my tomatoes too much in advance, the tomatoes would lose all the flavour... I took care of all this. But I didn't know anything about good food.

And I thought about enrolling in a cooking school. I wanted to go and try— and I tried, and they accepted me. I was 19.

My first years, I was a bit disappointed when I went to the school. I said, wow, I'm not sure if I like professional cooking at this time. But I'm talking about 19 years ago, you know— and at that time it was very classical, and schools didn't have the same development potential of today. It was very closed about everything. You went to the school to learn about traditional French cooking, and you had recipes for à la Florentine, and you took frozen spinach to make this recipe and you took frozen fish to make that recipe— and you went to the fridge and you had something fresh you'd say, "Why? Why would you buy something frozen when you had something good and fresh in your fridge?

At this time— I grew up in my young life with fresh food— and I said, why do you take this? I didn't have the feeling to cook this. It wasn't my way. I didn't like this food. I was very insecure at this time and I didn't know lots about gastronomy, but I started to learn about gastronomy. You know, I bought my dictionary, my vieux Escoffier and just for me, everything is new. One thing I knew was that I liked cooking, and something in the school was good, and I said I'd try two years, two years in the market, working, to see, to learn more, to decide if I liked it or not.

When I finished, I began to work at a small fish restaurant in Quebec City, and the chef, Jacques Le Pluart— and at this point I realized I liked cooking... just the first night with him. Just the first night.

What happened?

I don't know... for me, everything was new; there was lots of respect for the food in everything. I didn't learn about this in school— there, it was, get frozen fish, put the fish in the water to start it cooking. I knew that wasn't good, but when you're young and you see something for the first time, you think, maybe this is normal; but inside me, I thought, I don't want to make this. It's not the work I like. And then, when I started to work with Jacques the first day— he took so much time for everything to taste good, things were very fresh, and he made it fresh every day, and he changed the menu every day. He'd say, oh, the chives are no good— pih... it's finished, and you know, he'd use some other thing. It was very hard to work with him, but I learned lots and lots and lots— I've got a lot of respect for him. This chef gave me a passion for food. And one teacher I had in technique also gave me a passion for food— he talked about food and instilled in me the spirit to keep going to school. To try to know more, to say, okay, now I'm a chef, but I don't know everything, it's possible to know more and more. Sometimes the class finished at 11 o'clock, and at one o'clock or 1:30 we were still in the classroom talking about food, about some gastronomic experience, with a good spirit that told me it's possible to have a good life with food— and it's very important to like it.

The chef in Quebec City worked you very hard— did you ever think being a chef might be too difficult?

Sometimes I said, wow, what's the problem? But some chefs are bad just to be bad. Some chefs you work for do something and don't give you a good reason. But this chef... sometimes he pushed you, but every time, he gave a good reason. If he said, it's this way, I said, you're right; I felt okay all the time; it was very hard, but very right. Two-thirds of the chefs right now are rough just because they have the idea that a chef is supposed to be rough.

No, no one is yelling in my kitchen, though I learned there were chefs who yelled a lot. I tried all the time to do the best job possible, and if I made some error, I said, yes, chef, I'm sorry I made a mistake. I tried to respect my chef and I think it energized me a lot.

I remember lots about discipline: all the time it was possible to make something better and better. You ask me about being tired doing two sittings for the last 10 days— yes, I'm tired, but I'm not too tired to make my last table very good— for me, it's very important, it's the way I learned. Every customer of mine— from the first one to the last one, is important, and I try to give the maximum for the last one— more than the first one. With this chef I learned this. You never stop. You stop when it's finished. Consistency? I learned consistency with him. Never up and down. And for me in the kitchen here, it's very important— I don't have to ask the team to push too much, I have consistency.

Have any other chefs influenced you?

Gérard Oulley— I never worked for him very long, but he's a good chef. He's an Alsatian, from Quebec. One teacher, Guy Auclair, gave me patience. And the chefs working at Café de la Paix, Jean Marc Bass and Monsieur Abraham. He's a different chef than Jacques Le Pluart— he's a French chef— very hard— and this restaurant was very busy and prepared a lot of food— you know, 200 customers a night. I went to work there to learn more about the practical end— the speed. I like to make good food, but I like to be practical, too— to understand a large service, what's possible. I remember, he said to me, P'tit— he called me P'tit— he said, you know, when you're young, you like to go fast— to go in the line— and he said to me, P'tit— you know people always like to go to the hot line— and he said you work with me tonight— and all the time you have the hot tables— the potatoes, broccoli, the gratin. Everything was fresh, every 10 to 15 minutes, very fast. And I remember plating— my job was to plate the vegetables— and I took my time. You're very young and nervous and I took my time to plate the carrots and when he saw this, he took clarified butter for the vegetables, and just put it on my hands to burn me... yeah... I put out my hand— and the chef says, you know, P'tit, when you're faster, I'd never burn you.

You know, it's not the method I'd like to use— but I remember with him— he didn't do this every day, but just when he felt I was a little bit slow— just to push me. I don't think I'd use this method today, but I learned a lot from this chef.

I'd never seen people work very fast and do a good job. Not just fast but bang bang bang... and do a good job. This chef gave me a lot... and I've worked with a lot of good chefs.

Normand Laprise

How important is travel for you?

Travel is important— I don't travel enough, I think. It's the choice you make— you work or you travel, and I work a lot. But yeah, I do take the time to travel. I've gone to Asia, I've gone to Italy, to France. I worked in France with a very good chef. I didn't work with him for a long time, but this chef was very good for very typical French cooking. It was very different from the food I make now. He took a lot of time to make a good product— the food was very simple, but to make this food simple took a lot of work. We had 15 people working in the kitchen for 40 customers. This told me something important. It told me I wouldn't do this in my brigade— 12 or 13 people in the kitchen for 40 customers. Every night, every night, every lunch— yelling in the kitchen. The first table to the last table, all the time, all the time... I said, oh, wow, how's it possible to have 12 cooks and still be able to fit in? You have too many people in the kitchen. I never understood why... but the quality of the produce and everything was perfect. But I thought it was possible to do the same job with half the people. I was sure.

I said, the day I run my kitchen, I won't like to do this. I like to be soft in the kitchen. I never yell in my kitchen, and if one person *is* yelling, it's me. My cook never talks very loudly; everybody respects everybody. I like to make the food very sensitive, very feminine. Now, if you start yelling and fighting— where does it go? You stress the cooks. If you stress the cooks, they don't do a good job.

Some chefs are very aggressive and make good food. But for me— for my kind of food, it's important not to use aggressiveness. You're working too much, you know... some cooks work 12 or 13 hours. If I start yelling, I don't think it's very helpful to getting the job done better. But if I just push him in a good way, he comes back tomorrow. Yeah, if he makes something very bad and doesn't respect the food, I'm very upset, but if he makes a good product, good food, and he makes a little mistake... it's okay; I'm here to see the mistake and to reorganize. I help.

I say to all my cooks— the best commis in the brigade is me— if you have something that's not okay— if the plating is too hard for you, you call me, you call the chef, I am everywhere, I'll help you. I'm here for this. You're lucky, I never had this in my career. And I say, I prefer this than to be on the other side saying, c'mon, c'mon, c'mon.

You've been interested in the evolution of Quebec cuisine towards a cuisine of terroir— but now you have things like baby bok choy. Is there something specifically you'd would call— a cuisine montréalaise or québécoise?

I'd like to say North American. You live in North America— some produce is from here, some is from Ontario, now the fish is from the East Coast— Maine, Cape Cod, Massachusetts and further south— Maryland. The produce influences my food. I follow the seasons everywhere. You see the weather here now [December], it's not possible to work with the local produce. Some root vegetables, yes. Some growers produce lots of root vegetables for us— crosnes, yellow carrots, white carrots— they save it for me on the farm throughout the year and that gives me a real spirit to cook. Ten years ago, you didn't find this— you found celery, potatoes— and now, there's more and more, but it's the chefs who asked for it. And I encourage them to go further.

Mr. [Pierre-André] Daignault— one of the growers— he puts straw on the fields to protect the produce. You know, sometimes there's not a big snowfall before January— and it's possible to save some of the beds. The most important thing is that he's very close. So, it's much fresher. When you get roots from California, how many weeks does it take?— two weeks, three weeks sitting in cases. You lose the natural flavour.

Today, I try to buy very local produce, but the first priority is the freshness, the quality of the produce. Influences on my food? That was a chef from Bretagne. He cooked with lots and lots of cream and lots of butter and every night when I finished working, I just felt bad. You work a double shift— lunch and dinner— and I like to taste— and all the time, in the casseroles— now good is good, but after one week doing doubles, it was too much. When I was at home, what did I make? I would eat vegetables all the time— veg, veg, veg... and this influenced my food a lot. I use a lot of vegetables in my food— you talk about bok choy— any vegetable that's possible to find, I put in my food. I'm not a vegetarian, but I like food that is very simple and very light. I like it when my customers leave here and they say I ate well, but lightly— I feel good inside. And I take care, but it's not about being a purist in one thing. Sometimes, if I like to use cream, I use cream— just for the feeling— if the cream goes well in a dish, I use it, but, sure, I cook a lot with vegetables.

Like this dish with bok choy, semolina and salmon. I try to play with things I've learned. With the salmon, the bok choy gives a bit of crunchiness— it's a little bit fat— and some grain to go with the salmon to play with the taste of the salmon. And the eggplant is a little bitter and the bok choy is a little bit sweet. I don't know why I put everything together, but in my head I felt good making this, to say, wow, this is good with *this*... and mix it all together.

And your smoked eel? That's not québécois— and with the roasted red pepper and grilled eggplant... and the texture...

Ah... the eel was from a breakfast I had in Japan. I stayed for two or three days in a ryokan in Kyoto, and I remembered this. In the morning you wake up and... Canadians here... they don't eat the same food, eh? But breakfast was a very good time. They started to grill the small fish... grilled it and glazed it, and when you ate it there was a smoky taste and I felt good. I remember the first breakfast I had. I said, wow, where's my coffee, where's my jam? But I ate at 8:00 in the morning and at noon I was downtown, and I said, wow, I don't feel hungry, I had a lot of good energy. It's a very good balance of nutrients... in the food... green tea with seaweed— very typical.

And so the idea for the eel came from that part of my travels. Now, the grilled peppers and eggplant, this is a dish I have now on my lunch menu— and I didn't have enough when you arrived. This is an escabeche of mackerel, done in sake, rice vinegar and court bouillon. I didn't have enough of the escabeche, so I said, wow, I'd like to make the eel— because I'd just received the eel for the night menu. I just went with the feeling. I had lots of grilled eggplant, and I wanted to use that. The garlic chive oil and clementine juice sounded very good... and I liked the peppers and all these other ingredients at the same time. I'd never made it before. I just said, what should I make now? Tchih, tchih, tchih... I just made it all together. It's the play in life when you do this kind of thing, I'm sure. If I tried to learn about this dish and tried to balance it perfectly, it would be possible to make it better, but when I first made it, I felt comfortable. I said, wow.

And the textures?

Yeah... the crunchiness of the pepper, the eggplant is very soft, and this is after the eel, which is a little bit soft and smoky with the soya glaze. But when I made this, I went by my sense of the flavour. Texture comes after the flavours. If I make some dish and I think it's too soft, I'll try to find something to add or change. But if the taste is good, I feel comfortable with it. Taste is before texture.

Is this kind of food an expression of a Montreal or Quebec cuisine?

No, this is more personal. This is [slaps hands together] the inspiration of now. It's really when I say, what should I make? I look, I find this, I find this, and *yes*... And about some other things on my table, I'll say, no, just by reflex... My food is personal. I never make anything to try to follow a trend.

Sometimes there are trends in things, but I don't go that way. You hear that something is à la mode in Montreal, and then tomorrow it will be à la mode to make something crunchy, but I don't stop to make something crunchy. Right now, in New York, the big fashion is Indian food... and you'll start to find six or seven courses— spicy, spicy, spicy— and it's fun to cook with spices, oh, yeah, I like it, and it's fun to have cumin. And I might use it for one dish. But you won't find six spicy dishes on my menu. My food is not Indian food. It's normal to find that in an Indian restaurant, but if you go to a French restaurant?

It's a trend now. And in the next two years, what will be the new trend? You know, cuisine du terroir— some cooks make this cuisine, really from their inside. And when you go to those restaurants, you feel the cuisine du terroir. And some other people make this food to be à la mode. So you see, these are two different ways. It's possible to see two restaurants— cuisine du terroir and cuisine du terroir, and it's not the same food.

Normand Laprise

For you as a chef, you can sense this. But do you think other people can sense this?

Oh, yes... oh, yeah... maybe he doesn't sense that this is food and this is not food, but I'm sure when he goes to this one restaurant, he says, wow, this is very good here. It's better than the other one. He doesn't try to see why, but he's able to say it's better here. I'm sure about this. Some people say, I went to eat at this restaurant and it was very good, and I went to that other restaurant, and, oh, it was okay. Even though they make the same food. One makes the food very well, it's very true, and the other one plays with something and tries to be à la mode.

Do you think some people in Montreal and Quebec are thinking about a cuisine du terroir, a cuisine from here?

I think now you have a lot of good young cooks here. But Montreal is different from Quebec City. Montreal's very ethnic. I remember my focus before, when I opened Citrus, was to have fresh produce, the best produce it was possible to find. When it was hard, and there was less produce, and I didn't have a lot of contact with producers, where did I go? Chinatown. Indian. Small groceries to find something fresh. And I remember going down to Chinatown in January and you found everything. You know, Chinese people eat lots and lots of greens— and I found long beans and bok choy— at this time it was the big ones, though the small ones are better for the taste of my food. My food evolved a lot with this produce. I went and I bought everything. If I didn't know something, I bought it just to taste it and to see if it was good for my food or not. I tried lots and lots of different things, and I learned about that, and this influenced my food.

But one thing I respect is tradition: of all food. If you say classical French, the real classical French is very nice. But to make a good coq au vin— or bourgignon, you have a Charolais [beef from Burgundy, considered the best in France], you have wine from Burgundy, and then you have the terroir. How is it possible to make a beef bourgignon here in Quebec? But it's possible to make a similar thing. You take beef from here, and good wine— we're starting to have good wine from here— and if you take the wine from the area and you take some onions from here, it then becomes close to a beef bourgignon from France. But I just respect the classical name. If you make a sauce Périgourdine, make a true Périgourdine sauce. Don't put shit in the sauce. I never make sauce Périgourdine. I'm not classical, but I respect this. When I see someone trying to make something, and I say, wow, write something, but don't write perigourdin. Respect the base. In the same way, I don't make classical Japanese food, or put a Japanese dish on my menu. If I use a name, I like to respect it, and to respect the authenticity of the food. It's the reason I like to use the produce, you know— bok choy— or to use soya, but with my philosophy.

I write down what I put in my dish and I try to have as many different ethnic foods as it's possible to find.

I think more and more people in the world are open now. We travel a lot and travel fast, and you want to have something. I think now the most important thing is to communicate a spirit. I think it's important that you live in your country... What do you have around you? And after, if you don't find something, or if you find something else, you take that influence, but it's very important that you feel very comfortable in your place. Don't try to make one thing à la mode just to say, oh, wow, yeah... For me the most important thing is the food.

To be a chef is hard work. It's hard on family life?

Yeah. But if you like to be a chef, if you feel happy with it, it's not very hard. It's hard, yes, but it's not very hard if you think about yourself.

But if you think about family life and about normal life...

When you're working, your friends are playing and having a good time. When your friends are working, sometimes you're working, too, or, you try to play, but you're alone. And all the time you're with the same people. This is hard work with long hours, and when I get back tonight, my son will be asleep; maybe I'll go to sleep at one o'clock or two o'clock. He'll wake up before me tomorrow morning. Maybe I'll see him for one hour before I go to work. This is very hard. This is a big balance in my life; it's a big part of my life.

Sometimes, with work, I'll say, oh, yeah, it's too much, I'd like to take a break now. The reason I close Toqué! in December [for the last two weeks of the month] is because I know, if I close, my life will be quiet in every way. I have two problems. I'm a cook. Okay. If I just think— okay, I'll just forget about everything when I go home. But my big problem, which I'm struggling with, is that, for me, a good cook, it's very important that inside, you are a restaurateur. You restore people, you receive the people. I don't make the food just to say, I made this plate. No, I made this plate for you. For me this is very significant. I try to give my maximum to each guest. This is for my guests in my restaurant. I try to give all the energy I can find so that people will feel very happy. For me this is very important. I don't cook just to cook and to say this is my plate and that's it. If a customer doesn't like this...! This is very important.

I haven't had a family— my little boy— for very long. But sure, if my family isn't happy, this would influence me. But if I'm not happy here, and I go home, I don't think it's good for my family. If I'm very stressed and distracted and impatient— I don't like to see this. I like it when I go home and I'm just happy with everything and everything is good. And Sunday's my day off and I take all Sunday with my family. This is important. I try to find some other time in the week... I have a good opportunity, too, to have my time when I like to have my time. In December, in order to have a good time with my family, I close. The same for Christine, too, to take a break.

More and more women are entering cooking schools, but when you look at open kitchens, usually it's mainly men, with occasionally one woman in the line. How about women in your kitchen?

In France it's very macho... All the time, for me, it's very important to have a good balance in my brigade. My food is very feminine... and it's very important. Sometimes, when I have a period when I have more guys in my kitchen, the spirit is harder— a little bit more macho, and I don't like it this way. Sometimes I've experienced more women than guys, and I don't think that's better. I think when it's 50-50 it's good... 60-40.

But I don't try... I don't go looking... I try to find the best people in the market. But now I have the same constant number of women— for now I have five women and eight men. I have a mix all the time. It's very important. My sous chef is a woman.

I think more and more you're seeing women. People are more open. Women can do the same work as men. Sure, if she goes to work in a big hotel where they have 3,000 customers. It's important that the woman works very hard, but for the kind of food I make, she uses her head the same. I think she does the same job, maybe better— women are sometimes more sensitive, more feminine. You know sometimes, guys, some good chefs make good food, but it's a little bit too rough.

I asked Carol Chow about this at the Beach Side Café— and she likes to have a balance. And she said with women sometimes there's more co-operation, more collaboration.

Oh, yeah, oh, yeah... it's less macho. If you put six guys in the line... puh... they just try to push, and if you put a woman in the middle, they'll stop this pushing just out of respect. Yeah... she's right.

Now that you've moved into New York— do you think about your future— five years down the road?

I don't think like that. The year Christine and I opened Toqué! I didn't think about Toqué!. I don't like to think too much in advance— I think about things in the future, but I don't try to predict where I will be in two or five years. Sure, I think I'm here for a long time— I have a big mortgage. But in life, you never know. To think ahead is not a priority for me. Next week? Yes, that's a priority...

Now, I go to New York for my personal development. I like the spirit, and what I learn now. The New York experience, for me, I had the feeling to put inside, put inside, but it was too much. You know, too much work, too much food, too much cooking... But I just had the feeling right to take in lots, but not to explode with this new adventure. I know myself: in two years I'll explode from the pressure of this. Now, I have a great time. I'm working strongly, I'm having a great time. I'm very interested in seeing what these two years will give to me. It will give a lot to my philosophy. I understand my food more now. Before, I was just cooking and cooking. Now I take time to stop and ask, why did I make this? And why don't I like this?

Right now I'm in the process of something very intense within me, which I am going through with my cuisine, and really for myself, to understand all...

I talked about this a few days before. How a young cook comes here and says— "Oh, I understand everything. I know Toqué!'s food."— in just three months. I say, oh, wow— I took 19 years of my life and now I am beginning to understand the base... I want to take more time to learn more and more and more.

So cooking isn't any longer just passion, cooking with feelings?

It's very important to do it with passion, but I am starting to learn now that it's very important to have confidence in your food, and when you have confidence in your food, it's easier to go with your passion and still have control. Some cooks go with their passion, but they don't have the control. They will have the passion and the things they'll make are good, but the control of all the food, the consistency— don't forget, you don't make just one plate a night, you make 85 plates... 85 good plates, not just one with lots of things in that creation. You know, sometimes you go into a restaurant and the appetizer is very nice, and it goes downhill with the main course... for me, I said, one day, when I have my restaurant, I'd like the people to feel at Toqué!, this way— not high, not down— but this way, all the time.

The inspiration, the passion, is very important, but if you have confidence, it's better. I've just started to understand this now.

What other things outside cuisine inspire you creatively?

I read a lot, but the best inspiration is when my brigade is working during the service, and I have time for myself just to play. You know, I see all the produce on the table. I see everything and I say, wow— this with this and this— it's the best time. But this is not a good time to change something. One day, I'd like to have this facility in my kitchen— to be very free, make the dishes and that's it. I do this sometimes. I call in the brigade here, a deuxième [additional course or plate], a small deuxième— okay, the chef makes a deuxième— and it's very hard for the kitchen in normal life in the middle of the service.

And I said, it's a good friend, a good customer, I'll make these dishes— I take this, this, this and this. And cooks say, what are you making, chef?— it's not on the menu! And I say, continue your work, and I change a plate. But sometimes it disturbs the cooks. In New York, it's faster than here, and one night I did this and I never did it again— it's too fast. I made some change on the menu, just a small appetizer for a good customer and all the cooks stopped; they froze. Whew— what's that? It's not on the menu. You know, they were frozen because it was different. They said, where's this menu? It was just something I had a feeling to do, and they didn't understand. But for me, it was perfect food, perfect there, perfection there... and all that in my head.

Just like a jazz musician, the spontaneity, a collage—

Yeah. They asked me if the thoughts had been there for days. Was my idea there for days before I made that food? No. It was when I saw the produce— wow, that was it. That's it. For me, cuisine. I like it like that.

Normand Laprise

Normand Laprise graduated from Ecole Hôtelière Charles-bourg in Quebec, and studied at fine restaurants in Italy, France, and California. He has been executive chef and guest chef at many fine dining establishments, including the Granite Club in Toronto, Cena Restaurant in New York, and the James Beard Foundation. Normand Laprise is co-owner and chef of Toqué! Restaurant, which has been showered with awards and praise, including the *Table de Prestige* from the Société des Alcools du Québec, four stars from the *Guide Debeur*, and three stars by the *New York Times* in 1998, and first place (Montreal) from *Gourmet Magazine*'s America's Top Tables.

Normand Laprise's

GRATIN DE CHEVRE FRAIS TOURNEVENT, EPINARDS ET POIREAU-POMME DE TERRE AU JUS DE POIVRON JAUNE ET CONCASSE DE TOMATE AU THYM, FEUILLES BIOLOGIQUES [eight appetizer servings]

INGREDIENTS

TOMATO CONCASSÉ
19 oz yellow pepper juice*
2 1/2 oz organic** olive oil
4 oz fresh tomatoes, peeled, seeded and cut up
fresh thyme leaves
salt and freshly ground pepper

GRATIN
6 1/2 oz organic*** leeks, washed and cut in half-inch cubes
13 oz Yukon Gold potatoes, peeled and cut in half-inch cubes
1 oz butter
2 thyme sprigs
1 c chicken stock
1 c water
10 oz spinach leaves, washed and trimmed
10 oz Tournevent goat cheese
salt and freshly ground pepper
organic baby lettuces, such as mizuna and tatsoi

* Use a juice extractor— 1 big pepper yields about 5-6 ounces, so 4 peppers should do it
** You may substitute regular olive oil
*** You may substitute regular leeks

FOR CONCASSÉ
In small saucepan, bring pepper juice to a boil over high heat. Reduce heat to medium and gently simmer until reduced by half. Emulsify in blender with olive oil. Add tomatoes and thyme. Season to taste. Set aside. (Can be made one day ahead. Cover and refrigerate. Let stand at room temperature before serving.)

FOR GRATIN
Melt butter in medium saucepan over low heat. Add leeks, cover and sweat, about 10 minutes. Add potatoes, thyme, chicken stock and water. Bring to a boil, reduce the heat to medium and cook, half-covered, until tender, about 15 minutes.

Meanwhile, preheat oven to 350 F and soften cheese on top of double boiler. When potatoes and thyme are cooked, drain but do not discard cooking liquid. Season to taste and arrange in bottom of glass baking dish. Cook spinach in reserved liquid, drain, season to taste and arrange on top of leeks and potatoes. If desired, save broth for another use.

Whip cheese until creamy (it should look like whipped cream). Spoon over spinach and spread evenly with a spatula.

Bake for 15 minutes, then broil a few minutes. Arrange gratin in soup plate and surround with a few baby lettuces. Drizzle both gratin and lettuces with concassé.

Franca Mazza

Ristorante Il Mulino, Montreal, Quebec

When I moved to Montreal at the beginning of this last decade, I quickly realized that Montreal, besides being shaped not only by its Anglo and French roots, is a place where in food as in every aspect of social life, the Jews and Italians hold their own dominant sphere. Montreal clings fiercely to food traditions. When I asked some acquaintances of Italian background— a writing student of mine, my plumber, and the fellow who installed a window for me— where they would recommend for the best Italian food, they all named the same place: Il Mulino. When I returned to the city last year and began these talks, it became obvious that Ristorante Il Mulino would be among them. It is a special place, an anomaly these days— run as a real family operation spanning two generations in the kitchen. While mother, Maria Mazza does some of the cooking, the main cooking responsibilities fall to two chefs, Francesco Mazza and their daughter, Franca Mazza. The experience of Franca is unique. She works with the basis of true regional tradition, but as a young woman who has matured in North America, has travelled extensively, and thus tried a wide range of cuisines, she is bringing her own mark, transforming a familial cuisine. Pearl-hued scallop and asparagus from the grill and artichoke, lush from slow-roasting, with a presentation in harmony with the clarity of spectrum-crossing flavours, is how she has distilled her life in Italy and Canada.

When I planned to chat with her, I knew that it would be as much a rendezvous with family. By the time I arrived one morning, her father, whom I'd previously met, was already at market. Cappuccino in hand, I started by meeting her mother in the kitchen and peeking into the pots.

So we come in at eight o'clock. We start with the tomato sauce because it takes longer. This is canned tomatoes. We fry the onions and then throw in the canned tomatoes. And this is fresh tomatoes— just chopped up tomatoes, olive oil and onions. There are some orange ones and yellow ones, red ones.

I mix whatever I buy for salads and I can't use for salads. I'll make tomato sauce with it— you know they become very soft. We do that daily. So, it's a separate tomato sauce. Because some people like this one and some people like that one. Sometimes we mix, we have a nicer texture if we mix because it's canned tomato. You know, it's not the same. We're using the San Marzano, but it's still canned and I don't really appreciate that— it's not to my liking. It's not what a tomato sauce should look like— it's darker in colour and I don't like that. I like it when it's light.

Then we go on with the soup. Today, it's beans— pasta e fagioli— typical. Well, that's the first two things we do. Then, at nine o'clock, my mother starts on the foccacia and it'll be ready at 11:30. It's daily and by hand. And I start preparing my hot peppers and olives to put on the tables— we give that with foccacia and if we have an antipasto we put everything else. My father's probably at the market [Jean Talon Market is two minutes away] now so he'll bring in whatever fresh fruit or vegetables or fish or whatever. In the oven we have the goat which we put in first because it takes a few hours to cook. So that's in and it's been covered in wine and brandy and everything— so it's just cooking slowly. My onions will go with the goat— the cipollini— and I prepare my asparagus, a few peppers for lunch. I'm just waiting now, preparing my vegetables, and I'm just waiting to see what comes in fresh. And that's it and then I'll write my menu and take it from there. There's no more preparation except for the tomato sauce. That's it. And then we just do what the client asks us to do. We're four in here and in the evening we're four or five sometimes— myself, my father, my mother and Mike at lunch and in the evenings two or three helpers.

So whatever comes in— oyster mushrooms, portobella, porcinis— whatever's in season, whatever's nice— if that means fresh figs we'll have fresh figs and prosciutto— you know, we really work with the market. We don't prepare much.

That was right from the beginning?

Yeah. Because I figured a restaurant was not a place where you can have a big menu because you cannot keep the quality of the food, or the freshness of the food, if you have a big menu, because you have to prepare everything. And if you prepare it, it means you're freezing. Every day we do something different. Like on Wednesdays we'll do gnocchi and we'll serve them on Wednesday night and on Thursday. And if we don't sell them, we'll serve them on Friday. But that's as far as we go, you know? If we make fresh sausage on Thursdays, we'll make enough to last four, five days, but not to last for a month, you know? On Fridays sometimes we make stuffed pastas but we don't make enough to last a month or two— we just make it for a week or three days— whatever's needed. So, we do preparation, but not for a very long time.

If you eat something which has been frozen and you eat it fresh, it doesn't taste the same— more or less it might, but I don't think it's the same quality. Because I don't freeze anything. Even at home. I don't have a freezer and I don't want a freezer. All I have is a fridge, you know, and if I need something I'll go buy it and eat it. I think that's the way restaurants should be.

It requires for you to be awake— and we do everything— the calling, the ordering, the paying— everything. You can't, say, "Prepare this for a week and it's there," to someone. We do most of the preparation anyhow. It's more work because you have to verify what comes in because it has to be top quality otherwise it's bad. If you're buying, it's different, because you see it. But if it comes in— half the time they try to pass whatever they have or whatever's left over or whatever they can't sell. They say, well, it's a restaurant. They have to cook it. You know? But it doesn't work that way.

Do you make other charcuterie besides the sausage here?

Only sausage. The prosciutto and all those things are bought, of course. And now we have the Parma, which is a big thing now— the prosciutto di Parma that's in and bresaola and the cheeses we buy— the mascarpone and gorgonzola— and that's it. That's from suppliers and whatever comes in from Italy and it only comes in so many times a month and you have to jump on it, especially at Christmas time— special times of the year when you have to jump on it otherwise, forget about it.

Franca Mazza

So that's how the day has started.

Yeah. And then we go on, we read the menu, we see if there are any desserts
to prepare. We make our tiramisu here or apple pie or whatever fruit we have
and that's it and we wait to serve lunch. And whatever the client asks us to
do, because we really go with the client, with what people ask us to do.

**There's a long history of Italian restaurants in Montreal, but where did
you get this vision of what you do which is different from the bulk of
other restaurants?**

Because, I guess, I like things to be different when I do them, and I'm very
creative with whatever I do.

What's your background?

I grew up in Montreal. I was born in Italy, but I came here when I was nine.
It was in Calabria in a little town in a mountain area of Calabria— not even
a town. It was in the countryside, actually, the closest town, [laughing],
one-hour away, walking. And I went to school walking one hour every
morning with my brother. And that's how we grew up— out in the
countryside. So I like the stones, I like, you know, the flowers on the
balcony— on the— *mirador.*

I remember my father used to go hunting all the time so my mother
cooked a lot of game. So we really are from a big family— a big home in the
countryside where they really had to do with what they had, you know? They
had a lot of land and they lived off that, so that's maybe where the creative
part comes from. You have different trees, and different fruits and different...
So you've seen all these things. It's not that you see them on a rack, you've
seen them, the vegetation. I mean, you've seen them grow. You've seen them
in flowers.

That's what I miss the most. We were eating a lot of game, a lot of
vegetables. We had animals— we had cows, we had pigs, we had chicken,
we had rabbits— so that was our food— we had sheep. So, it was from the
growing to the killing, you know? And whatever the land gave. So it was
chestnuts... We were in an area where everything grows because it was

southern Italy— olives, oranges, lemons— and persimmons. That's my favourite fruit. Just plain. I think where you're born, where you come from, how you see things... You know, it's different when you see a fruit from flowering to being ripe, than just to see it on the stand in the market where, like, it's "How did it get there?" you know? It's very nice, it's very tasty, it's very good. But it's all you know. Where it grows, what did it look like— sometimes it's very difficult to imagine unless you see it. I guess that has a lot to do with your upbringing, with your culture. Then, you see the wine being made, you know?

So tell me about your background and where you grew up in Montreal.

In Little Italy— in this area right by the Jean Talon Market. Right across from the fish market, so I was always seeing food, it's always been around. Food was always very important in our household. My father would always buy the best and he still does. That's part of what made this restaurant, because he always bought what was good. If it wasn't the best, if it wasn't good, he wouldn't buy it. Even if he bought little, he always bought the best.

My parents were always in this business. Since 1969, when they came, they were always in this business. They worked for a restaurant on this same street, Frank's Restaurant. It was my father's sister. My mother and father worked for them for nineteen years, always in the same place, always in the kitchen, together as a team. I also worked there but never in the kitchen. But I've always seen food, you know. I've seen it but until they opened this restaurant here... I decided. I was working for Iberia but they needed help, so I used to do the buying in the morning— drop everything off, write my menu and go off to work, you know? And until I decided it was too much to hold two jobs and that I really help my dad here. But I was always exposed...

It was their work but I always... when it's family... we were always brought up to help. I was helping out because it was my parents and my husband, so I figured I had something to do with it as well.

I was a flight attendant... my world is the airlines. [laughs] I was a flight attendant for Canadian. I was in Vancouver for a while so maybe that's another exposure to food and to cultures, you know? So that's probably another one. And maybe that's what made me who I am today.

So you went to Iberia Airlines...

At the airport and then we opened here and I stayed 'til 1991. I was at Iberia over three years.

So you never thought about cooking the...

No, no, never. I just came in to help and somehow I got the hang of it. Like I figured, it's a family business, they needed help ahh... I know what's going on more or less... and it's probably easier if I got involved than have someone else there that will just come in from nowhere and not know anything. So I got involved and that's how I picked up cooking— from scratch actually. I was never a kitchen-oriented person. Never. And I'm not to this day if I'm home, I won't cook. I refuse to cook. It just happened, you know. Because when I do things I get involved, really involved.

It was difficult, very very difficult at the beginning because I knew nothing about actual real cooking. It was very difficult to learn. I mean, now it's one, two, three— it doesn't look like anything. It's nothing to be here, you know? In reality it is, if you don't know what you're doing.

So your training is from here?

From here, under someone who's not easy ahh... My father is very picky, very difficult. And it was very hard, especially the relationship. Also you know, working directly with your father because there are only so many things you can say and do. It's not a colleague.

I didn't expect that. I had no idea what he was like. I just got involved, I do that, you know. I'm a character who gets involved in things, not knowing what I'm getting involved in. But I won't give up. I always figure a way out. I'm a very easy person to get along with and I always try to maintain things as nice and neat as possible, as agreeable as possible. It has to be, otherwise you can't work in a kitchen. It has to be pleasant. Otherwise you have the rest of the personnel to deal with, too. Not just deal with yourself and your father.

It wasn't the learning, it was the relationship that was hard. The learning was actually not so hard because I pick things up very easily. I see it once and that's it. I have to see it. I cannot copy things. You cannot explain to me how something is done. I cannot read a recipe and do it. I have to see it done or try it myself or figure it out— my own way— but I'll figure it out. That's what makes me creative— I cannot follow someone else. So I looked at what he did and did it my own way. There was a little bit of friction, of course, because he said it's made this way, but this way looks better and if the client likes it then you know, it's nice. I cannot do two things the same way. So I don't consider myself a real cook because a real cook should follow, you know? I cannot follow. Like, I'll pull out two plates [laughing] not looking the same. Or the same food will not look the same taken out two three times a night. I'll alter it— I'll put a different leaf or, you know...

Was there a point when he realized that's the way you were?

[Laughing] No, no, no— he's still like, ah... "You, you, you cook like the French" or "You cook like the Spanish..." or "You did this this way..." and I say, "It's okay, it's okay, no problem..." [laughing] "Let's go on... let's just pull out the table..."

Nobody gets involved with anybody else. That would create a major storm. No, it's okay, it's been good. I mean we've been here eleven years so...

So how important is this experience with the family?

Very important. It's important because you... First of all, it's family and you can't leave that out, and second of all, you work together so the relationship has to be good or otherwise you can't work together and nothing will come out. If you're not agreeing on things then your plates or your food will show it.

And your husband is here.

He's in the dining room. For him it's not the same because he's in the dining room. He was always in the restaurant business. He's from Calgary and he's always been in this business. I think for him it's been his life and he doesn't see anything else.

It's not an easy task— it's very difficult because you have to work and then you have your work-related problems and then you have to deal with family issues which... and you can only say so much to your mom and dad and you have to respect the relationship. You cannot go overboard. Whereas if it's a colleague, then you can say, go to hell, today— tomorrow is another day. Whereas, family is family. It's there and you can't just avoid it, you know?

Well, in a usual kitchen there can be lots of yelling with a chef who rules...

Oh, we don't have that here. As bad as it may seem, it never goes to that extent. It's a very different kind of relationship. In a way it's nicer if you respect the family ties and... you know? You have to be a psychiatrist at the same time— the psychologist— and you have to keep everybody happy. It's very difficult.

Well, we're here, so it's different. The kids will, once in a while, complain about this— that we're never at home. But husband and wife relationship? We're together, we're not really away from each other, we're together and it's quite different.

I wouldn't work in any other kitchen but mine. If one day this place is sold or closed up, I don't intend to work in another kitchen. I did this really because it was family. I saw the need for it. But would I go in as a chef? I don't see it. I really worked here because it was family.

I enjoy what I'm doing here, but I can't see myself working in the kitchen with anyone else but my father. I say, the day he retires, I retire with him and I always said that. It's a very difficult job and I don't see me doing the same job with someone else.

I don't know, maybe. For now, I don't see the possibility of going... I'm really good at it. I've done a lot in this kitchen with my mom and my dad and Antoine too— because sometimes he has ideas too and we try them— but for now, I don't see it. Maybe later on, but for now I don't see it. It's a hard job for a woman.

Most of your staff is men. It's difficult because I run this place alone at the same time as the kitchen. It's a difficult task. Then there's the cleaning, and you still have to keep everything spotless every night; you have to clean; and every morning you come in and there's more... It's not just the cooking, you know. It's not as if you come in and just cook and leave.

So what do you think about the difference in kitchens these days with more women becoming chefs?

Women, I think, have more creativity than men in this... There are more women, yes. First of all, women are more understanding so they're easier to get along with. That's one thing. It makes the workplace more pleasant, I think... because I see it when I'm around— when I'm not around it's like... So it's different, you know?

At night I'm alone with the men and I see the difference— if I'm around everyone's smiling and everybody's happy because I'm around— I don't know if it's character.

But you've never brought other women into the kitchen?

No, no. Maybe I should, maybe [laughing] they'll tell me to stay at home! [both laugh] They'll tell me, go home. We don't need you any more. But I like what I'm doing. I enjoy what I'm doing and what I like is the creative side and I'm always looking for new things. I don't like to work with the same things over and over because I get bored and it's monotonous. You have your odd days when you don't feel like... But, generally, I'm very happy to be here. I just do what I have to do and that's it.

For me, it's like being at home, really. Like being at my own house and everybody comes... It's a regular clientele. Most clients come into the kitchen and say, how are you? What're you doing? So there's that human relationship. It's not just cooking. This restaurant is very personal because we know everybody we cook for. No mass production— we cook for someone because he eats this way or because he doesn't like that or he doesn't eat this or he doesn't eat salt or... He's special. So everyone is kind of special that you're cooking for and that makes it interesting.

It's very difficult because it's like you're cooking at home for six people— and one doesn't eat potatoes, and he doesn't eat... and you're trying to please everybody. But that's the way we function here most of the time. We're really cooking for somebody, for a certain person. And it's nice because you're not always doing the same thing.

But then, as a restaurant, you must have a certain standard...

Well, you keep the standard, but trying to please the client, that makes it even more difficult. That's what makes our job so difficult here at times. Because you keep the standards but you're trying to accommodate the way he's eating or supposed to be eating or is liking. So it's a very special place. It's not the typical chef-client relationship at all. There's a personalised aspect of it you know? If someone says here, one likes his pasta this way, and someone says here he likes it that way... So it's very personalised, really. It's like every individual has a different requirement.

Nowadays, go into any restaurant and there's pasta and there's an explosion of trendy pizza and pasta places, very often of questionable standard and people get used to that. Does that affect you?

No. If pasta is not al dente it doesn't come out of the kitchen. If the client wants it well done I say, I'm sorry sir, this is the way you take your pasta, otherwise eat something else 'cause that's the way my pasta is. My father sometimes says, "You can stick it in his nose," you know? [both laughing] The client will be hurt eating it. But that's the way I serve it. But in other little things, where you really have to, then I'll do it, but not in overcooking pastas. I refuse to do that. That's a rule. I'll never bend that. Definitely, definitely.

There's a way pizza and pasta should be made. I don't think everybody who opens pizza and pasta places will do it the right way, but you can't take that away from them, you can't take the right of these people to open. It does bring down the... makes it commercial, but it won't affect a restaurant like ours. It brings down... especially if you're going to a place where the pasta's overcooked and the lasagne's been frozen for a month and half and they just cut it and put it in the oven. But they're there and there's nothing you can do about it.

You're all from Calabria. Your parents have been cooking traditional food, but you're into the creative... is there a formula you strive for?

A little bit traditional and a little bit creative, but you can't take away the traditional because that's what makes the taste of the food. Then there's the way you present it, which makes it different— but the traditional has to be there.

The way we make our gnocchi— apparently our gnocchi... people talk about them as if they're gold— there's nothing to them. They're just gnocchi. [laughs] I guess it's the way they're made. First of all, the right quantity of... if you're supposed to use 24 eggs and we put 15, it won't be the same, the texture would change, so you have to keep that in mind. That's important.

Home-made sausage is tradition. But it depends how you present it on the plate. I mean, sausage is sausage. It could be fried, roasted or grilled, but then it's the presentation which makes them different. If I fry sausage and stick it on the plate, are you going to cut it up, are you going to put figs with it...?

So when do you think about it?

On the spot. Most things are done on the spot— were brought up on the spot. Oh, sometimes we're here and we try things— I wonder what this would taste like with that— you know.

I don't read about food. I like to have it in front of me and try things. If I would read about it, I wouldn't retain much because I can't follow. Can't follow a recipe. I can't bake. That's the reason why they tell me to put six eggs and I'll put twelve. [laughing]

You travelled a lot. Do your ideas for your cuisine come from other cuisines, eating in other restaurants?

I like Thai cuisine— but I'd have to go to Thailand to learn that. I think it's very difficult to do. I don't know if it's easy or difficult to do but they come out with amazing mixtures of... That's the one and only cuisine I'd like to learn.

You know, I'd never used ginger before, and now I use ginger. I used to use normal rice and now I use basmati rice. It's like— the Oriental, the

Oriental influence. But I like things from the Orient that we normally won't find. Like, we don't use ginger in Italy— ginger? What is that?— you know?

What did your father think when you brought that in?

He's very into that, very into that. He likes new things. He picks up whatever he finds and says, what is this? Do you know this? Let's taste this. Or we use bok choy, the vegetable— which is not Italian at all. We just boil it and put olive oil or garlic, or as a salad— just chop it up very very fine and we put onion and mint— so it's, yeah we use what we find, really. So, it's not what we know, it's what we knew. But whatever we find we'll try to make use of. You can't change drastically from whatever you know to a whole complete different cuisine because, for instance, you'll never really know what Spanish cuisine is all about unless you live there and cook with them for three years— or Thai cuisine, unless you live there and work with them. But you know, you have all kinds of little influences and we try to use them— and we do try to use all kinds of things— and that's exciting— finding out new things and what we can do with them. That's exciting.

We don't go to other restaurants to eat— very rarely— especially since we're always here and it's hard to find the time. And when you're not here you don't want to be in another restaurant. But what we find in the market... My father's usually good for that. What was the other thing? It was a zucchini, but round... we grill it. Celery root— we grill it, too. All kinds of things in Italy we don't use. But we've picked up here and there— they're not part of Italian cuisine but they go with things that we make. We find ways.

So when you make a dish, what values are important to you?

It's when the plate looks nice, and when the client comes back and says to me, it was amazing. It was really good. That's what I value. I can tell before it's out there because it depends how much you put into it— how much work you put into it, how much love you put into it. If you're cooking because you're just cooking, because it's your job and you're getting paid for it, it's one thing. But if you're doing it because you enjoy what you're doing, you care about what you're doing, you'll get that answer from whoever was eating it.

If you really take good care with what you're doing, if you really have it figured out, it will come out.

I think it's the creative part. It's all to do with creativity and if you can create and if you can create elsewhere, you can create in the kitchen too. I think you have to have the creative instincts. And I guess it's part of the culture— the natural— we grew up with that. And my kids too. They see all that, it's part of their everyday life almost. Because I'll have something here and I'll bring it home or there's new fruit and I'll bring it home.

And they do enjoy food. They're picky about their little things, they don't like everything. They have tastes of their own, but in general, yeah, they do enjoy food. And they're used to home cooking from their grandmother because I'm never home so it's my mother who does the cooking at night. It's real home cooking and they see that every day.

Are there any specific ingredients that make your mouth water and inspire you?

I really like fruits and vegetables— that's what I like working with. I don't like working with meats, really, or fish, but vegetables... If I can find a funny vegetable or spring vegetables to mix it with a meat or whatever, that will turn me on. But it's different things— for different salads.

In spring, I'm waiting for cherries and figs and, you know, all that spring produce that will come in— especially figs because we do a lot with figs. Like, we make a plate here— it's veal with prosciutto and then we put figs on top, which is amazing because the taste of the salt and sweet with the prosciutto and the fig— and the fig is grilled. The meat is fried, finished off with butter and wine and brandy and then the figs on top and then when you're eating it— it mixes the salt and sweet and it's amazing. And that's something we just came up with.

Also grilled figs and roasted peppers, which is very nice. Figs— I love figs. We use chestnuts as soon as they come in— middle of September until after Christmas— until they really end. We're the place that uses chestnuts. We make chicken with chestnuts— the small Cornish hens with chestnuts— chestnuts and orange— that might sound strange. It's oven roasted and while it's roasting— well you have to boil your chestnuts, and then you put your Cornish hens in the oven— you put all your herbs— thyme, a little bit of rosemary, salt— and you put it in the oven with olive oil and, while it's cooking, you put just the juice of your oranges and the peels inside. And then when it's half-cooked you put in your chestnuts because your chestnuts are cooked. Then you cook it until it's all done and once it's all done what I do is I grate up the orange and put it all over the chicken and add brandy to it and a touch of balsamic vinegar and a touch of butter and that's it— it's amazing. It gives it sweet... chestnuts are sweet so it's very nice. What else do we do? We have a chestnut soup with boiled chestnuts as well. I make tiramisu with chestnuts. Chestnut soup is a big thing in Northern Italian cuisine. We did use it in Southern Italy as well— even if it's not major. We make chestnut bread— that's very southern Italian. When they had nothing else to eat during the war that's what kept them alive. Because they made flour out of the chestnuts. They used to grind them and make flour and chestnut flour and make bread with it. And chestnut cookies— just fry them. There are a lot of things you can do with chestnuts.

Where did you learn about this?

That's through my mother. Through my parents, because her parents still... something they've done since 15, 20 years ago in Italy. It's a part of it. Yeah, because once in a while they talk about something they used to do— here or there to survive or whatever, you know. I mean, it's a stupid thing— but you know, people actually lived off of that and are still alive on their love and still alive today and it sounds... ridiculous things. They're there and they're part of whatever influence you have because they do talk about it. You know all these stories. You don't think about them, but they're there. It's special, very special. Because you hear all these stories you know— even through my grandfather because— he passed away in November— they tell me stories and that. We grew up as a very close family and even if... I've been living it. I'm back every year and my kids too, you know. It's part of— part of the culture.

Food has always been special. Every occasion has its special thing, you know. There's a lot of family tradition. Like certain foods, certain things that are baked at a certain time every year. They're probably baked in ten cities, you know, but in every city, they're baked differently. Like Christmas cookies my mother makes that are filled with nuts and chocolate and cooked wine. I mean, you have to cook the wine— when you're making the wine you have to prepare that in advance. So you're preparing this in September then to bake your cookies in December or... They're half-moons which are filled and this filling is prepared in advance and it's got tangerine peels, and chocolate— it's a funny mixture— and raisins, but everything is home-made— like the raisins are home-dried, the wine is home-cooked— it's a family tradition. And she still does it. And we do it [in the restaurant] at Christmas time. And it's a tradition— or honey, little squares with honey.

So that's part of what the restaurant is...

It's history. It's part of the home. It's like being home. I wouldn't run a restaurant with mass production or with ten chefs... I wouldn't be able to. Because that's not my idea of a restaurant.

But it is hard. It's hard because you can't— at one point you don't measure food costs, you can't think of food costs because you're doing things that are... out of proportion... that you would not normally do in a restaurant. You can't calculate food costs on certain things. You're doing them because it's something special and you're doing it once or twice and you just forget about it.

That must be hard in balancing your books— factoring in these things?

It's difficult. [laughs] It's really difficult. But we're doing it. And they do it in Europe. And that's how a lot of restaurants in Europe are... especially family-owned. It's a very different way of seeing things, a different attitude towards food. It's not so much how much you're going to make out of it, it's what you're going to make of it.

You'll calculate, but not on all items. You still work and you're here to make a living, but it's a different way.

Franca Mazza

We've talked about the influence of Southern Italy in your food, but you grew up mainly in Montreal. Did you grow up eating the typical Montreal things, and québécois, too?

Mostly family food. I know very little of their cuisine. I know— what's it called— pain de viande? but, I have no particular interests in that. The odd hot dog, I don't consider it part of my culture. We always grew up around the family table, cooking...

It never made me feel like an outcast. My father's never had a hot dog in his life, you know?

And you tell him hot dog and "yeccchhhh." [laughing] He says it's crushed bone, you know? My kids still eat the home food. The odd time they'll have a hamburger. They still eat my mother's food. It's not what you eat that will change who you are and where you come from.

You've done this, changing your career. How possible is that for others? Some people will think about going to hospitality schools...

It depends who they are and where they come from. I've done it, but I don't know. You can, but I think you have to have the proper background or the knowledge first. I think everyone who works in a kitchen should know where food comes from before they work with it.

To know what this is, what can be done with it. Where does it grow— is it in a field or on a tree? To know where basil comes from or where chives come from— where bananas come from— they could be in water— where rice comes from. That's what everybody should know before they get involved. If you're taking cooking lessons... I think cooking lessons should be the last thing they take. You should first have a background into nature, into where things are grown and where they come from. I mean, do they grow under the earth— is it a tree, is it a bush? Where do raspberries grow, how are they picked, what do you do with them, or what season? When does it come out, when is it ripe— is it in August, is it in June, March?

How does a chestnut... how is it on a tree, what does it look like? It has something around it— full of thorns— and then it opens when the chestnuts fall down and then you pick them. You wouldn't go in the tree and pick them because you can't. So, I think those should be the first courses a chef should take. I mean most people come out of school and go— what is this? Where does it come from? What part of the world does it come from, you know? I think everybody should know that.

One chef I know from France spoke of how the animal arrived and they had to do everything— skin the whole thing...

That's what we do here. We have the sheep and all the goats and that's what my father still does. When the sheep come in they're open but with the fur, the goats and... Yeah, he says that if the skin is on it keeps the freshness. So they come in every Wednesday but they'll leave them in a cold room with the skin on for two or three days before he cleans them completely. So it's part of the culture, I think. It's part of the way of seeing things. Not being portioned, or frozen... being on the counter for a week you know.

But I really think that everybody should be sent away to the country on a kind of a farm because I think everybody should know where things come from before you use them. Because unless you... What is an olive? Does it grow black? Is this the way it is... or how does it get there to what it is? It's like seeing how wine is made from beginning to end, rather than just drinking a bottle of wine. It's fine to just drink it but where does it come from? How's it made? How you have to cut the vines to give so many grapes, how you have to clean it— it's an art. Once you know that then you can apply that in the kitchen. Like you should know that before... For instance, this young man who works with us at night. He comes from cooking school and the thing I try to teach him as much as possible is where things come from— how they got there. That's what my father was telling me— what do they teach in school? Do they just teach them how to hold a frying pan? Once you know where products come from then you can cut it up— you don't have to know how to cut or hold a frying pan or roast— that's not a problem— that comes with time. It's not an important thing... for him.

Do you find a change in the quality of products in Canada?

No, not really. It's very hard to find the good products. It's very hard— there's a lot more than we had 20, 25, 30 years ago, definitely, and there's more influence— Oriental and European. I think we get our tomatoes from Holland all year now, and we get yellow, we get orange— and endives we get tend to be white, but it's still hard to find good quality products because Canada's not ready to pay. We're not a paying— we don't have a... consumer's not ready to pay. We're not ready to pay so a little comes in, but not as much as we should get, because we're not ready to pay for it.

It's coming, but slowly.

But if you understand about food, you'll know what's best for you. There's a difference if you're paying 15 or 20 dollars for pasta than if you're paying five dollars, definitely there is— it cannot be the same. It's like you're buying Gucci and Joe Blow from the corner— why are you paying Gucci $10,000 and this guy $100? It's the same dress— it looks the same, but maybe he put something else there— quality maybe is different. If you know what you're doing, if you know what you're buying, if you know what you want, I think you know where you want to eat. It all depends on your principle of life or what you can afford to— it all depends on everybody's willing or has the budget to go out and eat $80 a person in a restaurant, spend that much. Some people can't spend $10— it depends on your way of life too— and status— are you trying to impress someone? Are you taking out your girlfriend? You're not going to take her out to McDonald's— you have to go out and impress her.

Franca Mazza

Franca Mazza was born in Carlopoli, Calabria in 1961 and came to Montreal at the age of eight. She tells that her experience with food began in Italy living on a farm in the countryside. While attending school in Montreal, she then would daily visit Restaurant Frank, where her parents worked, and she would have lunch. Trained as a flight attendant, she was working in the airline industry when her parents opened Il Mulino, and in 1989 began doing the buying at market for them. A year later, she came into the restaurant full-time to cook, learning from her father while also developing her own individual style and techniques which have added to Il Mulino's food, legendary in Monteal's Little Italy.

Franca Mazza

Franca Mazza's
BALSAMIC SHRIMP (WITH SALAD) [for four]
(Note: Franca Mazza originally gave this recipe for a single serving.
Quantities were simply multiplied by four to keep exactly to her
measurements.)

FOR THE SHRIMP
2 dozen large shrimp, butterflied
4 cloves garlic, mashed
4 tbsp extra virgin olive oil
black pepper
4 small knobs of butter
4 tsp brandy
2 oranges
8 tsp balsamic vinegar

FOR THE SALAD
Use any salad green, such as lettuce, arugula, mache, frisée or endive, finely sliced
as for coleslaw

1 red onion, thinly sliced
8-12 fresh mint leaves
8 tbsp extra virgin olive oil
4 tbsp balsamic vinegar
juice of the oranges
salt and pepper

Preheat the oil in a frying pan. Put in the garlic cloves and shrimp at the same time. Sautée over high heat, adding black pepper. Once the shrimp are done (just opaque), drain off all the remaining oil from the pan. In the same pan, blend in the butter and away from the heat, carefully stir in the brandy. Freshly grate the orange zest into the shrimp. Add balsamic vinegar and reduce the sauce until it is brownish and of a syrupy consistency.

Meanwhile, in a large bowl, prepare the salad with the leaves and onion. Add remaining ingredients and toss well.

To plate, place a serving of salad in the centre of each dinner plate. Arrange six shrimp and sauce around it.

An Afterword

Gerry Shikatani

People who discover I am a food writer are immediately envious of the
wonderful meals I get to eat as part of my job. Now, I wouldn't deny how
special such privilege is. And this has always reminded me that to write about
gastronomy, I must, above all, convey as directly and concretely as possible
these experiences of food.

But in a certain respect, because most of us can, even if only rarely, go
out and eat at our favourite restaurants, I've always felt that the greater privilege
has been to meet chefs from time to time— ask questions, learn about
techniques, share at a table or by a cookstove, the congeniality of their
company and their visions and vigour.

It's that passport I've held wherever I've set down my bags in the world—
be it in Chicago, when I once sat with Michael Foley, one of the early stalwarts
of the New American Cooking, or a chef whose name I know simply as
Godart, after I'd shared exhilarating hours of talk with this dedicated humble
man at his unheralded auberge I'd fortuitously bicycled by in Ruffey-les-
Beaune in Burgundy.

With each such encounter, I have gradually found myself schooled in the
course of the chefs' working lives, to learn about their dedication and their
artful generosity in a profession that allows them to satisfy for us in a concrete,
elemental way what we've understood, beginning from infancy— the need
and desire to replenish our empty tummies, to eat what we crave as much as
what nutritionally satisfies.

While I sip my coffee at meal's end and then often to their surprise, tell
them what I do, a light is often struck in their eyes. They will then show and
tell things in ways which seem to express a deep-centred complicity with me,
a contract of pleasure which forgets the discordant sound of money. It's the
best dessert of all.

These moments I've often wanted to share with friends, with readers,
because I do hold a privileged post, and for the love of good food, for their

sake and the lineage of gastronomy, the more we as salivating eaters know, pushes the perimeters of the whole loop from producer to cooker to diner.

There's no doubt that every prospective reader will think of their favourite chefs who've been excluded from this book, as much as the *kinds* of chefs who are absent.

Anyone who regularly eats restaurant meals has pretty strong opinions of their favourite chefs. Interviews with many of these could have equally illumined these pages.

How can this book pass over the inspirational and bold Karen Barnaby in Vancouver or Michel Jacob, the Alsatian chef, who, at Le Crocodile, educated two generations of BC diners to what real French cuisine was? There is the long-respected Bruno Marti, whose talent and vision laid much of the groundwork for the best that Vancouver's tables now have to offer.

Top chefs in Montreal suggested James MacGuire of Le Passe-Partout, the wise wizard baker and master chef of NDG (Notre-Dame-de-Grace), who reminds Montrealers how the proper execution of classic French cooking can meet any trend head-on. Youthful Claude Pelletier at Mediterraneo is one chef who has brought as much real substance as mode to boulevard St. Laurent.

Renee Foote of Mercer Street Grill and pastry genius Joanne Yolles are not the only outstanding women chefs neglected in my all-male troupe from Toronto. Indeed, pastry chefs, who have very particular gifts, were not part of the parameters of this book. Where we've passed by Michael Stadtländer, let's hope for a book of his own to render justice to his uncompromising brilliance beyond the simple praise a scribe can bring. Consider Arpi Magyar, Mark McEwan and Chris McDonald, three of Toronto's elite chefs who come to mind when we tap the letter "M" on this keyboard.

The fact that diners in every province and territory in Canada would add so many more names than even these, attests to the passion Canadians on both sides of the kitchen's doors have developed in the last two decades.

The chefs you've met here are not necessarily the most celebrated stars— indeed star-making is not what this book is about. But all are outstanding chefs of utmost integrity in the kitchen. All have something to tell.

They are among the very best in their cities and if you live elsewhere, you would have recognized in them the finest definitive qualities possessed by the best chefs where you live. It's something of what I saw in my late father, who was once a cook in an old-fashioned Inner City Toronto *'spoon*, where he made pies, soups, stews and cakes from scratch. It might be evident in the steakhouse grillman who, intimate with the propensities of hardwood coal heat, timing and placement, delivers consistency of crusting and jus, while buried under order upon order. Such virtues too define the masters of the asadors of suckling pigs and lambs in Castille.

Once into the process of these talks, and still deliberating over my selections, I was faced with another dilemma, the more so since my eating history from birth ladled out equal portions of miso soup and beef stew. The exclusion of Portuguese, Polish, Pakistani chefs and the diverse population palette in a Canada struggling to construct a more inclusive syncretic culture was leaving a bad taste in my mouth.

I was in Vancouver and my food contacts advised me to see Tojo, the master Japanese chef, and Vikram Vij, whose modern, stylish and very personal Indian cooking has reaped praise across the continent.

In the end, I limited my scope to what we conventionally identify as part of North American fine dining style— essentially French and contemporary North American, with a nod to Italian to acknowledge what from fast-food court to grunge café and home-sweet-home kitchen, we love to eat. In Montreal and Toronto Italian food is only one way Canadians of Italian heritage have influenced the character of those cities.

These interviews open rather than close the menu to what we can reap from other chefs and from other cuisines as we end a Millennium's meals.

To those fine chefs and foodlovers elsewhere in Canada, I apologize. But do call me up, set the finery in order, I'm always a touch peckish. And I'll tote along my laptop. Promise.

It was on a bus going across the Lion's Gate Bridge to North and then West Van to see Carol Chow that I became aware of how these encounters would inevitably be a quite personal quest along on which I was inviting readers for the ride.

I'm writing this in Toronto, to where I've recently moved back. It's where I was born, have spent most of my life, and first began writing about food.

Where as a 12-year-old, I convinced some schoolmates to check out the local "European" restaurant at Spadina and College and their "famous wiener schnitzel"— only to be served a sausage-less plate. In between, I've lived in Montreal and Paris, the former where I worked as a restaurant reviewer.

I never lived in Vancouver. Yet, it dawned on me that in spite of my Central Canada upbringing, I virtually began with a taste of the Pacific Northwest in my mouth. I come from pre-World War II Skeena River fishing family roots. In the '50s, our family would regularly receive shipments of seafood— from seaweed to salmon roe— from the West Coast, so that Skeena River salmon is more gustatorily defining of me than any food, and I knew about smoked Alaska black cod decades before it became fashion in today's Vancouver cuisine.

Spending time with these 12 chefs and letting them speak about their passions allowed me to speculate further on personal self-definitions through food in the way that writers and painters who express their specific visions from a deeper place, magically ignite a common wick of insight within us, and nudge us open in larger ways.

There are central common concerns to these chefs, though their backgrounds reach across the country and globe. Tenacity in the best sense is common among these chefs no matter where they're from.

It's as easy to be dismissive as awe-struck of chefs— especially in a time when our *mediatique* world has often forced their hand to be as much hawker and clown or lofty artist as cook. Even though fame and fortune are further determined by factors beyond the fundamental objectives of chefs, the relationship chefs engage in with food, as gifted mediators between us and the world at the plane of hospitality, can't be denied.

Some chefs we know talk lots on the screen. Some loudly shout and bang pots and pans. But, it's at the moment of their work, where they face the fridge and then the stove, give themselves over to the material, forget virtually all else but the ingredients, that their the magic begins.

Their reverence for the freshness and beauty of the products places them in league with the farmers and fishermen who are grounded to food not as market-fresh, but at a deeper level of intimacy felt in their hands of how fleeting peak quality is: the natural process of life, as ephemeral as it is. In all these chefs at some point in their lives, usually very early on, there was something pivotal, an experience which has remained with them.

Chefs realize, too, what is profoundly human. That beauty inspires them into the magic of transforming, and something at some point made them marvel at the magic that makes food "special," be it a simple club sandwich. The transformative is above all else.

Why have they come to possess such a commitment to transmit their own astonishment before the larder and their own private pleasure? We know that while they have cooked with the most luxurious foods in the world, cooking, for them, is an honouring of the dignity of all foods, not just the deluxe, nor is it a glib rhyming off of a fashion, but their chance to show the raw materials at their best. Here they have much to teach us.

Simplicity is echoed over and over in the course of these talks, but that is deceptive. Simplicity in the various ways these chefs cook arrives in many forms, be it simple salt and pepper seasoning or the complex layering of tastes and textures in a process that nevertheless yields sophisticated harmony. They all seek to define harmony for themselves, and it is a matter of which approach to choose, which feels best for them.

But the layers of their cooking are not simply restricted to taste and texture, but include a distillation of knowledge and history.

Chefs know they are grounded in a culinary history, the techniques handed down from many cultures, and they express excitement about the heirloom vegetable and the artisanal producer who grows it. A sense of history, personal and otherwise, also inspires a dedication to hospitality. So, why do they want to give the better part of their lives to giving their customers pleasure? The commitment to this profession is rooted in love and passion for the full spectrum of cuisine, and it is this which drives them to communicate.

They all have an instinctive understanding of the way they can educate. Educate our bodies, our senses, to new sensations, to surprise. All of which fundamentally helps us get closer to ourselves and pleasure, and then experience richer lives. It's not to suggest something far-flung from real daily living. Instead, their attention helps us regain a wisdom we may be lost, disconnected from: the connection to seasons and landscape and the basic goal to create and build from these sources.

An Afterword

The passing on to us of passion makes us more aware. And the next step in that food-chain of events? They can work with and nurture further food producers with whom they share commitment, for they have created in us the demand.

Eating the foods of good chefs seems often expensive but, like buying anything from a CD to a house, value is really the what we both— chef and client— must carefully consider, these chefs seem to be telling us. Anne Desjardins refers directly to the notion of the restorative in the restaurant experience, whether the client regularly eats fine cuisine or it is a rare experience one saves long and hard for. It is on that special occasion that Robert Feenie brings pleasure to his diners and allows him to continue his passionate pursuit.

To dine at such tables we are treated to a value— their knowledge and experience and understanding of the range of what we mean by palate— and to their inspiration, which is driven by the products they choose and their desire to share and celebrate the occasion of food. In many instances it is a transmission of local and family culture, a simplicity and purity which is at the vision of every chef on these pages.

They all speak the same vocabulary of hospitality. They all know that if they were to sit down at a table over something like a fresh tomato with a guest, if that guest was a farmer, even penniless, who proclaimed ignorance over fancy cooking, they would speak the same language and then enjoy together something more refined by the chef, because they begin standing upon the same ground. Food, as these chefs live it, is not about class or money, even if the patronage of customers who define cuisine more by status, trend and expense must impinge on their work.

As I sat listening and editing these interviews, I found how what I've learned continues past the meetings I had and will have.

Early this past spring I was in Madrid on a cold, wet shivery afternoon. I was in the mood for *pimientos de padron*, which grow in the extreme Northwest region of Spain called Galicia. Simply fried, they are quite popular in many places throughout Spain. The peppers are small and green and are of such a variety of size and shape to tell of nature's idiosyncratic difference. Some are thumb-sized and oblong, others like small marbles. All share, in the end, the same destiny of a dip in hot oil. It is the astonishing simplicity of the taste of good peppery extra virgin olive oil, a dash of sea salt to draw out the pepper's sweetness, the crisp skin and tender flesh— even the light brittle of delicate stems.

While some tapas bars had these displayed on their counters, I saw that they had been pre-fried. While they suggested a different pleasure, wilted with good oil, I waited to find a place where they would be cooked on order.

So, I had become damp and chilled until I was there on the Calle Fuencarral in an Asturian bar in a barrio of Madrid, where a number of Galician and Asturian establishments are to be found. And as I sat munching with a little beer, my pleasure at eating these peppers, I realized, had a lot to do with the ways chefs have changed me. Dreamily and deliciously reflecting on the idea of layers and levels of taste, there was a changed, more considerate way of finding humble temporal pleasure within the small architecture of the mouth.

I have passed years eating with open mind as well as open mouth, but now I possess more the passionate comprehension of what occurs in us. I feel that these chefs and others have brought my life closer to Nature and to history. And as I look at the words of these splendid chefs across Canada, my experience in Spain tells me their words will be now part of the way I experience food, comprehend my relationship to the environment, to the last bite.

It's my hope that after listening to the words of these chefs, for you, eating henceforth might also not be the same. Like the many hard-working chefs not included here, these 12 are all successful— in their enduring commitment to give their customers pleasure.

Patrick Alléguède's words do speak for all these chefs when he says that food is a message. As any magic or spiritual awakening, it is a transmission of pleasure, a moment of their lives— the duet of John Higgins and Normand Laprise, who receive the morning fish delivery and can only blurt out, "Wow."

October 1999, Toronto

Acknowledgements

My sincere thanks to:

Donald and Beverley Daurio, my publishers and editor who first came to me to consider the feasibility of this project and have enthusiastically supported it throughout its progress. All those who assisted in the transcription of these interviews. Gordon Robertson, for sharing his genius as designer of the cover.

Starting with my parents, both wonderful and caring cooks, our family has always placed utmost importance on good food in meals and snacks taken both in home and out.

They and the following individuals and organizations deserve my gratitude.

Writers, editors and producers who have offered support and friendship in my work as a food writer— in particular, Elizabeth Baird, Dali Castro, Carol Ferguson, Jane Giffen, Bruce Steele, and above all, Carolyn Jackson and Liz Primeau.

The Toronto and Madrid offices of the Instituto Comercio de Exterior (ICEX)— the Trade Commission of Spain— Trade Commisioner Arturo Pina and particularly José Luis Atristáin, Deputy Trade Commissioner, in Canada.

In Toronto, friends Margaret Christakos and Bryan Gee, Cathy and Sandra Hogan, Larry Sherman and especially Maria Muszynska in whose homes some of the work in this book was done; Tamsen Tillson for assistance and timely encouragement. In Montreal, Annie St. Aubin and Julie Gagné whose home was mine during workstays in Montreal; Richard Poirier at L'Eau à la Bouche; Christine Lamarche and Patricia Hovington; Marla Master; and multi-talented word and music craftsman Fréderic Gary Comeau and flamenco artist Marie Parisella for their duende. My aunt Atsuko Shikatani, and my cousin Patsy Shikatani Clever and her husband Howard Clever and to the memory of my cousin Dennis Shikatani for their many years of ongoing hospitality in Surrey; artists Karen Lee and Henry Tsang, who welcomed me during my work in Vancouver. Sue Alexander for her assistance on the Carol

Acknowledgements

Chow talk and whose miracle efforts facilitated my visit with Robert Feenie upon short notice; Leanne Chan also for the Feenie conversation; Tanis Fritz at the Metropolitan Hotel; and Victoria Pratt, astonishing source and advisor on Vancouver's culinary scene who assisted in my talk with Michael Noble. Highly respected chef/vineyard owner Mara Jernigan in Cobble Hill, Vancouver Island, whose own words would have graced these pages had my project ventured beyond Vancouver.

Dedicated chefs everywhere I've eaten, who've shared their genius and of course, passion, none more than the soft-spoken Jean-François Casari, a magnificent and large-hearted chef whose premature passing was a great loss to Toronto dining.

Finally, all the chefs who kindly consented to these talks to make this book possible. Their generosity with their time, wisdom, and candour will, I know, nurture and propel the evolution of Canadian cuisine and gastronomy in many directions.

About the Author

GERRY SHIKATANI is the author of *Lake & Other Stories, Aqueduct, 1988: Selected Poems and Texts, A Sparrow's Food, The Book of Tree*, and the co-editor of *Paper Doors: Japanese-Canadian Poetry in English*. Journalist, performance artist, film-maker, poet, fiction writer, sports and gourmet expert, Gerry Shikatani's international reputation is growing. He divides his time between Montreal, Paris, Vancouver and Toronto.